*Female Crime,
Criminals and Cellmates*

Female Crime, Criminals and Cellmates

An Exploration of Female Criminality and Delinquency

by R. BARRI FLOWERS

McFarland & Company, Inc., Publishers
Jefferson, North Carolina, and London

British Library Cataloguing-in-Publication data are available

Library of Congress Cataloguing-in-Publication Data

Flowers, Ronald B.
    Female crime, criminals and cellmates : an exploration of female
criminality and delinquency / by R. Barri Flowers.
      p. cm.
    Includes bibliographical references (p.) and index. ∞
    ISBN 0-7864-0069-2 (lib. bdg. : 50# alk. paper)
    1. Female offenders—United States. 2. Female offenders—United
States—Statistics. 3. Women prisoners—United States. 4. Women
prisoners—United States—Statistics. I. Title.
HV6046.F56 1995
364.3'74'0973—dc20   95-5633
                                                      CIP

Manufactured in the United States of America

McFarland & Company, Inc., Publishers
  Box 611, Jefferson, North Carolina 28640

To law-abiding members of the fairer sex:
H. Loraine, Julie, Linda, Lara, Grayson,
Kathy, Jayne, Oksana, Surecka, Carol, Barbara,
Connie, Bette, Marcia, Racquel, Vivian, Whitney,
Susan, Jackie, Marjah Aljean, and Miss Kitty

Contents

Figures and Tables   ix

Preface   xiii

Introduction   1

Part I : The Dynamics of Female Criminality

Chapter 1   The Extent of Female Crime   5

Chapter 2   The Nature of Female Crime   26

Chapter 3   Female Crime in Comparison to Male Crime   44

Part II : Causal Approaches to Female Crime and Delinquency

Chapter 4   Theories on Female Criminality   65

Chapter 5   Factors in Female Delinquency and Crime   72

Part III : Women and Crime

Chapter 6   Homicidal Women   81

Chapter 7   Women and Domestic Violence   90

Chapter 8   Incestuous Women   96

Chapter 9   Women and Prostitution   101

Chapter 10   Women and Drug Abuse   115

Contents

Chapter 11 Female White-Collar Criminals   125

Chapter 12 Female Rapists and Con Artists   131

Part IV : Girls, Crime, and Delinquency

Chapter 13 Runaway Girls   141

Chapter 14 Girl Prostitutes   148

Chapter 15 Girls, Alcohol, and Drugs   157

Chapter 16 Girl Thieves   168

Chapter 17 Girls in Gangs   178

Part V : Females Behind Bars

Chapter 18 Girls in Custody   187

Chapter 19 Women as Jail Inmates   199

Chapter 20 Women Prisoners   215

Notes   241

Selected Bibliography   267

Index   275

Figures and Tables

FIGURES

1-1 Female Arrest Trends, 1988–92   18

1-2 Female Arrest Trends for Crime Index Offenses, 1960–92   19

2-1 Distribution of Female Property Crimes, 1992   36

2-2 Distribution of Female Violent Crimes, 1992   37

2-3 Distribution of Female White-Collar Offenses, 1992   38

2-4 Distribution of Female Alcohol- and Drug-Related Offenses, 1992   39

2-5 Distribution of Female Sex Offenses, 1992   40

3-1 Female and Male Offenders, by Arrests and Correctional Facilities, 1992   47

3-2 Violent Crime Arrest Patterns, by Gender, 1992   51

3-3 Property Crime Arrest Patterns, by Gender, 1992   52

3-4 Drug- and Alcohol-Related Arrest Patterns, by Gender, 1992   53

3-5 Juvenile Offenders by Sex, Arrest, and Type of Facility, in Recent Years   54

3-6 Violent Crime Arrest Trends, by Gender, 1960–92   57

3-7 Property Crime Arrest Trends, by Gender, 1960–92   59

6-1 Female Murderers, by Age, 1992   82

6-2 Victims in Female Perpetrated Murders, by Race and Gender, 1992   83

9-1 Women's Prostitution and Commercialized Vice Arrests, by Age Groups, 1992   104

10-1 Trends in Women's Arrests for Drug Abuse Violations, 1983–92   117

10-2   Percentage of Men and Women Illicit Drug Users, by Drug
Type, 1991   118

11-1   Trends in Women's Arrests for White-Collar Crimes,
1977–92   126

11-2   Distribution of Female Arrests for White-Collar Offenses,
1992   127

13-1   Female Arrest Trends for Running Away and Juvenile
Prostitution, 1983 and 1992   142

13-2   Female Runaways, by Age, 1992   143

14-1   Girl Prostitutes, by Age, 1992   151

15-1   Girls and Alcohol-Related Offenses, 1992   158

15-2   Girls and Substance Abuse Offenses, 1992   159

15-3   Girl Arrests for Substance Abuse Violations, by Age, 1992   160

15-4   Female Juvenile Arrest Trends for Alcohol- and Drug-
Related Offenses, 1983–92   161

15-5   Most Recent Alcohol Use by Female High School Seniors,
1992   162

16-1   Girls and Theft Crimes, 1992   169

16-2   Girls Arrested for Larceny-Theft, by Age, 1992   171

16-3   Trends in Girl Arrests for Larceny-Theft and Other Theft
Crimes, 1983–92   172

16-4   Women and Theft Crimes, 1992   175

16-5   Trends in Women's Arrests for Theft Crimes, 1983 and 1992   176

18-1   Girl Admissions to Local Jails, 1983–91   188

18-2   Juveniles Held in Private Facilities, by Sex, 1991   190

18-3   Juveniles Held in Public Facilities, by Sex, 1989   191

18-4   Girls Held in Public and Private Juvenile Facilities, 1979–89   192

18-5   Girls in Private Juvenile Facilities, by Type of Facility, 1991   193

19-1   Women Held in Local Jails, 1983 and 1992   200

19-2   Distribution of Female Jail Inmates, by Race and Ethnic
Origin, 1989   202

20-1   Female State and Federal Prisoners, 1981–93   216

20-2   Racial Distribution of State and Federal Female Prisoners,
1991   224

20-3   Ethnic Distribution of State and Federal Female Prisoners,
1991   225

20-4   Female New Court Commitments to State and Federal
Prison, by Type of Offense Incarcerated For, 1991   230

20-5 Drugs Used by Women State Prisoners in Month Before
         Offense, by Type of Drug, 1991   231

20-6 Female Recidivists in State Prison, 1991   232

TABLES

1-1 Female Arrests, 1992   6

1-2 Percent Distribution of Female Arrests, by Offense, 1992   9

1-3 Rate of Female Arrests, by Age and Offense, 1992   11

1-4 Arrests of Females, by Community Type, for Crime Index
        Offenses, 1992   12

1-5 Arrests of Females, by Community Type, for Nonindex
        Offenses, 1992   14

1-6 Female Arrest Trends, 1983–92   16

1-7 Females in Correctional Facilities in Recent Years   21

1-8 Percent Distribution of Single- and Multiple-Offender
        Victimizations Where Offender Was Perceived to Be
        Female, 1992   24

2-1 Female Arrests, Distribution by Age, 1992   28

2-2 Total Arrests, Percent Distribution by Race and Female
        Arrestees, 1992   32

2-3 Female Arrests, Ranked by Offense, 1992   34

2-4 New Court Commitments of Females to State Prison and
        Federal Prison by Offense, 1991   41

3-1 Total Arrests, Percent Distribution by Gender, 1992   45

3-2 Male–Female Arrest Ratios for Selected Crimes, by Offense
        and Age, 1992   48

3-3 Most Frequent Arrests, by Gender and Offense, 1992   50

3-4 Most Common Arrests of Juveniles, by Gender and Offense,
        1992   56

3-5 Property Crime Arrest Trends, by Gender, 1983–92   60

3-6 Juvenile Arrest Trends, by Gender, 1983–92   61

10-1 Most Serious Offenses of Women Inmates in Prison, by
         Drug Use History, 1991   122

15-1 Most Recent Drug Use by Female High School Seniors, by
         Drug Type, 1992   164

16-1 Percent of Female Arrests for Larceny-Theft, of Crime Index
          and Total Offense Arrests, by Age, 1992   170

18-1 Girls Held in Public Juvenile Facilities, by Type of Offenses
          and Reasons for Detention, 1989   194

19-1 Detention Status and Sentence Length of Female Jail
          Inmates, 1989   201

19-2 Children of Female Jail Inmates, by Race, 1989   204

19-3 Type of Offense Female Jail Inmates Held For, by
          Conviction Status and Race, 1989   206

19-4 Criminal History of Female Jail Inmates, by Most Serious
          Current Offense, 1989   208

19-5 Drug Use History of Convicted Female Inmates, 1989   210

20-1 Women in State or Federal Prisons, 1993   218

20-2 Sentenced Female Prisoners Admitted to State or Federal
          Jurisdiction, by Type of Admission, 1991   220

20-3 Sentenced Female Prisoners Released Conditionally or
          Unconditionally from State or Federal Jurisdiction, by
          Type of Release, 1991   221

20-4 Movement of Female Prisoners Under Sentence of Death,
          by Race, 1991   222

20-5 Characteristics of State Female Prison Inmates, 1991   226

20-6 Most Serious Offenses of Women in State Prisons, 1991   228

Preface

Fear of crime and victimization has become an epidemic in America. With the easy access to guns, drugs, and alcohol in the past few decades, we have seen a rise in violent crimes, property crimes, sex crimes, domestic crimes, white-collar crimes, and hidden crimes. A crime bill was finally passed, and signed on September 13, 1994. Even this new weapon against crime will not bring criminality to a halt. With too few law enforcement officers to go around, prison overcrowding forcing early release of repeat offenders, and ever-expanding means for perpetrating criminal acts, *real* crime control in the foreseeable future is tenuous at best.

Not too surprisingly, much of the research on crime and criminals has focused on male crime, since 8 out of every 10 persons arrested for crime in the United States are male. In addition, at least as high a percentage of the offenders are not identified or detected by authorities. However, female crime has grown steadily since the 1960s and at a rate higher than male crime. Criminologists, sociologists, psychologists, and other crime authorities have failed to keep pace in adequately addressing this increase in female crime and delinquency. The dearth of study on the female offender has left a void in our knowledge of the disparities in female and male criminality, the changing nature and scope of female criminal behavior, the differences between adult female and juvenile female crime, the characteristics of female criminals and delinquents, the factors and causes of female deviance, and the scope and dynamics of female inmates in juvenile and adult correctional facilities.

This book examines the participation of females in criminal and delinquent activities as we move toward the twenty-first century. It was written to promote a greater understanding and knowledge of women's and girls' crime, its dimensions, separateness, and relationship to male crime, and the situational and social-psychological variables that affect, influence, and deter female crime.

The work is suitable for undergraduate and graduate level study in the fields of women's studies, juvenile studies, criminology, criminal justice, sociology, psychology, human behavior, and related disciplines. *Female Crime, Criminals and Cellmates* was also written with a professional readership in mind, particularly researchers, legislators, social scientists, criminologists, medical practitioners, those in law enforcement, and others with a keen interest in female behavior and misbehavior. In addition, the book will appeal to the general reader who seeks educational, informational, and substantive discussion on the expanding female role in crime and delinquency in America.

I would like to acknowledge my administrative assistant, Bell Jar, for her tireless work in typing the text and countless tables and figures. Her devotion and professional expertise will shine brightly across the pages of this book for years to come.

Introduction

Female criminality has long been overshadowed by male criminality in terms of incidence, magnitude, seriousness, research, and recognition. As a result, we know relatively little about the modern female criminal: her motivations, diversity, complexities, incarceration, and victims. This is not to say that female crime has gone virtually unnoticed through the years. On the contrary, certain crimes have historically been considered largely female crimes, such as prostitution and shoplifting. However, these conclusions were often drawn from weak or sexist methodologies. Other crimes such as violent or white-collar crime that once seemed almost off-limits to female offenders may in fact be much more representative of female criminal behavior than previously believed. The reality is that women's and girls' crimes and delinquencies, similar to male criminality, are heterogeneous in nature. Equally, female offenders are neither easily nor singularly characterized, but in fact are varied in dimension, age, race, ethnicity, background, and their criminal behavior.

This study offers a multifaceted exploration of female criminals and delinquents—who they are, where they come from, what crimes they commit, why they perpetrate criminal and delinquent acts, and what elements characterize the incarceration of female offenders. It is complemented with relevant figures and tables.

Part I focuses on the extent of female crime in the United States: its nature and comparison to male crime. Part II examines early and influential theories on female criminality, and significant factors that relate to female delinquency and crime. Part III explores the criminality and deviance of women offenders, including homicidal women, women and family offenses, incestuous women, prostitution, drug

1

abuse, female white-collar criminals, female rapists, and women as con artists. Part IV concentrates on the criminality and delinquency of female juveniles, including runaways and prostitutes, their involvement with drugs and alcohol, juvenile thieves, and girls in gangs. Finally, Part V offers a comprehensive examination of females in the custody of correctional authorities, including girls in adult correctional institutions and juvenile detention facilities, and women in jails and prisons.

PART I

The Dynamics of Female Criminality

1. The Extent
of Female Crime

As we reach the mid–1990s, it is clear that female crime and delinquency can no longer be regarded in terms of them being insufficient, negligible, passive, or nonviolent. Although female criminality continues to be outdistanced by male criminality, females are committing more crimes today and are more heterogeneous in the types of offenses they commit. The trend toward equality of the sexes has not only given females access to more legitimate opportunities than ever before but also more illegitimate opportunities.

This chapter will examine the magnitude of female crime in the United States as seen through arrest, prisoner, and victimization data.

GAUGING THE SCOPE
OF FEMALE CRIMINALITY

To date, the most significant source for gathering and assessing information on female offenders is the Uniform Crime Reporting Program. Established in 1930 by the Federal Bureau of Investigation (FBI), the program collects crime statistics nationwide through voluntary reporting by city, county, and state law enforcement agencies representing 95 percent of the U.S. population. The data, which include arrest statistics, are presented annually through the FBI's *Crime in the United States: Uniform Crime Reports (UCR)*.

The *UCR* dichotomizes offenses into two classifications: part 1

TABLE 1-1
Female Arrests, 1992

Offense Charged	Ages under 15	Ages under 18	Ages 18 and over	Total all ages
TOTAL[a]	178,007	446,272	1,813,072	2,259,344
(Percent distribution[b])	(7.9)	(19.8)	(80.2)	(100.0)
Murder and nonnegligent manslaughter	35	159	1,740	1,899
Forcible rape	61	111	309	420
Robbery	1,317	3,447	9,635	13,082
Aggravated assault	3,933	10,497	54,042	64,539
Burglary	5,413	10,904	22,225	33,129
Larceny-theft	52,862	118,404	296,844	415,248
Motor vehicle theft	3,629	9,382	9,134	18,516
Arson	552	847	1,336	2,183
Violent crime[c]	5,346	14,214	65,726	79,940
(Percent distribution[b])	(6.7)	(17.8)	(82.2)	(100.0)
Property crime[d]	62,456	139,537	329,539	469,076
(Percent distribution[b])	(13.3)	(29.7)	(70.3)	(100.0)
Crime Index total[e]	67,802	153,751	395,265	549,016
(Percent distribution[b])	(12.3)	(28.0)	(72.0)	(100.0)
Other assaults	15,928	35,148	121,436	156,584
Forgery and counterfeiting	404	2,449	28,351	30,800
Fraud	1,236	3,959	141,989	145,948
Embezzlement	31	299	4,261	4,560

Stolen property; buying, receiving, possessing	17,077	13,178	3,899	1,339
Vandalism	29,625	19,531	10,094	5,283
Weapons; carrying, possessing, etc.	15,319	12,023	3,296	1,394
Prostitution and commercialized vice	56,808	56,244	564	81
Sex offenses (except forcible rape and prostitution)	7,020	5,817	1,203	711
Drug abuse violations	151,344	143,183	8,161	1,765
Gambling	2,087	2,011	76	15
Offenses against family and children	15,213	13,828	1,385	566
Driving under the influence	182,041	180,363	1,678	82
Liquor laws	85,316	57,419	27,897	4,164
Drunkenness	71,912	69,424	2,488	596
Disorderly conduct	124,690	100,604	24,086	9,459
Vagrancy	2,834	2,314	520	219
All other offenses (except traffic)	505,488	444,287	61,201	21,469
Suspicion	2,673	1,544	1,129	487
Curfew and loitering law violations	19,997		19,997	7,110
Runaways	82,992		82,992	37,866

[a] Based on 10,962 agencies; 1992 estimated population 213,392,000.

[b] Because of rounding, the percentages may not add to total.

[c] Violent crimes are offenses of murder, forcible rape, robbery, and aggravated assault.

[d] Property crimes are offenses of burglary, larceny-theft, motor vehicle theft, and arson.

[e] Includes arson.

Source: U.S. Federal Bureau of Investigation, *Crime in the United States: Uniform Crime Reports 1992* (Washington, D.C.: Government Printing Office, 1993), p. 231.

(Crime Index offenses) and part 2 (nonindex offenses). Part 1, the *Crime Index*, measures fluctuations in the total volume and rate of crime. It consists of eight offenses believed to represent the most serious, frequent, and reported crimes, including the violent crimes of *murder and nonnegligent manslaughter, forcible rape, robbery*, and *aggravated assault*; and property crimes of *burglary, larceny-theft, motor vehicle theft*, and *arson*.

Part 2, *nonindex offenses*, consists of 21 less serious crimes, including *simple* or *other assaults, fraud, vandalism, use of weapons, and carrying, possessing of such, prostitution and commercialized vice, driving under the influence, drug abuse violations*, and *runaways*.

According to the *UCR*, there were 2,259,344 female arrests in 1992 (see Table 1-1). More than 80 percent of the arrestees were age 18 and over, while just under 20 percent were under 18 years of age, and nearly 8 percent were under the age of 15.

More than 8 of every 10 arrests for violent crimes were of females age 18 and over; while over one-third of the females under 18 arrested for violent crimes were younger than age 15. For property crimes, female arrestees 18 and over accounted for just over 70 percent of the total arrests and those under 18 nearly 30 percent.

For Crime Index offenses, 72 percent of the female arrestees were age 18 and over, 28 percent under the age of 18, and 12.3 percent under 15.

Arrests of females in 1992 totaled 1,710,328 for nonindex offenses, representing 76 percent of all female arrests.

THE DISTRIBUTION OF FEMALE CRIME

Measuring how female arrests are distributed by crime can help us to understand the nature of female criminality and delinquency. Table 1-2 reflects the percent distribution of total female arrests in 1992. Nearly 25 percent of all arrests were for Crime Index offenses, including more than 20 percent for property crime. Among Crime Index offenses, arrests were highest for larceny-theft, accounting for 18.4 percent of total arrests for part 1 and part 2 offenses.

The highest overall percent of female arrests was for *all other offenses* (violations of state or local laws, excluding those related to vagrancy and traffic offenses). Over 22 percent of the total arrests were in this category. Other nonindex crimes were responsible for the next most common arrests of females, including driving under the influence

TABLE 1-2

Percent Distribution of
Female Arrests, by Offense, 1992

Offense Charged	Percent distribution[b]
TOTAL[a]	100.0
Murder and nonnegligent manslaughter	0.1
Forcible rape	[c]
Robbery	0.6
Aggravated assault	2.9
Burglary	1.5
Larceny-theft	18.4
Motor vehicle theft	0.8
Arson	0.1
Violent crime[d]	3.5
Property crime[e]	20.8
Crime Index total[f]	24.3
Other assaults	6.9
Forgery and counterfeiting	1.4
Fraud	6.5
Embezzlement	0.2
Stolen property; buying, receiving, possessing	0.8
Vandalism	1.3
Weapons; carrying, possessing, etc.	0.7
Prostitution and commercialized vice	2.5
Sex offenses (except forcible rape and prostitution)	0.3
Drug abuse violations	6.7
Gambling	0.1
Offenses against family and children	0.7
Driving under the influence	8.1
Liquor laws	3.8
Drunkenness	3.2
Disorderly conduct	5.5
Vagrancy	0.1
All other offenses (except traffic)	22.4

Table 1-2, *continued*

Offense Charged	Percent distribution[b]
Suspicion	0.1
Curfew and loitering law violations	0.9
Runaways	3.7

[a] Based on 10,962 agencies; 1992 estimated population 213,392,000.
[b] Because of rounding, the percentages may not add to total.
[c] Less than one-tenth of 1 percent.
[d] Violent crimes are offenses of murder, forcible rape, robbery, and aggravated assault.
[e] Property crimes are offenses of burglary, larceny-theft, motor vehicle theft, and arson.
[f] Includes arson.

Source: U.S. Federal Bureau of Investigation, *Crime in the United States: Uniform Crime Reports 1992* (Washington, D.C.: Government Printing Office, 1993), p. 234.

(8.1 percent), other assaults (6.9 percent), drug abuse violations (6.7 percent), and fraud (6.5 percent).

THE RATE OF FEMALE ARRESTS

Another way in which crime and criminals are measured is through crime and arrest rates. The *UCR* compares arrest and crime rates—relating the incidence of arrest or crime to population—for index offenses per 100,000 population. The rate of female arrests for total and serious crime in 1992 can be seen in Table 1-3. For all females, the rate of arrest was highest for larceny-theft, followed by aggravated assault. The arrest rate for property crime was nearly six times greater than that for violent crime.

Females aged 18 and over had a higher arrest rate than those under 18 for every offense except motor vehicle theft, where the rate was essentially the same. For all Crime Index offenses, the rate of arrests for females 18 and over was more than 2.5 times greater than that for females under 18.

For total crimes, the rate of female arrests was more than four times the rate for Crime Index arrests.

TABLE 1-3

Rate of Female Arrests, by Age and Offense, 1992

Offense	Rate per 100,000[a]		
	Total all ages	Ages under 18	Ages 18 and over
Murder and nonnegligent manslaughter	0.9	0.07	0.8
Forcible rape	0.2	0.05	0.1
Robbery	6.1	1.6	4.5
Aggravated assault	30.2	4.9	25.3
Burglary	15.5	5.1	10.4
Larceny-theft	194.6	55.5	139.1
Motor vehicle theft	8.7	4.4	4.3
Arson	1.0	0.4	0.6
Violent crime	37.5	6.7	30.8
Property crime	219.8	65.4	154.4
Crime Index total	257.3	72.1	185.2
Total Crimes	1058.8	209.1	849.6

[a] Rates are based on Crime Index offenses in which females were arrested in 1992.

Source: Adapted from U.S. Federal Bureau of Investigation, *Crime in the United States: Uniform Crime Reports 1992* (Washington, D.C.: Government Printing Office, 1993), p. 234.

COMPARISON OF FEMALE CRIME IN DIFFERENT TYPES OF COMMUNITIES

Like crime in general, female crime occurs in varying degrees of frequency in every geographic region and community in the United States. However, studies show that crime rates in Metropolitan Statistical Areas (MSAs)—including a central city or urbanized area of at least 50,000 inhabitants—generally have a higher volume and rate of crime than suburban and rural areas.[1]

TABLE 1-4

Arrests of Females, by Community Type, for Crime Index Offenses, 1992

Offense Charged	City	Community Size[a] Suburban County[b]	Rural County	Suburban Area[c]
Murder and nonnegligent manslaughter	1,401	302	196	481
Forcible rape	295	62	63	135
Robbery	11,647	1,211	224	2,834
Aggravated assault	51,374	9,209	3,956	19,574
Burglary	25,809	4,908	2,412	10,737
Larceny-theft	359,249	44,850	11,149	145,223
Motor vehicle theft	14,733	2,807	976	5,868
Arson	1,616	360	207	798
Violent crime	64,717	10,784	4,439	23,024
Property crime	401,407	52,925	14,744	162,626
Crime Index total	466,124	63,709	19,183	185,650
Total arrests	1,761,075	334,286	163,983	812,698

[a] Totals are based on different numbers of reporting agencies and population figures.
[b] Counties within an MSA, including the county containing a central city and other contiguous counties with strong socioeconomic ties to the central city.
[c] Includes cities with under 50,000 inhabitants and unincorporated areas within the MSA.

Source: Compiled from U.S. Federal Bureau of Investigation, *Crime in the United States: Uniform Crime Reports 1992* (Washington, D.C.: Government Printing Office, 1993), pp. 243, 252, 261, 270.

Table 1-4 compares Crime Index arrests of females in different community sizes in 1992. As we see, arrests in the city outpaced those occurring in the suburbs and rural counties. Arrests for crimes of violence were more than 14 times as likely to occur in cities than rural areas, and 6 times as often as in suburban counties.

An even greater disparity can be seen for property crime, where female arrests in cities were 27 times greater than those in rural counties, and 7.5 times that of arrests in suburban counties. The gap is not as great between arrests in cities and suburban areas, where the differential is 2.5 to 1 for all Crime Index offenses.

For total arrests, females were nearly 11 times more likely to be arrested in the city than rural counties, and better than 5 times as likely as in suburban counties.

Similar differences in female arrests by community type can be seen for nonindex offenses in 1992 (see Table 1-5). Despite the relationship between crime volume and rates and community size, specifically the more urbanized communities, some studies have shown crime in suburbia and rural America to be growing at a faster rate than inner city crime.[2]

TRENDS IN FEMALE CRIMINALITY

Arrest trends indicate that female crime is on the rise. Between 1983 and 1992, total female arrests increased 37.5 percent (see Table 1-6). Arrests for violent crimes grew nearly 73 percent. Motor vehicle thefts rose the most among Crime Index offenses during the period, increasing almost 105 percent.

Most nonindex offenses showed significant growth in female arrests over the ten years, including nearly a 145 percent increase in other or simple assaults and a 235.5 percent rise in arrests for offenses against family and children.

For females under 18 years of age, total arrests climbed 25.6 percent from 1983 to 1992. Arrests for Crime Index offenses grew by almost 31 percent, and violent crime by nearly 83 percent. Motor vehicle theft arrestees rose 148.5 percent; while arrests for forcible rape and aggravated assault increased by more than 91 percent.

Notable increases in arrests for nonindex offenses during the period of females younger than 18 can be seen in other assaults (+129.1 percent), carrying or possessing weapons (+147.4 percent), offenses against family and children (+200.7 percent), and runaways (+28.8 percent).

TABLE 1-5

Arrests of Females, by Community Type, for Nonindex Offenses, 1992

Offense Charged	Community Size[a]			
	City	Suburban County[b]	Rural County	Suburban Area[c]
Other assaults	123,647	22,380	10,557	54,996
Forgery and counterfeiting	22,680	5,382	2,738	11,577
Fraud	77,624	40,423	27,901	67,778
Embezzlement	3,373	816	371	1,557
Stolen property; buying, receiving, possessing	13,982	2,250	845	6,354
Vandalism	23,933	3,536	2,156	10,618
Weapons; carrying, possessing, etc.	12,573	2,090	656	4,734
Prostitution and commercialized vice	54,696	2,007	105	5,040
Sex offenses (except forcible rape and prostitution)	5,861	758	401	1,649
Drug abuse violations	117,861	24,175	9,308	46,410
Gambling	1,777	220	90	387
Offenses against family and children	11,346	2,483	1,384	5,389
Driving under the influence	116,249	38,480	27,312	83,985
Liquor laws	66,780	10,013	8,523	33,664
Drunkenness	60,127	6,335	5,450	22,734
Disorderly conduct	110,927	8,090	5,673	38,909
Vagrancy	2,571	208	55	613

All other offenses (except traffic)	380,499	88,842	36,147	194,620
Suspicion	2,480	153	40	461
Curfew and loitering law violations	18,820	670	507	6,490
Runaways	67,145	11,266	4,581	29,083
Total Nonindex Arrests	1,294,951	270,577	144,800	627,048
Total Arrests	1,761,075	334,286	163,983	812,698

[a]Totals are based on different numbers of reporting agencies and population figures.
[b]Counties within an MSA, including the county containing a central city and other contiguous counties with socioeconomic ties to the central city.
[c]Includes cities with under 50,000 inhabitants and unincorporated areas within the MSA.

Source: Adapted from U.S. Federal Bureau of Investigation, *Crime in the United States: Uniform Crime Reports 1992* (Washington, D.C.: Government Printing Office, 1993), pp. 243, 252, 261, 270.

TABLE 1-6
Female Arrest Trends, 1983–92

Offense Charged	Total			Under 18		
	1983	1992	Percent change	1983	1992	Percent change
TOTAL[a]	1,464,023	2,013,342	+37.5	318,775	400,241	+25.6
Murder and nonnegligent manslaughter	2,033	1,744	−14.2	129	149	+15.5
Forcible rape	245	359	+46.5	47	90	+91.5
Robbery	8,848	12,331	+39.4	2,068	3,245	+56.9
Aggravated assault	31,075	58,529	+88.3	4,871	9,527	+95.6
Burglary	25,412	30,611	+20.5	9,594	9,995	+4.2
Larceny-theft	297,414	376,906	+26.7	86,483	107,397	+24.2
Motor vehicle theft	8,373	17,147	+104.8	3,470	8,622	+148.5
Arson	1,838	1,961	+6.7	539	738	+36.9
Violent crime[b]	42,201	72,963	+72.9	7,115	13,011	+82.9
Property crime[c]	333,037	426,625	+28.1	100,086	126,752	+26.6
Crime Index total[d]	375,238	499,588	+33.1	107,201	139,763	+30.4
Other assaults	57,587	141,028	+144.9	13,961	31,984	+129.1
Forgery and counterfeiting	21,765	27,960	+28.5	1,940	2,212	+14.0
Fraud	87,490	115,006	+31.5	4,294	3,097	−27.9
Embezzlement	2,292	4,082	+78.1	122	262	+114.8
Stolen property; buying, receiving, possessing	11,234	15,590	+38.8	2,238	3,576	+59.8
Vandalism	16,909	26,380	+56.0	6,608	8,934	+35.2

Weapons; carrying, possessing, etc.	10,728	13,885	+29.4	1,226	3,033	+147.4
Prostitution and commercialized vice	72,911	54,600	-25.1	1,576	544	-65.5
Sex offenses (except forcible rape and prostitution)	5,089	6,615	+30.0	675	1,028	+52.3
Drug abuse violations	76,487	141,278	+84.7	10,552	7,576	-28.2
Gambling	3,499	1,836	-47.5	44	72	+63.6
Offenses against family and children	3,981	13,356	+235.5	410	1,233	+200.7
Driving under the influence	159,280	158,111	-0.7	2,741	1,417	-48.3
Liquor laws	57,580	70,176	+21.9	23,812	23,081	-3.1
Drunkenness	76,377	64,497	-15.6	4,019	2,239	-44.3
Disorderly conduct	81,283	110,692	+36.2	13,380	21,285	+59.1
Vagrancy	2,891	2,583	-10.7	351	479	+36.5
All other offenses (except traffic)	267,291	450,417	+68.5	50,630	54,254	+7.2
Suspicion	1,646	2,600	+58.0	530	1,110	+109.4
Curfew and loitering law violations	14,186	18,026	+27.1	14,186	18,026	+27.1
Runaways	58,279	75,036	+28.8	58,279	75,036	+28.8

[a] Based on 8,054 agencies; 1992 estimated population 185,616,000; 1983 estimated population 169,243,000.
[b] Violent crimes are offenses of murder, forcible rape, robbery, and aggravated assault.
[c] Property crimes are offenses of burglary, larceny-theft, motor vehicle theft, and arson.
[d] Includes arson.

Source: Calculated from U.S. Federal Bureau of Investigation, *Crime in the United States: Uniform Crime Reports 1992* (Washington, D.C.: Government Printing Office, 1993), p. 222.

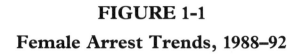

FIGURE 1-1

Female Arrest Trends, 1988–92

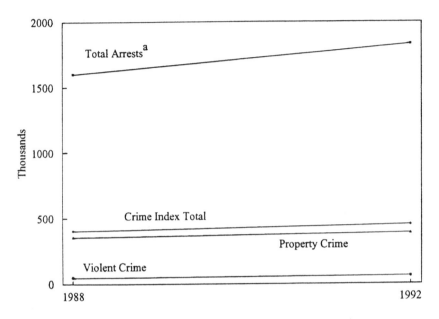

[a] Based on 7,937 agencies; 1992 estimated population 171,002,000; 1988 estimated population 165,051,000.

Source: Adapted from U.S. Federal Bureau of Investigation, *Crime in the United States: Uniform Crime Reports 1992* (Washington, D.C.: Government Printing Office, 1993), p. 224.

The five-year arrest trends from 1988 to 1992 also reveal an increase in female arrests, though not quite as high (Figure 1-1). Overall arrests over the period rose 14.4 percent, violent crime arrestees grew 32.5 percent, and arrests for Crime Index offenses increased more than 12 percent.

Long-term arrest trends put crime fluctuations in a more meaningful perspective. Figure 1-2 charts female arrest trends from 1960 to 1992 for serious crimes. Between 1960 and 1992, female arrests for Crime Index offenses increased 922.7 percent, property crime arrestees grew by 1007.4 percent, and females arrested for violent crimes rose by 619.6 percent.

FIGURE 1-2

Female Arrest Trends for Crime Index Offenses, 1960–92

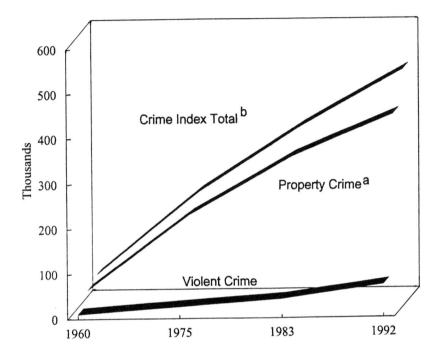

[a] Arson was added in 1979 and thus is included in the property crime figures for 1983 and 1992.

[b] The number of law enforcement agencies reporting data on arrests may vary from year to year.

Source: Constructed from U.S. Federal Bureau of Investigation, *Crime in the United States: Uniform Crime Reports 1960, 1975, 1983, 1992* (Washington, D.C.: Government Printing Office, 1961, 1976, 1984, 1993).

What these trends tell us is that female involvement in violent, property, and nonindex crimes and arrests have risen steadily over the years. What they do not tell us is why. Subsequent chapters will address this issue. We can assume that while females are undoubtedly committing more offenses in the 1990s than in previous decades, the relative weight of those crimes on society is still small compared to

their male counterparts. Nevertheless, this should not distract from the severity of the growing problem of female crime and delinquency.

CRITICISM OF *UNIFORM CRIME REPORTS*

In spite of the importance of official statistics in law enforcement administration and management as well as the study of arrest patterns, crime, and offenders, the Uniform Crime Reporting Program is not without its weaknesses.

Edwin Sutherland and Donald Cressey point out the unreliability of official statistics in measuring criminality:

> The statistics about crime and delinquency are probably the most unreliable and most difficult of all statistics. It is impossible to determine with accuracy the amount of crime in any given jurisdiction or any particular time. Some behavior is labeled "delinquent" or "crime" by one observer, but not by another. Obviously a large proportion of all law violations go undetected. Other crimes are detected but not reported and still others are reported but not officially recorded.[3]

Charles Shireman and Frederic Reamer advanced that official data's limitations exist in the "unknown relationship between the number of crimes actually committed, the number of those reported to the police, and the number of those so reported actually recorded and reported by the police."[4]

The most common criticisms directed toward *Uniform Crime Reports* and official statistics include the following:

- Official data reflect only those offenses law enforcement agencies are aware of.
- Statistics are not gathered for all crimes.
- For various reasons (that is, fear or lack of knowledge), many people fail to report crime and victimization.
- Law enforcement agencies may be politically motivated or have other reasons in underreporting crime or inflating arrest statistics.
- The overreliance on percent changes in the total volume of Crime Index offenses.
- The overlapping of defining a crime (that is, arrest, charged, guilty, and incarceration).

TABLE 1-7

Females in Correctional
Facilities in Recent Years

Type of Institution	Year	Female Inmates
State prison	1992	44,010
Federal prison	1992	6,399
Local jail	1992	40,674
Total		91,083
Public juvenile facilities	1989	6,680
Private juvenile facilities	1991	10,389
Total[a]		17,069
Total Females in Custody[a]		108,152

[a] Since figures from the same year were not available for comparison, the total is an approximation.

Source: Derived from U.S. Department of Justice, *Prisoners in 1992* (Washington, D.C.: Government Printing Office, 1993), p. 4; U.S. Department of Justice, *Jail Inmates 1992* (Washington, D.C.: Government Printing Office, 1993), p. 2; U.S. Department of Justice, *Sourcebook of Criminal Justice Statistics—1992* (Washington, D.C.: Government Printing Office, 1993), pp. 577, 579.

- The variance of *UCR* statistics.
- The differential enforcement of criminal statistics.
- The voluntary nature of reporting arrests and crime data.
- Insufficient information on crime victims and victimization.

In addition, the *UCR* Program is based entirely on crime figures and fluctuations reported by local law enforcement agencies, ignoring other national and local data and reports that could provide for a more complete picture of crime and criminals in the United States.

FEMALES IN CUSTODY

A second means for identifying female criminals and assessing female crime is through females being held in adult and juvenile correctional facilities. Table 1-7 shows the number of female prison and jail inmates in the United States in 1992, and the number of females in U.S. public and private juvenile facilities in 1989 and 1991, respectively.

In 1992, there was a total of 91,083 females in prison or jail in this country, including 50,409 state and federal prisoners. This represented nearly a 6 percent increase over the female prison inmate population in 1991. The rate of incarceration for sentenced females in 1992 was 35 per 100,000 females in the resident population. Women made up 5.7 percent of the nation's prisoners in 1992.[5]

Women in jails increased 3 percent between 1991 and 1992. More than half the female jail population during 1992 was convicted of a crime. An estimated 1 in every 2,417 women in the United States were in a local jail on June 30, 1992.[6]

The data for females held in juvenile detention indicate that more females are in private juvenile than public juvenile facilities. In total, more than 108,000 females were in custody for the years shown. Refer to part 5 for further discussion on the extent and nature of female incarceration.

The Shortcomings of Female Inmate Data

Similar to official arrest statistics, prisoner statistics have drawbacks with respect to measuring female criminality. Since most females who commit crimes are never detected, arrested, and incarcerated, female prisoners are not entirely representative of all female offenders. Additionally, differential enforcement of the law, and race, social class, and other biases may affect the makeup of the female prison population, limiting its relationship to female crime in the general population.

Information on female juveniles in custody is flawed by the lack of current data available, as well as the fact that most such data concentrate on females in juvenile facilities, though many female juvenile offenders spend some time in jails and/or prisons.

FEMALE OFFENDERS
AND VICTIMIZATION DATA

Crime victimization surveys provide a third methodology for gauging the nature and extent of female criminality. The most comprehensive victimization survey is conducted by the U.S. Department of Justice's Bureau of Justice Statistics. Begun in 1972 and administered by the Bureau of the Census, the annual national survey is entitled: *Criminal Victimization in the United States: A National Crime Victimization Survey (NCVS)*. Using a representative sample of about 110,000 respondents age 12 or over living in approximately 66,000 housing units, the *NCVS* focuses its survey on specific crimes and crime victims who "not only are willing to report the crime but also understand what happened and how it happened."[7]

The *NCVS* measures victimization and victim and offender characteristics associated with certain criminal offenses, including the *personal crimes* of *rape, robbery, assault,* and *larceny;* and the *household crimes* of *burglary, larceny,* and *motor vehicle theft.* According to the *NCVS* released in 1994, 13.1 percent of approximately 4.6 million single-offender violent crime victimizations in 1992 were perceived by victims to have been committed by female offenders (see Table 1-8), representing over 600,000 such victimizations attributed to female perpetrators.

For completed single-offender crimes of violence, 14.5 percent of the offenders were perceived to be females. Nearly 15 percent of the 3.9 million single-offender assaults reported to the *NCVS* were believed to have been committed by females. The percent of female offenders was highest for simple assaults at 16.7 percent of the total.

Over 114,000 or 6.2 percent of the multiple-offender violent victimizations in 1992 were perceived to be perpetrated by female only offenders. More than 10 percent of the simple assaults by multiple offenders were reported as having been committed by all female perpetrators.

Of the multiple-offender violent victimizations in which the offenders were perceived as female and male, there were more than 264,900 victimizations, or 14.4 percent of all multiple-offender victimizations. Over 16 percent of the multiple-offender completed crimes of violence were believed to have been committed by both female and male offenders.

The Limitations of Victimization Surveys

Victimization surveys are an important complement to official data in examining crime fluctuations and circumstances. However, there are serious limitations that weaken the data such surveys supply.

TABLE 1-8

Percent Distribution of Single- and Multiple-Offender Victimizations Where Offender Was Perceived to Be Female, 1992

Type of Crime	Number of single-offender victimizations	Percent of perceived female offenders	Number of multiple-offender victimizations	Percent of perceived female only offenders	Percent of perceived female and male offenders
Crimes of violence	4,587,560	13.1	1,839,780	6.2	14.4
Completed	1,495,370	14.5	837,810	4.1[a]	16.4
Attempted	3,092,180	12.5	1,001,960	7.9	12.8
Rape	97,700	3.6[a]	40,120	8.4[a]	11.3[a]
Robbery	593,290	3.9[a]	591,830	3.3[a]	12.3
Completed	370,880	4.3[a]	406,360	3.2[a]	15.4
With injury	147,920	3.7[a]	166,910	3.1[a]	9.7[a]
Without injury	222,950	4.7[a]	239,440	3.2[a]	19.4
Attempted	222,400	3.1[a]	185,470	3.5[a]	5.3[a]
With injury	33,100[a]	0.0[a]	61,920	0.0[a]	5.2[a]
Without injury	189,300	3.7[a]	123,550	5.2[a]	5.4[a]
Assault	3,896,560	14.8	1,207,810	7.5	15.6
Aggravated	1,098,860	9.9	658,090	5.1[a]	13.8
Simple	2,797,700	16.7	549,720	10.4	17.8

Note: Figures may not add to total due to rounding.

[a] Estimate is based on about 10 or fewer sample cases.

Source: Derived from U.S. Department of Justice, *Criminal Victimization in the United Staes, 1992: A National Crime Victimization Survey Report* (Washington, D.C.: Government Printing Office, 1994), pp. 59, 63.

The most obvious is that any survey must rely on the honesty of the respondent as well as their willingness to cooperate and the accuracy of interpretation (for example, perception of offender characteristics).

A second drawback is the fact that only respondents age 12 and over are interviewed, leaving many younger victims and their perceptions unaccounted for. *NCVS* surveys further exclude serious crimes such as murder and kidnapping, and so-called "victimless" crimes like prostitution and drug abuse. Finally, the *NCVS* staffers do not attempt to validate reported victimization by cross-checking it with police records or other data.

2. The Nature
of Female Crime

Now that we have explored the extent of female crime, we need to examine its nature. What age groups are responsible for the most female crime? What racial or ethnic groups commit the most female crimes? How does class relate to female crime? What types of crimes are females most and least likely to commit?

AGE AND FEMALE CRIMINALITY

We know that more than 80 percent of the females arrested for crimes are 18 years of age and over. What does this mean in terms of specific age groups, arrests, and offenses for which females of different ages are charged? Table 2-1 distributes female arrests in 1992 by various age groupings from under 10 to 65 and over. We can see that among individual ages, the highest percentage of overall arrests were of females aged 15 and 16 at 14.1 percent, with arrest percentages fairly even between the ages of 17 and 24. Arrest figures indicate that female arrests peak at age 16, drop only slightly through age 29, and decline with each succeeding age group.

For Crime Index offenses, most arrests of females are in the age 15 to 18 category, with arrests peaking at age 15, comprising 5.5 percent of the total arrests. The next highest age group for Crime Index offense arrests were those ages 19 to 24, each age accounting for more than 3 percent of all arrests. Violent crime arrests were highest for ages 15 and

21 but show a pattern of consistency and comparable percentages for females aged 15 to 29.

The patterns for nonindex crime arrests are generally similar to that for Crime Index offenses, that is, many of the arrests fall into the 15 to 29 age groups, with younger, preteen females and those 40 and over showing the lowest percent of arrests for all offenses. The exception is arrests as runaways, where the peak ages were 13 to 16, with all arrests of females ages under 10 to 17.

For other nonindex offenses, the peak age groups for arrests tend to vary with the offense. For example, arrests for prostitution and commercialized vice peaked in the 25 to 29 age group; while arrests for driving under the influence peaked at ages 30 to 34.

FEMALE CRIME, RACE, AND ETHNICITY

Official data does not break down female arrests by race or ethnicity. However, studies have shown that patterns of arrest tend to be similar for females and males along racial and ethnic lines.[1] Table 2-2 reflects the racial distribution for arrests in 1992, along with the percent of females arrested for all offenses.

We see that of persons arrested, nearly 68 percent were white, while black arrestees accounted for more than 30 percent of arrests. Other racial groups such as American Indians and Asians made up about 2 percent of the persons arrested.

Blacks comprised almost 45 percent of the violent crime arrestees, while whites constituted nearly 54 percent of the arrestees. Blacks were arrested disproportionately in relation to their population figures.

Nineteen percent of all arrestees were female in 1992. For Crime Index offenses this percentage rose to just over 22 percent, while 25.5 percent of all arrests for property crimes were of females.

Some studies have compared the criminality of white and black women. Marvin Wolfgang found black female crime to be closer to black male crime than white female crime to white male crime.[2] Another study concluded that "the black female's criminality exceeds that of the white female by a much greater margin than black males over white males."[3] In a study of female prisoners in 14 states, R. W. Glick and V. V. Neto found that though black women constituted only 10 percent of the adult female population in those states, they accounted for 50 percent of the women incarcerated.[4]

According to the Bureau of Justice Statistics, 49.1 percent of the

TABLE 2-1

Female Arrests, Distribution by Age, 1992

Offense Charged	Under 10	10–12	13–14	15	16	17	18	19	20	21
AGE										
TOTAL[a]	6,598	36,856	134,553	93,653	92,182	82,430	80,875	82,938	82,452	83,783
Percent distribution[b]	0.3	1.6	6.0	4.1	4.1	3.6	3.6	3.7	3.6	3.7
Murder and nonnegligent manslaughter	0	7	28	34	43	47	66	60	83	69
Forcible rape	6	17	38	24	10	16	14	20	13	17
Robbery	12	195	1,110	833	685	612	579	505	512	522
Aggravated assault	104	791	3,038	2,192	2,269	2,103	2,065	2,148	2,228	2,484
Burglary	411	1,496	3,506	2,023	1,836	1,632	1,436	1,408	1,200	1,118
Larceny-theft	2,250	14,134	36,478	22,528	22,331	20,683	18,200	16,027	14,146	13,777
Motor vehicle theft	31	420	3,178	2,387	2,006	1,360	855	697	575	548
Arson	72	167	313	124	102	69	47	41	42	53
Violent crime[c]	122	1,010	4,214	3,083	3,007	2,778	2,724	2,733	2,836	3,092
Percent distribution[b]	0.2	1.3	5.3	3.9	3.8	3.5	3.4	3.4	3.5	3.9
Property crime[d]	2,764	16,217	43,475	27,062	26,275	23,744	20,538	18,173	15,963	15,496
Percent distribution[b]	0.6	3.5	9.3	5.8	5.6	5.1	4.4	3.9	3.4	3.3
Crime Index total[e]	2,886	17,227	47,689	30,145	29,282	26,522	23,262	20,906	18,799	18,588
Percent distribution[b]	0.5	3.1	8.7	5.5	5.3	4.8	4.2	3.8	3.4	3.4
Other assaults	547	3,649	11,732	7,000	6,494	5,726	5,388	5,358	5,501	6,018
Forgery and counterfeiting	16	73	315	405	618	1,022	1,292	1,519	1,614	1,429

Offense										
Fraud	25	183	1,028	958	656	1,109	2,816	4,514	5,799	6,639
Embezzlement	1	10	20	10	63	195	183	236	293	287
Stolen property; buying, receiving, possessing	24	228	1,087	849	834	877	872	883	790	800
Vandalism	516	1,490	3,277	1,637	1,638	1,536	1,112	1,063	1,057	1,050
Weapons; carrying, possessing, etc.	33	268	1,093	682	627	593	562	524	537	634
Prostitution and commercialized vice	9	3	69	71	129	283	982	1,603	1,808	2,536
Sex offenses (except forcible rape and prostitution)	94	221	396	184	160	148	177	217	245	265
Drug abuse violations	32	206	1,527	1,494	2,134	2,768	4,156	4,681	5,012	5,728
Gambling	2	2	11	9	20	32	26	28	27	41
Offenses against family and children	56	112	398	308	268	243	399	430	515	593
Driving under the influence	25	6	51	103	483	1,010	2,603	3,554	4,591	7,149
Liquor laws	54	365	3,745	5,061	7,887	10,785	13,658	12,271	9,400	2,546
Drunkenness	11	60	525	511	601	780	1,326	1,583	1,605	2,243
Disorderly conduct	357	2,055	7,047	5,015	4,944	4,668	5,043	4,910	4,946	5,663
Vagrancy	0	35	184	113	100	88	126	119	79	102
All other offenses (except traffic)	1,273	4,032	16,164	11,900	13,283	14,549	16,825	18,478	19,781	21,410
Suspicion	17	78	392	304	279	59	67	61	53	62
Curfew and loitering law violations	80	997	6,033	4,867	4,886	3,134	0	0	0	0
Runaways	540	5,556	31,770	22,027	16,796	6,303	0	0	0	0

TABLE 2-1, *continued*

AGE

Offense Charged	22	23	24	25-29	30-34	35-39	40-44	45-49	50-54	55-59	60-64	65 and over
TOTAL[a]	81,370	77,824	78,909	387,827	349,705	235,830	128,452	65,253	33,325	17,800	11,168	15,561
Percent distribution[b]	3.6	3.4	3.5	17.2	15.5	10.4	5.7	2.9	1.5	0.8	0.5	0.7
Murder and nonnegligent manslaughter	85	82	56	343	311	223	156	87	57	30	12	20
Forcible rape	14	12	10	71	65	44	13	5	2	1	0	8
Robbery	477	442	534	2,446	1,930	1,066	382	147	41	23	11	18
Aggravated assault	2,458	2,414	2,393	12,013	10,842	7,237	3,650	1,963	1,014	509	264	360
Burglary	1,111	1,035	1,038	4,947	4,072	2,613	1,237	551	246	99	53	61
Larceny-theft	12,762	11,898	12,345	56,650	50,207	35,112	20,872	12,138	7,415	4,931	3,890	6,474
Motor vehicle theft	473	555	485	1,979	1,525	813	350	148	66	23	15	27
Arson	49	50	30	265	263	194	126	87	32	29	17	11
Violent crime[c]	3,034	2,950	2,993	14,873	13,148	8,570	4,201	2,202	1,114	563	287	406
Percent distribution[b]	3.8	3.7	3.7	18.6	16.4	10.7	5.3	2.8	1.4	0.7	0.4	0.5
Property crime[d]	14,395	13,538	13,898	63,841	56,067	38,732	22,585	12,924	7,759	5,082	3,975	6,573
Percent distribution[b]	3.1	2.9	3.0	13.6	12.0	8.3	4.8	2.8	1.7	1.1	0.8	1.4
Crime Index total[e]	17,429	16,488	16,891	78,714	69,215	47,302	26,786	15,126	8,873	5,645	4,262	6,979
Percent distribution[b]	3.2	3.0	3.1	14.3	12.6	8.6	4.9	2.8	1.6	1.0	0.8	1.3
Other assaults	5,840	5,479	5,501	27,298	23,296	15,192	7,997	4,081	2,013	1,027	591	856
Forgery and counterfeiting	1,491	1,218	1,312	6,413	5,443	3,361	1,804	848	301	166	63	77
Fraud	6,683	6,740	6,864	31,223	26,903	20,073	11,850	5,885	2,858	1,351	785	1,006
Embezzlement	254	205	218	816	676	462	332	151	78	38	18	14
Stolen property; buying, receiving, possessing	707	591	593	2,772	2,293	1,501	752	328	162	60	33	41

Vandalism	1,062	964	931	4,383	3,458	2,166	1,099	528	308	150	71	129
Weapons; carrying, possessing, etc.	604	548	521	2,487	2,113	1,508	884	494	283	134	92	98
Prostitution and commercialized vice	2,968	2,880	3,046	16,303	13,617	7,058	2,476	688	172	61	20	26
Sex offenses (except forcible rape and prostitution)	319	292	275	1,514	1,197	702	347	141	55	33	14	24
Drug abuse violations	6,004	6,142	6,298	35,484	33,214	20,861	9,553	3,601	1,349	573	273	254
Gambling	44	32	41	259	272	301	270	233	177	122	56	82
Offenses against family and children	606	624	590	3,007	3,002	2,127	1,017	444	230	104	59	81
Driving under the influence	7,162	7,099	6,962	37,657	38,573	27,426	17,022	9,823	5,042	2,691	1,563	1,446
Liquor laws	1,703	1,273	1,094	4,570	4,046	2,827	1,751	1,038	528	310	188	216
Drunkenness	2,186	2,210	2,348	13,852	15,850	11,656	6,735	3,825	1,895	951	566	593
Disorderly conduct	5,351	5,038	4,999	23,394	18,494	11,530	5,879	2,869	1,527	773	478	710
Vagrancy	113	89	127	519	445	312	147	55	33	21	5	22
All other offenses (except traffic)	20,781	19,842	20,211	97,803	87,267	59,246	31,665	15,054	7,421	3,582	2,026	2,905
Suspicion	63	70	87	359	331	219	96	41	20	8	5	2
Curfew and loitering law violations	0	0	0	0	0	0	0	0	0	0	0	0
Runaways	0	0	0	0	0	0	0	0	0	0	0	0

[a]Based on 10,962 agencies; 1992 estimated population 213,392,000.
[b]Because of rounding, the percentages may not add to total.
[c]Violent crimes are offenses of murder, forcible rape, robbery, and aggravated assault.
[d]Property crimes are offenses of burglary, larceny-theft, motor vehicle theft, and arson.
[e]Includes arson.

Source: U.S. Federal Bureau of Investigation, *Crime in the United States: Uniform Crime Reports 1992* (Washington, D.C.: Government Printing Office, 1993), pp. 231, 232.

TABLE 2-2

Total Arrests, Percent Distribution by Race and Female Arrestees, 1992

Offense Charged	Total arrests	Percent female	Percent Distribution by Race				
			Total	White	Black	American Indian or Alaskan Native	Asian or Pacific Islander
TOTAL	11,876,204	19.0	100.0	67.6	30.3	1.1	1.0
Murder and nonnegligent manslaughter	19,463	9.7	100.0	43.5	55.1	0.5	0.8
Forcible rape	33,332	1.3	100.0	55.5	42.8	0.9	0.9
Robbery	153,246	8.5	100.0	37.7	60.9	0.4	0.9
Aggravated assault	434,471	14.8	100.0	59.5	38.8	0.8	0.8
Burglary	359,306	9.2	100.0	67.8	30.4	0.8	1.0
Larceny-theft	1,290,278	32.1	100.0	66.2	31.4	1.1	1.4
Motor vehicle theft	171,136	10.8	100.0	58.4	39.4	0.8	1.4
Arson	16,275	13.4	100.0	76.4	21.9	0.8	0.8
Violent crime[a]	640,512	12.5	100.0	53.6	44.8	0.7	0.8
Property crime[b]	1,836,995	25.5	100.0	65.8	31.8	1.0	1.3
Crime Index total	2,477,507	22.1	100.0	62.7	35.2	0.9	1.2
Other assaults	911,374	17.2	100.0	64.2	33.8	1.2	0.9
Forgery and counterfeiting	88,573	34.7	100.0	64.8	33.6	0.6	1.0
Fraud	345,768	42.1	100.0	64.6	34.4	0.4	0.5
Embezzlement	11,699	39.0	100.0	68.6	29.7	0.4	1.3

Offense	Number		Total				
Stolen property; buying, receiving, possessing	136,411	12.5	100.0	56.9	41.7	0.6	0.9
Vandalism	262,084	11.3	100.0	76.2	21.9	1.0	0.9
Weapons; carrying, possessing, etc.	203,739	7.5	100.0	56.6	41.8	0.5	1.1
Prostitution and commercialized vice	86,932	65.3	100.0	62.0	36.3	0.6	1.1
Sex offenses (except forcible rape and prostitution)	91,454	7.7	100.0	79.1	18.9	0.9	1.0
Drug abuse violations	919,561	16.4	100.0	59.4	39.6	0.4	0.6
Gambling	15,021	13.9	100.0	47.9	45.0	0.4	6.7
Offenses against family and children	83,770	18.0	100.0	67.0	29.2	1.2	2.6
Driving under the influence	1,317,968	13.8	100.0	87.7	10.1	1.4	0.9
Liquor laws	441,781	19.3	100.0	85.6	10.7	2.7	0.9
Drunkenness	663,573	10.8	100.0	80.6	17.1	2.1	0.3
Disorderly conduct	604,612	20.6	100.0	65.2	32.9	1.3	0.6
Vagrancy	28,611	9.8	100.0	50.9	47.5	1.3	0.4
All other offenses (except traffic)	2,950,424	17.1	100.0	61.7	36.2	1.0	1.1
Suspicion	15,336	17.4	100.0	49.4	49.8	0.2	0.7
Curfew and loitering law violations	74,428	26.8	100.0	76.3	21.0	0.9	1.8
Runaways	145,578	56.8	100.0	78.5	17.3	1.1	3.1

Note: Because of rounding, percentages may not add to total.

[a]Violent crimes are offenses of murder, forcible rape, robbery, and aggravated assault.
[b]Property crimes are offenses of burglary, larceny-theft, motor vehicle theft, and arson.

Source: Derived from U.S. Federal Bureau of Investigation, *Crime in the United States: Uniform Crime Reports 1992* (Washington, D.C.: Government Printing Office, 1993), pp. 234, 235.

TABLE 2-3

Female Arrests, Ranked by Offense, 1992

Rank	Most Frequent Arrests by Offense	Rank	Least Frequent Arrests by Offense
1	All other offenses (except traffic)	1	Forcible rape
2	Larceny-theft	2	Murder and nonnegligent manslaughter
3	Driving under the influence	3	Gambling
4	Other assaults	4	Arson
5	Drug abuse violations	5	Suspicion
6	Fraud	6	Vagrancy
7	Disorderly conduct	7	Embezzlement
8	Liquor laws	8	Sex offenses (except forcible rape and prostitution)
9	Runaways	9	Robbery
10	Drunkenness	10	Offenses against family and children

Source: Compiled from U.S. Federal Bureau of Investigation, *Crime in the United States: Uniform Crime Reports 1992* (Washington, D.C.: Government Printing Office, 1993), p. 234.

female prisoners under state or federal jurisdiction in 1991 were black, 46.4 white, 1.1 Native Americans, and 0.4 percent Asian or Pacific Islander.[5]

Hispanic women are also overrepresented in the prison population, accounting for 11.6 percent of all female prisoners in 1991.[6]

FEMALE CRIME AND CLASS

There does not appear to be a strong relationship between female criminality and class differences. However, some researchers have found that female arrestees and inmates are disproportionately poor and undereducated.[7] In general, an inverse relationship has been established between social class and adult street crime.[8] In a review of 46 studies that used official arrest statistics, it was found that lower-class adults had consistently higher crime rates than middle- and upper-class adults.[9]

Similarly, a review of studies examining the relationship between class and delinquency found that in 44 of 53 studies using official data, lower-class juveniles had higher rates of delinquency than did middle-class juveniles.[10]

THE FREQUENCY OF FEMALE CRIMES

Females are arrested far more often for nonviolent than violent crimes. Many of the female arrests tend to be for offenses related to alcohol and drug use or abuse. Table 2-3 lists the 10 most frequent and least frequent offenses in which females were arrested in 1992. Females were arrested most often for the category "all other offenses," or violations of state and local laws. Larceny-theft accounted for the second most frequent arrests, comprising nearly 20 percent of all female arrests. Four of the top 10 most common arrests of females involved alcohol or drugs.

Females were arrested least often for four of the Crime Index offenses, including murder and nonnegligent manslaughter and arson. Other offenses among the lowest in female arrest figures included gambling, vagrancy, and suspicion.

FIGURE 2-1

The Distribution of
Female Property Crimes, 1992

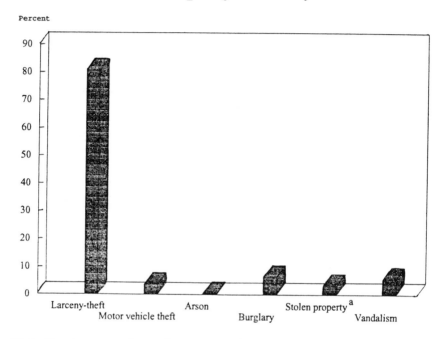

Note: Based on arrest figures for property crimes in 1992.

[a] Buying, receiving and/or possessing.

Source: Calculated from U.S. Department of Justice, *Crime in the United States: Uniform Crime Reports 1992* (Washington, D.C.: Government Printing Office, 1993), p. 231.

PROPERTY CRIME

Property crimes account for more female arrests than any other type of violation of the law. The distribution of female property crime arrests in 1992 can be seen in Figure 2-1. More than 8 of every 10 female arrests for property crimes was for larceny-theft. Burglary and vandalism constituted the second and third highest percentage of arrests respectively, combining for just over 12 percent. Motor vehicle

FIGURE 2-2

The Distribution of
Female Violent Crimes, 1992

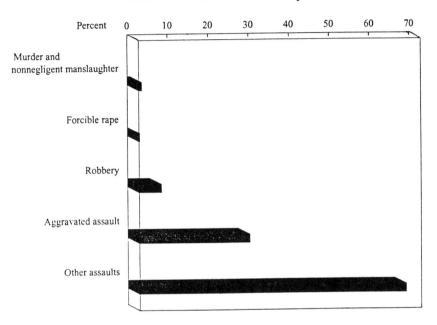

Note: Based on arrest figures for property crimes in 1992.

Source: Calculated from U.S. Department of Justice, *Crime in the United States: Uniform Crime Reports 1992* (Washington, D.C.: Government Printing Office, 1993), p. 231.

---

theft and stolen property offenses accounted for less than 7 percent of all female property crime arrests; while the fewest arrests came for arson at less than 1 percent.

VIOLENT CRIME

Relatively few female crimes are of a violent nature. Most such crimes tend to be assaultive crimes (see Figure 2-2). Other assaults, or

FIGURE 2-3

The Distribution of Female
White-Collar Offenses, 1992

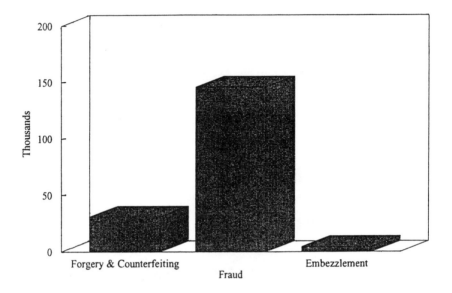

Note: Based on arrest figures for property crimes in 1992.

Source: Calculated from U.S. Department of Justice, *Crime in the United States: Uniform Crime Reports 1992* (Washington, D.C.: Government Printing Office, 1993), p. 234.

nonaggravated assaults, accounted for 66 percent of all female arrests for violent or personal crimes in 1992. Aggravated assaults constituted just over 27 percent of female arrestees, robbery under 6 percent, and murder and forcible rape 1 percent combined.

WHITE-COLLAR OFFENSES

Female white-collar offenses have soared since the 1960s (see chapters 3 and 11). As shown in Figure 2-3, arrest statistics for 1992 reveal that more than 80 percent of the female arrests for white-collar crimes (including forgery and counterfeiting, fraud, and embezzlement)

FIGURE 2-4

The Distribution of Female Alcohol- and Drug-Related Offenses, 1992

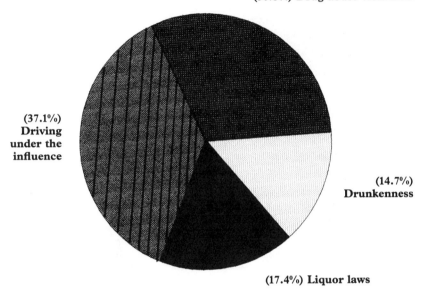

(30.8%) Drug abuse violations

(37.1%) Driving under the influence

(14.7%) Drunkenness

(17.4%) Liquor laws

Source: Calculated from U.S. Department of Justice, *Crime in the United States: Uniform Crime Reports 1992* (Washington, D.C.: Government Printing Office, 1993), p. 234.

were for fraud. Forgery and counterfeiting accounted for 17 percent of the arrests, while embezzlement made up only 2.5 percent of the white-collar offense arrests.

ALCOHOL- AND DRUG-RELATED OFFENSES

Studies indicate most female crime is related to use of alcohol and/or drugs.[11] Female arrests for drug- and alcohol-related offenses in 1992 can be seen in Figure 2-4. Alcohol-related crimes accounted

FIGURE 2-5

The Distribution of
Female Sex Offenses, 1992

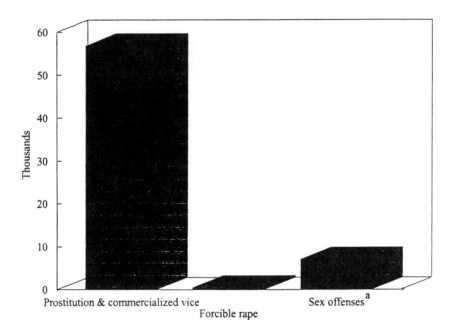

Note: Based on arrest figures for property crimes in 1992.

[a] Except forcible rape and prostitution.

Source: Calculated from U.S. Department of Justice, *Crime in the United States: Uniform Crime Reports 1992* (Washington, D.C.: Government Printing Office, 1993), p. 231.

---

for nearly 70 percent of the female arrests, while driving under the influence made up over 37 percent of the arrests for drug- and alcohol-related crimes. Drug abuse violations were responsible for nearly 31 percent of all arrests for substance abuse offenses. Liquor law violations and drunkenness constituted 17.4 percent and 14.7 percent of the female arrests, respectively.

TABLE 2-4

New Court Commitments
of Females to State Prison and
Federal Prison by Offense, 1991

Most Serious Offense	Percent of New Court Commitments[a] to State Prison[b]
All offenses	100.0
Violent offenses	16.7
Homicide	4.4
Murder/nonnegligent manslaughter	2.5
Murder	1.8
Nonnegligent manslaughter	0.6
Negligent manslaughter	1.8
Unspecified homicide	0.1
Kidnapping	0.2
Rape	0.2
Other sexual assault	0.4
Robbery	5.3
Assault	5.2
Other violent	1.0
Property offenses	35.4
Burglary	5.2
Larceny/theft	15.1
Motor vehicle theft	0.9
Arson	0.7
Fraud	11.7
Stolen property	1.3
Other property	0.4
Drug offenses	40.9
Possession	9.5
Trafficking	23.1
Other/unspecified drug	8.3
Public-order offenses	5.7
Weapons	0.7
Driving while intoxicated	1.1
Other public-order	3.9
Other offenses	1.3

Table 2-4, *continued*

Most Serious Offense	Percent of New Court Commitments[a] to Federal Prison[c]
All offenses	100.0
Violent offenses	3.4
Homicide	0.3
Kidnapping	0.1
Rape	0.0
Other sexual assault	0.0
Robbery	2.2
Assault	0.8
Other violent	0.0
Property offenses	33.0
Fraud Offense	26.2
Embezzlement	6.3
Fraud	16.4
Forgery	2.6
Counterfeiting	0.9
Nonfraud offense	6.8
Burglary	0.1
Larceny/theft	6.0
Arson	0.1
Motor vehicle theft	0.1
Other property	0.6
Drug offenses	42.4
Possession	1.9
Trafficking	25.4
Other/unspecified drug	15.0
Public-order offenses	20.7
Regulatory offense	1.2
Nonregulatory public-order	19.5
Weapons	2.2
Immigration	9.9
Tax law violations	1.0
Racketeering and extortion	2.0
Other public-order	4.4
Other offenses	0.5

[a] New court commitments are females incarcerated in State or Federal prisons for the first time on one or more new sentences.
[b] Total number of admissions to state prison was 21,109.
[c] Total number of admissions to federal prison was 3,796.

Source: Adapted from U.S. Department of Justice, *National Corrections Reporting Program, 1991* (Washington, D.C.: Government Printing Office, 1994), pp. 12, 55.

SEX OFFENSES

Female sex offenses predominantly reflect prostitution and commercialized vice (see Figure 2-5). In 1992, female arrests for prostitution and commercialized vice accounted for nearly 90 percent of all female sex offense arrests. Almost 11 percent of arrests were for sex offenses other than forcible rape and prostitution. Forcible rape accounted for less than 1 percent of arrests, yet such arrests are increasing at a higher rate than other female sex offenses.

FEMALE PRISONERS

Another means of assessing the nature of female crime is by looking at the crimes of recently confined female prisoners. Table 2-4 distributes the types of offenses perpetrated by female new court commitments to state and federal prisons in 1991. Drug offenses such as possession and trafficking accounted for the highest percentage of new female state and federal prisoners, at over 40 percent. Over 33 percent of the new court commitments to state and federal prisons were for property crimes such as fraud and larceny-theft.

In state prisons nearly 17 percent of the new court commitments were for violent crimes, including homicide and robbery. More than 20 percent of the federal prison female commitments were for public-order offenses such as weapons and immigration charges.

3. Female Crime in Comparison to Male Crime

In recent years much has been made of the rise and changing nature of female criminality and a possible narrowing of the gap between male and female offenders. How do females compare to males in their crimes and delinquency? Does age make a difference in relation to the criminality of males and females? What do long-term trends tell us about the gender disparities or similarities in arrest patterns, crime fluctuations, and the distribution of offenses? In this chapter we will examine these issues.

GENDER AND CRIME

Arrest statistics indicate that the vast majority of crimes are committed by males. As shown in Table 3-1, male arrestees constituted 81 percent of all persons arrested in 1992, compared to 19 percent for females arrested. Nearly 9 of every 10 persons arrested for violent crimes were male, while 3 out of 4 property crime arrestees were male. The only offenses where females outnumbered males arrested were in prostitution and commercialized vice, and runaways, where 65.3 percent and 56.8 percent of the arrestees, respectively, were female.

Statistics on males and females incarcerated reflect an even wider differential as shown in Figure 3-1. Over 90 percent of jail and prison inmates in 1992 were male, with the percent of female inmates ranging from 5.7 percent of federal and state prisoners to 9.2 percent of jail inmates.

TABLE 3-1

Total Arrests, Percent Distribution by Gender, 1992

Offense Charged	Total arrests	Percent male	Percent female
TOTAL[a]	11,893,153	81.0	19.0
Murder and nonnegligent manslaughter	19,491	90.3	9.7
Forcible rape	33,385	98.7	1.3
Robbery	153,456	91.5	8.5
Aggravated assault	434,918	85.2	14.8
Burglary	359,699	90.8	9.2
Larceny-theft	1,291,984	67.9	32.1
Motor vehicle theft	171,269	89.2	10.8
Arson	16,322	86.6	13.4
Violent crime[b]	641,250	87.5	12.5
Property crime[c]	1,839,274	74.5	25.5
Crime Index total[d]	2,480,524	77.9	22.1
Other assaults	912,517	82.8	17.2
Forgery and counterfeiting	88,649	65.3	34.7
Fraud	346,314	57.9	42.1
Embezzlement	11,707	61.0	39.0
Stolen property; buying, receiving, possessing	136,765	87.5	12.5
Vandalism	262,477	88.7	11.3
Weapons; carrying, possessing, etc.	204,116	92.5	7.5
Prostitution and commercialized vice	86,988	34.7	65.3
Sex offenses (except forcible rape and prostitution)	91,560	92.3	7.7
Drug abuse violations	920,424	83.6	16.4
Gambling	15,029	86.1	13.9
Offenses against family and children	84,328	82.0	18.0
Driving under the influence	1,319,583	86.2	13.8

Table 3-1, *continued*

Offense Charged	Total arrests	Percent male	Percent female
Liquor laws	442,985	80.7	19.3
Drunkenness	664,236	89.2	10.8
Disorderly conduct	605,367	79.4	20.6
Vagrancy	29,004	90.2	9.8
All other offenses (except traffic)	2,954,440	82.9	17.1
Suspicion	15,351	82.6	17.4
Curfew and loitering law violations	74,619	73.2	26.8
Runaways	146,170	43.2	56.8

[a] Based on 10,962 agencies; 1992 estimated population 213,392,000.
[b] Violent crimes are offenses of murder, forcible rape, robbery, and aggravated assault.
[c] Property crimes are offenses of burglary, larceny-theft, motor vehicle theft, and arson.
[d] Includes arson.

Source: Adapted from U.S. Federal Bureau of Investigation, *Crime in the United States: Uniform Crime Reports 1992* (Washington, D.C.: Government Printing Office, 1993), p. 234.

Victimization survey data yield a similar disparity between male and female offenders. In the *National Crime Victimization Survey 1992 (NCVS)*, males were perceived as the offender in 86 percent of all single-offender violent crime victimizations, compared to females in 13 percent. Over 75 percent of the perpetrators of multiple-offender violent crimes were believed to be all male, with all female offenders accounting for just over 6 percent of such victimizations.[1]

ARREST RATIOS AND GENDER

The differential in male–female arrests can be seen in gender ratios in arrests (see Table 3-2). For total offenses males were arrested 4.2 times for every female arrested in 1992. The male–female ratio of

FIGURE 3-1

Female and Male Offenders, by Arrests and Correctional Facilities, 1992

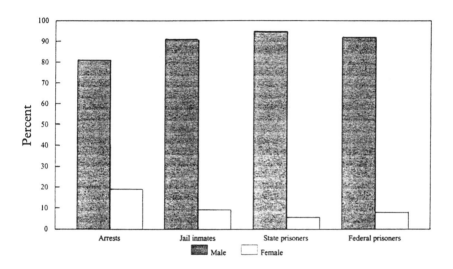

Note: Figures represent the total number of arrests and prisoners in each institution.

Source: Constructed from U.S. Federal Bureau of Investigation, *Crime in the United States: Uniform Crime Reports 1992* (Washington, D.C.: Government Printing Office, 1993), p. 234; U.S. Department of Justice, *Jail Inmates 1992* (Washington, D.C.: Government Printing Office, 1993), p. 2; U.S. Department of Justice, *Prisoners in 1992* (Washington, D.C.: Government Printing Office, 1993), pp. 2, 4.

arrests for violent crimes was 7.0 to 1, and property crimes 2.9 to 1. Males were more than 78 times as likely to be arrested for forcible rape as females; however, the differential is nearly cut in half for persons under 18 years old, though the ratio of 44.5 is still considerable.

Among nonindex crimes, the male–female ratio of arrests was 12.3 to 1 for weapons-related charges, 5.1 to 1 for drug abuse violations, and 7.9 to 1 for vandalism. Arrest ratios favored female arrestees for prostitution and commercialized vice at 1.9 to 1, and runaways at 1.3 female arrests for every male arrested.

TABLE 3-2

Male–Female Arrest Ratios for Selected Crimes, by Offense and Age, 1992

(Numbers refer to male arrests in comparison to one female arrest)

Offense	Total	Ages under 18	Ages 18 and over
Total Offenses	4.2	3.3	4.5
Murder and nonnegligent manslaughter	9.3	16.3	8.6
Forcible rape	78.5	44.5	89.7
Robbery	10.7	10.7	10.7
Aggravated assault	5.7	5.2	5.9
Burglary	9.9	9.9	9.7
Larceny-theft	2.1	2.4	2.0
Motor vehicle theft	8.2	6.9	9.5
Arson	6.5	8.4	5.3
Violent crime	7.0	7.0	7.0
Property crime	2.9	3.3	2.7
Crime Index total	3.5	3.7	3.5
Other assaults	4.8	3.1	5.3
Forgery and counterfeiting	1.9	1.9	1.9
Vandalism	7.9	10.7	6.4
Weapons; carrying, possessing, etc.	12.3	13.4	12.1
Prostitution and commercialized vice	1.9[a]	1.2[a]	1.9[a]
Drug abuse violations	5.1	7.9	4.9
Driving under the influence	6.2	6.3	6.2
Offenses against family and children	4.5	1.8	4.8
Runaways	1.3[a]	1.3[a]	0.0

[a] These ratios are for female-male arrests.

Source: Derived from U.S. Federal Bureau of Investigation, *Crime in the United States: Uniform Crime Reports 1992* (Washington, D.C.: Government Printing Office, 1993), pp. 226, 229, 231.

When relating age to gender and arrest ratios, the male–female ratio of arrests was higher for persons ages 18 and over, at 4.5 to 1, than persons under 18, at 3.3 to 1, and total arrests, at 4.2 to 1. The ratio of arrests relative to age and gender are generally consistent from offense to offense, except for certain offenses such as motor vehicle theft, drug abuse violations, and vandalism which show a greater male–female ratio of arrests for persons under 18 than those age 18 and over.

HOW FEMALE AND MALE
CRIMES ARE DISTRIBUTED

In addition to the raw numbers that differentiate female and male crime, it is important to distinguish the relative gender differences in types of offenses most often committed, including violent crimes, property crimes, and drug- and alcohol-related offenses. Table 3-3 lists the 10 most frequent offenses in which males and females were arrested in 1992. All other offenses ranked first and disorderly conduct seventh for both sexes. Otherwise, the patterns of arrest differed by gender. Males were arrested second most often for driving under the influence, while the second most common offense of arrest for females was larceny-theft.

Three of the top 10 offenses for male arrestees were Crime Index offenses, compared to only 1 of the offenses for female arrestees. Both males and females were arrested most often for drug- and alcohol-related crimes in 4 of the 10 rankings.

Violent Crimes

Arrest patterns for violent crimes show that more than 80 percent of female arrests in 1992 were for aggravated assault, compared to only 66 percent of the male arrests (see Figure 3-2). Male arrests tended to be more distributed than female arrests for crimes of violence. One in every four male arrests was for robbery, whereas robbery constituted 16.4 percent of the female arrests. Murder and forcible rape accounted for the lowest percentages of violent crime arrests for males and females; however, the male percentage of arrests was more than 3 times that of female arrests.

TABLE 3-3

Most Frequent Arrests, by Gender and Offense, 1992

Rank	Male	Rank	Female
1	All other offenses (except traffic)	1	All other offenses (except traffic)
2	Driving under the influence	2	Larceny-theft
3	Larceny-theft	3	Driving under the influence
4	Drug abuse violations	4	Other assaults
5	Other assaults	5	Drug abuse violations
6	Drunkenness	6	Fraud
7	Disorderly conduct	7	Disorderly conduct
8	Aggravated assault	8	Liquor laws
9	Liquor laws	9	Runaways
10	Burglary	10	Drunkenness

Source: Compiled from U.S. Federal Bureau of Investigation, *Crime in the United States: Uniform Crime Reports 1992* (Washington, D.C.: Government Printing Office, 1993), p. 234.

FIGURE 3-2

Violent Crime Arrest
Patterns, by Gender, 1992

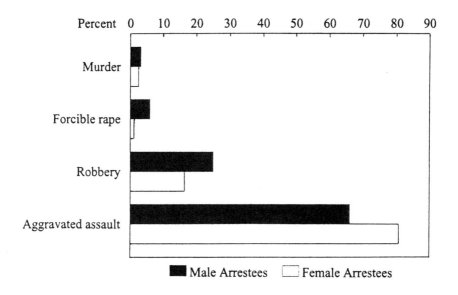

■ Male Arrestees   ☐ Female Arrestees

Source: Constructed from U.S. Federal Bureau of Investigation, *Crime in the United States: Uniform Crime Reports 1992* (Washington, D.C.: Government Printing Office, 1993), p. 234.

Property Crimes

Property crime arrests also reflect differences by gender (see Figure 3-3). More than 8 in 10 female arrests were for larceny-theft in 1992, whereas larceny-theft accounted for just over half the male arrests for property crime. Nineteen percent of male arrests were for burglary, compared to under 7 percent of the female arrests. More than twice as high a percentage of males were arrested for vandalism and stolen property–related offenses than females. Arson arrests had the lowest percentage of property crime arrests for males and females.

FIGURE 3-3

Property Crime Arrest Patterns, by Gender, 1992

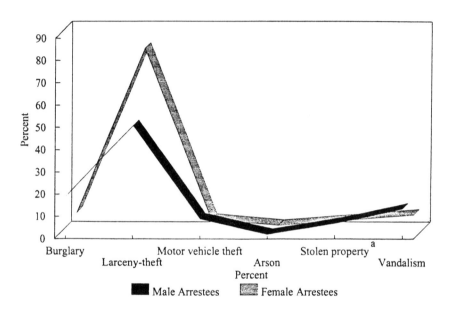

[a] Includes buying, receiving and/or possessing.

Source: Derived from U.S. Federal Bureau of Investigation, *Crime in the United States: Uniform Crime Reports 1992* (Washington, D.C.: Government Printing Office, 1993), p. 234.

Drug- and Alcohol-Related Offenses

The distribution of drug- and alcohol-related crimes was similar between female and male arrestees in 1992 (see Figure 3-4). Driving under the influence accounted for nearly 40 percent of the male and female arrests. Over 30 percent of the female arrests came for drug abuse violations, compared to under 27 percent of the male arrests. Just over 20 percent of all male arrests were for drunkenness, while liquor law violations were responsible for more than 17 percent of the female arrests.

FIGURE 3-4

Drug- and Alcohol-Related
Arrest Patterns, by Gender, 1992

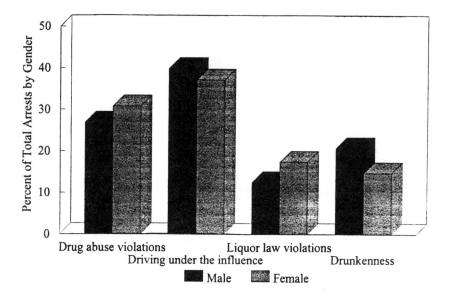

Source: Derived from U.S. Federal Bureau of Investigation, *Crime in the United States: Uniform Crime Reports 1992* (Washington, D.C.: Government Printing Office, 1993), p. 234.

GENDER AND JUVENILE CRIME

Male juveniles are involved in more criminal activity than female juveniles, though the disparity is not as great as that for male and female adults. In 1992, there were 3.3 males under 18 years of age arrested for every female under the age of 18. For violent crimes, male juveniles were 7 times more likely to be arrested than female juveniles. Females younger than 18 were arrested slightly more than their male counterparts for prostitution and commercialized vice, and running away.[2]

Figure 3-5 reflects gender differences in juvenile arrests and persons held in juvenile detention facilities between 1989 and 1992. Nearly

FIGURE 3-5

Juvenile Offenders, by Sex, Arrests, and Type of Facility, in Recent Years

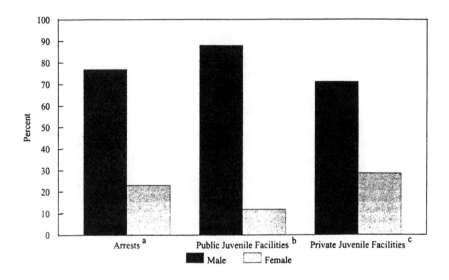

[a]Figures are for total persons under 18 years of age arrested in 1992.
[b]Based on 1989 figures.
[c]Based on 1991 data.

Source: Derived from U.S. Department of Justice, *Children in Custody 1989* (Washington, D.C.: Government Printing Office, 1991), p. 4; U.S. Department of Justice, *Sourcebook of Criminal Justice Statistics—1992* (Washington, D.C.: Government Printing Office, 1993), p. 579; U.S. Federal Bureau of Investigation, *Crime in the United States: Uniform Crime Reports 1992* (Washington, D.C.: Government Printing Office, 1993), p. 226.

---

77 percent of the persons arrested under the age of 18 in 1992 were male, compared to 23.1 percent female. In public juvenile facilities in 1989, over 88 percent of those being held were male; whereas in private juvenile facilities in 1991 more than 7 in 10 in custody were male.

The 10 most common offenses for which juveniles were arrested in 1992 can be seen in Table 3-4. Male and female juveniles were arrested most often for larceny-theft. Other assaults and disorderly conduct ranked fourth and sixth, respectively, for both sexes. Four of the top 10 offenses in which male juveniles were arrested were property crimes.

Female juveniles tended to be arrested most often for such crimes as running away and curfew and loitering law violations. However, 2 of the 10 most frequent offenses females were arrested for were assaultive crimes, including aggravated assault. Despite being the only one to place a violent crime in the top 10 arrests, females under 18 were still outnumbered by males under 18 in arrests for aggravated assault by more than 5 to 1.

Self-Report Surveys and Juvenile Crime

Self-report surveys have focused largely on juvenile delinquency in assessing differences between males and females. Such surveys have generally supported official statistics on gender ratios with respect to criminality and delinquency, though the differential has been shown to be smaller in self-report studies. Earlier surveys by Nancy Wise[3] and Ivan Nye and James Short[4] yielded male–female juvenile ratios of admitted criminal involvement of 2.3 and 2.4, respectively. More recent surveys by Stephen Cernkovich and Peggy Giordano[5] and Peter Kratcoski and John Kratcoski[6] found the gender ratio of delinquency to be 2.2 and 2.0, in favor of males.

IS FEMALE CRIME CLOSING THE GAP ON MALE CRIME?

Since the mid–1970s there has been much debate over the nature, extent, and rate of female crime in relation to male crime. Some have suggested the emergence of a "new" female criminal, more closely resembling the male criminal in terms of violent and aggressive criminality. Others have noted an increasing prevalence in female property crimes, outpacing male property crimes.

In *Sisters in Crime*, Freda Adler related the women's liberation movement, women's assertiveness, and the entry of females into nontraditional occupations with an increase in violent female crimes. She contended that "although males continue to commit the greater number

TABLE 3-4

Most Common Arrests of Juveniles, by Gender and Offense, 1992

Rank	Female	Rank	Male
1	Larceny-theft	1	Larceny-theft
2	Runaways	2	All other offenses (except traffic)
3	All other offenses (except traffic)	3	Vandalism
4	Other assaults	4	Other assaults
5	Liquor laws	5	Burglary
6	Disorderly conduct	6	Disorderly conduct
7	Curfew and loitering law violations	7	Liquor laws
8	Burglary	8	Drug abuse violations
9	Vandalism	9	Runaways
10	Aggravated assault	10	Motor vehicle theft

Source: Compiled from U.S. Federal Bureau of Investigation, *Crime in the United States: Uniform Crime Reports 1992* (Washington, D.C.: Government Printing Office, 1993), p. 226.

FIGURE 3-6

Violent Crime Arrest Trends, [a]
by Gender, 1960–92

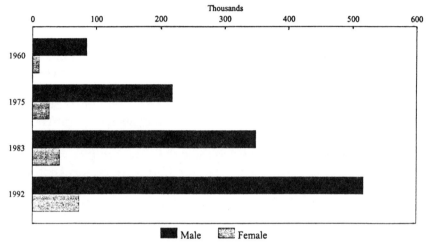

Between 1960 and 1992, female arrests increased by 619.6% compared to a 508.6% increase in male arrests.

[a] The number of law enforcement agencies reporting data on arrests may vary from year to year.

Source: Calculated from U.S. Federal Bureau of Investigation, *Crime in the United States: Uniform Crime Reports 1960, 1975, 1983, 1992* (Washington, D.C.: Government Printing Office, 1961, 1976, 1984, 1993).

---

of offenses, it is [females] who are committing those same crimes at yearly rates of increase now running as high as six and seven times faster than males."[7] Adler relied heavily on *UCR* data from the 1950s through the 1970s to reach her conclusions.

Critics have largely rejected Adler's findings. In a study of gender differences in adult crime, Darrell Steffensmeir found little change in female arrest patterns during the 12-year period examined.[8] Carol Smart also took issue with the notion of a new female criminal. After examining official statistics from the United States and England, she argued that increases in female crime were nothing new and further criticized the "tendency to fixate on monocausal explanations of female criminality such as the women's movement, when studies of male deviance indicate several possible etiological perspectives."[9]

In analyzing male and female arrest trends for violent crime from 1960 to 1992, as shown in Figure 3-6, we can see that female arrests increased 619.6 percent compared to an increase of 508.6 percent for male arrests over the period. However, the narrowing of the gap has been entirely in relative terms. The absolute figures indicate that the difference between male and female arrestees in 1992 was nearly six times greater than in 1960. The reality is that violent crime is still largely a male phenomenon, with little indication that females are making significant inroads in bridging the disparity.

An explosion in female property crime rates in recent decades has also led some researchers to believe that the male–female differential in property crimes is steadily shrinking. Rita Simon analyzed arrest statistics from 1953 to 1972. From these she advanced that should the present trends in female arrest rates for property crimes continue, "approximately equal numbers of men and women will be arrested for larceny and for fraud and embezzlement by the 1990s; and for forgery and counterfeiting the proportions should be equal by the 2010s."[10]

These conclusions have been challenged by others as inaccurate and methodologically unsound. For example, George Noblit and Janie Burcart argued that Simon failed to examine age categories in relation to her findings, was inconsistent in her use of official statistics, and did not allow for changes in the population.[11]

A current study of arrest trends for property crime fails to support Simon's contention. As shown in Figure 3-7, between 1960 and 1992 female arrests for property crime increased by 1007.4 percent, compared to a 270.7 percent increase in male arrests for property crime. Despite this relative differential in the growth rate of female– male arrests, the gender gap in quantitative terms remains far apart. Nearly three times as many males were arrested for property crimes as females in 1992.

A closer examination of property crime arrest trends from 1983 to 1992 indicates that female arrests for property crimes continue to increase at a higher rate than male arrests for property crimes (see Table 3-5). This rate of increase is cause for concern in the study of female crime. Nevertheless, we are still a long way from parity of the sexes in property criminality, particularly with respect to burglary, motor vehicle theft, stolen property–related charges, and vandalism. Even for larceny-theft, which accounts for the greatest number of property

FIGURE 3-7

Property Crime Arrest Trends,[a] by Gender, 1960–92

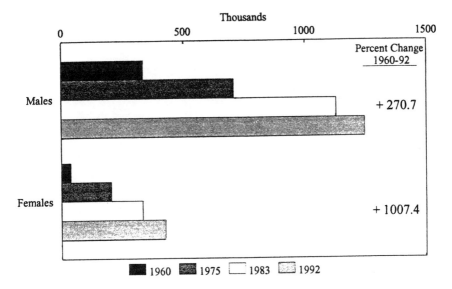

[a] Arson was added in 1979 and thus is included in property crime data for 1983 and 1992. The number of law enforcement agencies reporting data on arrests may vary from year to year.

Source: Calculated from U.S. Federal Bureau of Investigation, *Crime in the United States: Uniform Crime Reports 1960, 1975, 1983, 1992* (Washington, D.C.: Government Printing Office, 1961, 1976, 1984, 1993).

---

crime arrests for both sexes, males are more than twice as likely to face arrest as females.

COMPARING CRIME AND DELINQUENCY TRENDS OF GIRLS AND BOYS

Some criminologists believe that girls and boys are becoming more alike in their criminal and delinquent activities in both numbers and nature. Official statistics indicate that females under the age of 18

TABLE 3-5
Property Crime Arrest Trends, by Gender, 1983–92

Offense Charged	Male Arrests			Female Arrests		
	1983	1992	Percent change	1983	1992	Percent change
Larceny-theft	693,319	794,123	+14.5	297,414	376,906	+26.7
Burglary	337,659	297,651	−11.8	25,412	30,611	+20.5
Motor vehicle theft	84,957	142,316	+67.5	8,373	17,147	+104.8
Arson	12,968	12,691	−2.1	1,838	1,961	+6.7
Total[a]	1,128,903	1,246,781	+10.4	333,037	426,625	+28.1
Fraud	134,195	161,515	+20.4	87,470	115,006	+31.5
Embezzlement	4,640	6,440	+38.8	2,292	4,082	+78.1
Forgery and counterfeiting	43,052	52,123	+21.1	21,765	27,960	+28.5
Stolen property; buying, receiving, possessing	89,005	109,907	+23.5	11,234	15,590	+38.8
Vandalism	159,072	208,103	+30.8	16,909	26,380	+56.0

[a] Index property crimes.

Source: Derived from U.S. Federal Bureau of Investigation, *Crime in the United States: Uniform Crime Reports 1992* (Washington, D.C.: Government Printing Office, 1993), p. 222.

TABLE 3-6

Juvenile Arrest Trends, by Gender, 1983–92

	Males under 18			Females under 18		
	1983	1992	Percent change	1983	1992	Percent change
Total	1,162,826	1,339,049	+15.2	318,245	399,131	+25.4
Violent crime	59,181	91,126	+54.0	7,115	13,011	+82.9
Property crime	396,602	423,994	+6.9	100,086	126,752	+26.6
Crime Index total	455,783	515,120	+13.0	107,201	139,763	+30.4

Source: Derived from U.S. Federal Bureau of Investigation, *Crime in the United States: Uniform Crime Reports 1992* (Washington, D.C.: Government Printing Office, 1993), p. 222.

are being arrested at a faster rate than males under 18. Table 3-6 shows that between 1983 and 1992, juvenile female total arrests increased 25.4 percent, compared to a 15.2 percent increase for juvenile male arrests. Violent crime arrests increased nearly 83 percent for females and 54 percent for males. Arrests for property crime grew by nearly 27 percent for females over the period, compared to just under 7 percent for males. For total Crime Index offenses, female juvenile arrests rose more than 30 percent and male juvenile arrests increased by 13 percent.

While girls are now being arrested more often than in the past, the gains on boys arrested are still slight in actual figures. In total, more than three times as many male juveniles were arrested as female juveniles in 1992.

Self-report surveys generally give a more accurate account of the nature and incidence of juvenile crime and delinquency as well as gender differences and similarities in deviant behavior. In a self-report survey on delinquency from 1967 to 1972, Martin Gold and David Reimer found that while offenses among female teens had increased over the period, the increase was mainly in nonindex offenses such as drug and alcohol abuse. The researchers concluded that were these offenses omitted, they would "find no change over the five years in per capita frequency of offenses among girls."[12] Cernkovich and Giordano's 1977 survey of 822 Midwestern teenagers revealed that overall males were more likely to be involved in delinquent activities than females, though they found the male–female ratio of delinquency to be smaller than official indicators.[13]

More recently, Douglas Smith and Christy Visher compared male and female delinquency, using self-report and official data. They found that while the gender disparity appeared to be shrinking on the whole, it was more prevalent for status offenses and petty crimes than violent crimes.[14] A similar finding was made by Kratcoski and Kratcoski.[15]

In a study of self-report surveys over a 22-year period, Darrell Steffensmeir and Renee Steffensmeir found that the gender disparity in self-reported delinquency was generally stable for much of the period, with the exception of minor increases in female property damage and petty theft.[16] Michael Hindelang found the actual types of delinquent acts perpetrated by male and female adolescents to be resembling.[17]

Girls appear to be more varied today in their criminal and delinquent activities than do boys. However, the rise in female delinquency is less a reflection of an increase in nontraditional female criminality than in traditional female offenses such as running away, substance abuse, shoplifting, and minor assaults.[18]

PART II

Causal Approaches to Female Crime and Delinquency

4. Theories on Female Criminality

Attempts to explain female deviant behavior are not new. Many date back to the late 1800s and early 1900s and are rooted in age-old stereotypes, notions of female inferiority, and sexism. More modern concepts seek to associate female crime and delinquency with environmental and sociological causes. Some research focuses on why females are less apt than males to commit crimes or at least certain types of crimes. We will now explore the more prominent theoretical propositions on female crime and criminals.

BIOLOGICAL THEORIES

Italian psychiatrist Cesare Lombroso (1836–1909) was among the first to study scientifically female criminality. Referred to by some as the founding father of the biological-positivistic school of criminology, Lombroso collaborated with his son-in-law, William Ferrero.[1] They combined quantitative and qualitative data in an attempt to understand the female criminal. After examining the skeletal remains of female offenders (particularly the brain, face, jawbones, and cranium) and female prisoners for signs of atavism, Lombroso and Ferrero hypothesized that females were "born criminals" and thus biologically predisposed to criminality. Such females were believed to be atavistic, or throwbacks to primitive genetic traits—possessing certain physical anomalies absent in normal women. For instance, a prostitute was "likely to have very heavy lower jaws, large nasal spines, simple cranial sutures, deep frontal sinuses and wormian bones. A 'fallen woman' usually possessed occipital irregularities, a narrow forehead, prominent cheekbones, and a 'virile' type of face."[2]

Lombroso and Ferrero theorized that there were fewer females than males born criminal, but characterized females who were born criminals as

> even more immoral and menacing than male criminals . . . less compassionate and sensitive to pain, while possessing jealousy and capable of vengeful behavior. These "ladylike" characteristics tend to be mitigated by common female attributes such as weakness, piety, maternity, and insufficiently developed intelligence. . . . Women are simply overgrown adolescents who when bad, are far more frightening than men. These women lack maternal affection, illustrating their degeneracy and masculinity.[3]

Lombroso also studied the "occasional" female criminal, whom he believed accounted for most female offenders. "These women generally had none or few degenerative qualities and possessed 'moral equipment' near that of normal women."[4] The occasional female criminal committed a crime for reasons such as "male persuasion, higher education (preventing marriage and inducing want), and excessive temptation (for example, shoplifting because of the overwhelming display of goods in stores)."[5] Such women lacked the respect for property that men had and believed clothing to be essential for attracting a man.

The work of Lombroso and Ferrero has long since been rejected, due largely to the inadequacies of their methodology, the relatively small sample group, and the gender-based theory of atavism in relation to criminal behavior.

More recent biologically based research on female crime has studied the relationship between genetics and female delinquency. T. C. Gibbens found a high rate of sex chromosomal anomalies in female delinquents.[6] J. Cowie and colleagues identified genetic factors in female delinquency—relating obesity in girls to sexual promiscuity, and menstruation "to the distress females feel in recognizing that they can never be males, thereby making them more susceptible to delinquent conduct."[7]

Other studies have also linked menstruation and premenstrual syndrome (PMS) to female criminality, noting such related symptoms as increased aggression, irritability, and tension.[8] One sociologist suggested that the relationship between the arrests of women for violent crimes and PMS may be one of fatigue and slower reaction time during the commission of the crime.[9]

PSYCHOLOGICAL THEORIES

The psychological school of thought with respect to female criminality is believed by many to be rooted in the psychoanalytic writings of Sigmund Freud. Like Lombroso, Freud regarded females as biologically inferior to males. In 1933, he described female offenders as passive, narcissistic, and masochistic.[10] He attributed these defective qualities to a "masculinity complex" or "penis envy." As a result of this "physical deficiency," Freud theorized that women were unable to resolve the Oedipal conflict, making them "morally inferior" and less able to control their impulses, which in turn affected such areas as the female's intellectual sphere. Such females were characterized by jealousy, immorality, emotionalism, and bad judgment.

Although Freud did not directly relate female criminality to superego weakness, he believed that females were "inclined toward amorality because of their 'anatomical' deficiency."[11]

Critics of Freud's theories included some of his own psychoanalytic "disciples." Alfred Adler rejected the notion of penis envy in women when he advanced that a "sense of inferiority was created in women not because they felt less well endowed physically than men, but because an unnatural relationship of male dominance exists between the sexes."[12] Karen Horney contended that males and females were mutually envious, with the male envy of the female or men's femininity complex actually stronger than women's masculinity complex.[13] Horney suggested that girls did tend to envy boys' ease in urinating and masturbating.

Freud's propositions have been largely abandoned in modern day psychology and psychiatry.

In a study of delinquent females, Gisela Konopla identified four key psychologically and biologically based elements that are associated with female delinquency: (1) the uniquely female biological onset of puberty, (2) a complex process of identifying with their mothers, (3) changes in the cultural position of females, and (4) a "faceless" adult authority which results in low self-esteem and loneliness.[14] Indeed, psychological maladjustment and dysfunction have been associated with female crime and delinquency in some studies.[15]

SOCIOLOGICAL THEORIES

Sociologist William Thomas was among the first to relate female criminality to the social environment. In 1907, Thomas criticized anthropologists for their "assumption of the inferiority of women and their subsequent failure to distinguish between congenital and acquired characteristics."[16] He postulated that any gender differences in intellectual functioning were not a reflection of biological differences but social influences.

It was in his book, *The Unadjusted Girl*, published in 1923, that Thomas "established his eminence by fusing sociology and social psychology into the analysis of social organization and personality."[17] He saw the female criminal as a product of innate instincts in conjunction with influences within the social environment. Thomas developed a dyadic goals-means conflict theory in which he proposed that every human (particularly prostitutes) had four basic desires: security, recognition, new experience, and response. It was the desire for new experience and response that Thomas believed most influenced female criminality. "A woman entered prostitution to satisfy a desire for excitement and response; as a woman, prostitution in one form or another was the most likely avenue to satisfy those needs."[18]

Thomas's works were criticized for their liberal paternalism and unproven assumptions. Noted one critic: "He believed in manipulating people's lives 'for their own good' to conform to social norms that were not necessarily universal. His theories were sexist in that females were identified as offenders through sexual behavior."[19]

Sheldon and Eleanor Glueck's work in the field of female criminality was based on a detailed study, published in 1934, of 500 Massachusetts delinquent girls.[20] The Gluecks followed the girls from childhood through parole, tracing their backgrounds and social histories as well as comparing their physical and psychological traits. The researchers concluded that female delinquency was the result of biological and economic factors. They found that an extremely high percentage of delinquent girls came from abnormally large families where criminal behavior was intergenerational. Many of these girls were believed to be mentally defective and had been arrested primarily for illicit sexual behavior.

The Gluecks' findings were attacked as being methodologically sexist and influenced by biases. For example, they routinely examined the sexual histories of their subjects.

Otto Pollak's 1950 book, *The Criminality of Women*, was considered the definitive work on female crime during the postwar years.[21] Pollak, a sociology professor, analyzed data from a comprehensive survey of American, British, German, and French literature. He posited that female crime was primarily sexually motivated, while male crime was largely economically motivated, with the exception of crimes of passion.

Pollak further postulated that the incidence of crime among women was probably equal to that of men were it not for the "masked" or "hidden" female criminality. He contended that as a result, women's criminality was inadequately reflected in official statistics, giving such examples as shoplifting, illegal abortions, domestic thefts, and prostitute-perpetrated thefts of customers. According to Pollak, who was influenced by Lombroso and Freud's theories,

> women are particularly "addicted" to crimes that are easily concealed and rarely reported. ... The traditional social roles assigned to women (for instance, homemakers, caretakers of children, or the sick) are ideal for hiding crimes such as sexual offenses against children, which leaves no physical evidence and even less suspicion. ... Women are more deceitful than men in their commission of crimes and teach deceit through physiological tactics. ... Women disguise sexual response, fake orgasms, conceal their menstruation ... thus women are trained in deception.[22]

Pollak argued that women were given preferential treatment at every stage of the criminal justice system, arising in part from men's "chivalrous and paternalistic regard for women,"[23] allowing for fewer arrests, less prosecution, shorter sentences, and a lower rate of incarceration than male offenders. Recent studies have supported Pollak's views with regard to more lenient treatment of women in the criminal justice system.[24] However, other findings reject the argument; in some instances contending that females are treated more harshly than males in the criminal and juvenile justice systems.[25]

Much of Pollak's conclusions have been criticized as biased and unsubstantiated. One writer noted: "It is difficult to argue the existence of undetected crime since its very nature implies that it is unknown. Such a theory cannot be based on evidence, a weakness compounded by assertions that simply defy plausibility. ... His claims of sex offenses against children and female exhibitionism are boldly stated without evidence or even reasonable explanations."[26]

Some proponents of the hidden crime theory among females have cited evidence of a low reportability rate for such crimes as infanticide, prostitution, and illegal abortions.[27] Critics have countered this by pointing out that as many if not more, male crimes go unreported and undetected, such as domestic violence and rape.[28]

SOCIOECONOMIC THEORIES

A number of theories tied to social and economic forces have been proposed in explaining female criminality. Role or opportunity theorists reject the masculinization of female behavior as the cause of female crime but rather relate it to the "illegitimate expression" of role expectations.[29] These theorists also posit that females are most likely to engage in criminal behavior when legitimate avenues for reaching social goals are closed but illegitimate avenues are open. The criminality and delinquency of females is, therefore, directly related to female socialization and opportunities, and conversely, the lack of either of these elements.

In a study of delinquent girls and differential opportunity, Susan Datesman and associates found that perception of blocked opportunity was more closely related to female delinquency than that perception was to male delinquency.[30] Stephen Cernkovich and Peggy Giordano's study of self-report surveys of 1,355 female and male high school students found that blocked opportunity was a greater predictor of delinquency for both sexes than any other factor.[31]

Critics of sex-role and opportunity theories have argued that they offer "little understanding of actual women criminals and can easily slide into discussions of inadequate female socialization, implying that individual difficulties rather than structural problems are at issue."[32] Opportunity theory fails to examine the "structural origins of sex-role inequality or to deal with the inferior status of women in historical or cultural terms."[33]

Many believe that female criminality is by and large a reflection of economic need or necessity rather than such factors as sexual motivation. In a review of the literature on the etiology of female criminality, Dorie Klein found that poor and Third World women "negate the notions of sexually motivated crime," instead engaging "in illegal activities as a viable economic alternative."[34] Indeed, studies show that most female offenders tend to be economically disadvantaged, undereducated, self-supporting, and mothers, leading one researcher to comment that criminality may be a necessity for women "to provide for themselves and their families, a factor which makes it conceivable to view their larcenies, burglaries, and robberies in simple economic terms."[35]

Even in prostitution, which many link to promiscuity and other sexual motivations, economics play the larger role. In a study of prostitutes Jennifer James found that 84.9 percent of her sample were in the business primarily for the money or material goods.[36]

WOMEN'S LIBERATION MOVEMENT

The increase in certain female crimes in recent decades has been linked by some researchers to the "consciousness-raising" women's movement, which they credit for the increased participation of females in the labor force, changing women's identity and self-concept, and a parallel rise in female criminality. In her detailed study of women, crime, and the contemporary women's movement, Rita Simon advanced that "women have no greater store of morality than do men. Their propensities to commit crimes do not differ, but in the past, their opportunities have been much more limited. As women's opportunities to commit crimes increase, so will their deviant behavior and the types of crimes they commit will more closely resemble those committed by men."[37]

The alleged correlation between the women's liberation movement and women's criminality has been challenged by critics as naïve, methodologically weak, and inaccurate. Laura Crites pointed out that many female offenders are poor, single, unemployed, uneducated, and belonging to a racial minority, and thus they have not taken part in the women's movement and greater social and economic opportunities.[38] Based on a review of self-report and official data on female crime, Joseph Weis argued that a new, liberated female criminal is less an empirical reality than a social invention.[39]

There is no doubt that female crime has grown and spread out into new territory since the 1960s. However, the evidence does not support a strong relationship with women's advances in the workplace, nor is there any indication that the general nature or amount of female crime has dramatically changed or come closer to male crime (see chapter 3 for a more detailed discussion of this issue).

5. Factors in Female
Delinquency and Crime

In addition to theories on female criminality, criminologists have studied causative elements that have been shown to correlate with the crime and delinquency of females. Significant factors that have been linked to female criminality include broken homes, child abuse and neglect, the battering of women, substance abuse, race and/or ethnicity, mental illness, the menstrual cycle, male coercion, and recidivism.

THE BROKEN HOME

Much attention has been paid to broken homes with respect to female deviance. The term *broken home* is defined as a home in which one or both parents are absent due to desertion, divorce, separation, or death—thereby depriving the child or children of the benefits of a complete, stable family environment. Studies have shown that delinquent girls are more likely to come from broken homes than delinquent boys.[1] Maura Crowley found that 85 percent of the runaway girl prostitutes sampled came from homes where at least one parent was absent.[2] In the Huckleberry House study 70 percent of the girl prostitutes were products of broken homes.[3]

Research on females incarcerated also indicates a high rate of inmates who grew up in broken homes. In a survey of girl and boy delinquents in long-term juvenile facilities it was revealed that less than 3 in 10 grew up with both parents present.[4] Recent data on women in jail and prison have shown that more than half lived with only one or neither parent when growing up;[5] and the vast majority of female inmates were found to be single parents.[6]

CHILD ABUSE AND NEGLECT

Most women who abuse and neglect their children or parents were themselves the victims of child abuse, according to various studies. "Research postulates that children living in violent families are emotionally and psychologically vulnerable as adults to enacting the role of either the victim or abuser which they observed or experienced during their childhoods."[7] Vincent Fontana contended that the parents of these abusive parents were often unloving, brutal, and cruel.[8]

Other studies have linked juvenile female delinquency with violent child abuse. H. Simmons held that "a brutal parent tends to produce a brutal child;"[9] while D. Lewis and J. Pincus found that most violent juveniles had both witnessed and been the victims of severe physical violence by their own parents.[10] Most female prostitutes report being physically abused during their childhood. Over two-thirds of the prostitutes in Crowley's study and the Huckleberry House project were victims of physical child abuse.[11] And Martin Haskell and Lewis Yablonsky noted that juvenile correctional facilities are filled with teenagers who were victims of child abuse and other family pathology.[12] More than 4 in 10 women in jail or prison report being victims of child abuse.[13]

CHILD SEXUAL ABUSE

There is a strong correlation between female sex offenders and child sexual abuse. In the Huckleberry House study 90 percent of the female prostitutes reported being sexually abused.[14] In a study of prostitutes and sexual assault, Mimi Silbert found that nearly 66 percent of her sample were victims of incest and child abuse.[15] Studies on girl runaways indicate that a high percentage ran away from sexually abusive homes.[16] Other research has shown a relationship between incestuous women and their being victims of incest.[17] While a study of sexually abusive parents found that 75 percent had been sexually abused themselves as children.[18] Indeed, female inmates often tend to be the victims of childhood sexual abuse. About 33 percent of the women incarcerated reported that they had been sexually abused before the age of 18.[19]

CONJUGAL ABUSE

Battered wives and girlfriends often become husband or lover batterers and/or spouse or lover killers. It has been estimated that 65 percent of all married couples are physically violent toward one another over the lifetime of their marriage.[20] In 25 percent of the cases the violence is severe. In an extrapolation of a review of spouse abuse research, it was estimated that 2 million husbands in comparison to 1.8 million wives had experienced at least one severe form of spouse abuse.[21]

Other studies have found a correlation between unmarried couples' violence and woman battering. In a study of cohabiting couples, K. Yllo and Murray Straus found that this group reported more conjugal violence than did married couples;[22] and this is backed up by other reports showing a disproportionate number of unmarried couples engage in domestic violence.[23]

The majority of females who kill their spouse or boyfriend report doing so after repeated physical, sexual, and mental abuse by the male partner.[24] Women in prison for murder are almost twice as likely to have killed a spouse, ex-spouse, or other intimate person than other family members.[25] It is estimated that 1 in 5 violent female inmates perpetrated their violent crime against an intimate.[26]

Indeed, a relationship between the battering of women, female child abuse, and family violence has been well established in the literature.[27]

A FAMILY CYCLE OF ABUSE AND VIOLENCE

An intergenerational cycle of family abuse, neglect, crime, and violence has long been associated with such female crimes as child abuse and neglect, sexual abuse, prostitution, delinquency, and adult criminality. In the late 1800s and early 1900s, researchers such as Richard Dugdale[28] and Henry Goddard[29] studied the long histories of deviant behavior in certain families, including idiocy, prostitution, delinquency, fornication, and feeblemindedness. More recently,

Christopher Ounsted and colleagues held that abusive parents are often the product of families where violence has been passed from generation to generation.[30] In a study of neglectful families, Norman Polansky and associates suggested a "generation-to-generation transference of a lifestyle of neglect that comes from the sharing and passing on of family misfortunes."[31] Research by Maria Roy[32] and J. Gayford[33] revealed that a high percentage of women and men involved in domestic violence situations came from violent backgrounds. While other studies have established a link between female criminality and delinquency and a cycle of crime and delinquency within the family.[34]

SUBSTANCE ABUSE

Females who use and/or abuse alcohol or drugs are more likely than nonusers to become involved in or continue abusive or criminal behavior. Data indicate that female addicts are involved in a range of other criminal activities such as violent crime, property crime, drug trafficking, and family offenses.[35] Substance abuse is often associated with female sex crimes such as prostitution and child sexual abuse.[36] It is estimated that between 20 and 50 percent of all girl prostitutes use drugs regularly.[37]

Alcohol abuse by mothers has been linked to child abandonment and female drug abuse to child maltreatment.[38] Patricia Mrazek suggested that the "organicity associated with drug induced psychosis and other forms of toxicity may ... act as a trigger for incestuous relationships."[39] In studying family violence, Brandt Steele reported that the "chronic use of alcohol and the taking of hallucinogenic drugs can cause severe distortion of mental functioning with delusional thinking and the lowering of the threshold for the release of violence in many forms, including child abuse, homicide, and suicide."[40]

Eight of every 10 female inmates in state prison have used drugs at some point, with more than one-third being under the influence of drugs during the time of the offense for which they are incarcerated.[41]

RACE AND ETHNICITY

Race and/or ethnicity does appear to be a factor in certain crimes perpetrated by females. White, non–Hispanic females, for example, are more likely than racial or ethnic minorities to be runaways and prostitutes.[42] However, black and Hispanic women are overrepresented in violent crimes, arrests, and incarceration compared to whites and non–Hispanic women.[43] One study found the rate of husband abuse to be twice as high among black couples than white couples.[44] However, other research suggests that the rate of domestic violence is similar for blacks and whites.[45]

There is evidence to indicate that racism may play a role in differential enforcement of the law with respect to females, race, and ethnicity. Black and Hispanic women have been shown to be more likely to come into contact with the various stages of the criminal justice system (that is, arrest, courts) than white and non–Hispanic women.[46]

MENTAL ILLNESS

Mental illness is generally believed to be a factor in only a small percentage of female crimes. Nevertheless, studies have shown a relationship between various types of female criminality—including violent crimes, child maltreatment, and runaways—and mental disorders such as depression, schizophrenia, and psychosis.[47] In a study of child abuse, S. Zalba found that abusive mothers exhibited a number of mental dysfunctions, including impulse-ridden character disorder and violent and/or episodic schizophrenia.[48] Researchers from the New York Psychiatric Institute found that 41 percent of the runaways studied were characterized as depressed and antisocial, and 30 percent were depressed, while 50 percent had attempted suicide.[49] Female prostitutes were found to suffer from depression, schizophrenia, and emotional deprivation,[50] while incestuous and infanticidal women were characterized as severely disturbed.[51]

THE MENSTRUAL CYCLE

A biological factor explored in relation to female criminality is the role of the menstrual cycle. A number of studies have shown that female deviant behavior occurs most often during certain phases of the menstrual cycle—the 4 premenstrual days and the first 4 days of menstruation.[52] In a study of female inmates, J. H. Morton and associates found that 62 percent of the women convicted of unpremeditated violent crimes, such as murder and assault, had committed their crimes during the premenstrual week and 17 percent during menstruation.[53] K. Dalton's 1961 study of menstruation and female crime has perhaps been the most influential in associating women's criminality with the menstrual cycle. Over a six-month period at an English women's prison, Dalton interviewed 156 new inmates whose offenses had been committed within the prior 28 days. She found that 49 percent of all crimes were committed within the 8-day paramenstruum phase (the 4 premenstrual days and first 4 days of menstruation).[54] In interviewing 94 prisoners reported to the governor for behavioral problems within the prison, Dalton found that 54 percent had been disorderly during the paramenstruum.[55]

Recent studies on the relationship between menstruation and criminality have centered on the effects of premenstrual syndrome on female deviance, particularly with respect to violent and homicidal aggression (see chapter 6). Currently, however, most experts see other factors as more significant in contributing to female crime and delinquency.

MALE COERCION

Many believe that female criminality is often a reflection of male coercion or forced participation or coparticipation in criminal activities. Studies have shown that violence among females is related to violence by males, domestic violence, child abuse, and male psychological abuse.[56] Female runaways and throwaways are often forced to leave a male-dominated abusive environment.[57] Prostitutes have been found to be coerced into prostitution by pimps or other males, as well as involvement in other criminal activities such as drug abuse and dealing, theft, violent crimes, and child abuse.[58] Other research has shown a correlation between physically and sexually abusive women and physically and sexually abusive men.[59] The *National Crime Victimization Survey* shows that in more than 14 percent of the multiple-offender crimes of violence, the offenders are perceived as being male and female.[60]

RECIDIVISM

The majority of female criminals and delinquents are recidivists, or repeat offenders. More than 66 percent of the women imprisoned had prior criminal convictions as either an adult or juvenile.[61] Almost 50 percent of all female inmates in state prison had previously been given prison sentences or probation at least twice; 33 percent three or more times; and more than one in seven had prior convictions of six times or more.[62]

PART III

Women and Crime

6. Homicidal Women

Although the occurrences of homicidal women are relatively rare, history is replete with examples of murderous women or accused murderesses. Lizzie Borden, Bonnie Parker, and Jean Harris, who murdered her lover in a crime of passion, are perhaps three of the best known. Other female killers who have left their mark on the public's imagination include Elizabeth Ann Duncan, who was executed in 1962 for hiring two men to murder her son's pregnant wife; Margie Velma Barfield, who was executed in 1984 for poisoning her fiancé to death by lacing his beer with arsenic; and Bernadette Powell, who was convicted in 1976 of killing her ex-husband after unsuccessfully using a battered woman defense.

Infamous politically motivated would-be lady killers such as Lynette "Squeaky" Fromme and Sara Jane Moore, who attempted to murder Gerald Ford, have given way to more unpredictable homicidal women in recent years. In 1982, after agreeing to testify against her husband accomplice in the kidnapping-murders of 10 people (including a pregnant woman), Charlene Williams Gallego pleaded guilty to four murders in California and Nevada in what may have been the first case of husband and wife serial killers in the country. In 1992, Aileen Carol Wuormos, a lesbian prostitute, was sentenced to death in Florida's electric chair after confessing to the murder of seven of her male clients.

One of the more shocking and tragic cases of female homicide occurred in October 1994, when Susan Smith drowned her two young sons in South Carolina. She later confessed to the crime after first claiming the children had been abducted.

FIGURE 6-1

Female Murderers, by Age, 1992

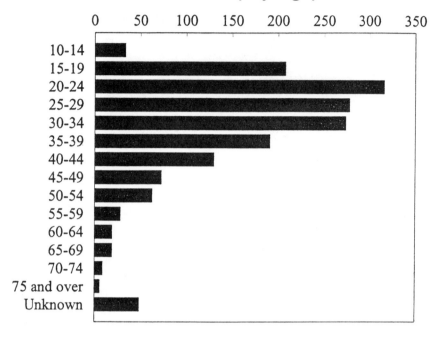

Source: Adapted from U.S. Federal Bureau of Investigation, *Crime in the United States: Uniform Crime Reports 1992* (Washington, D.C.: Government Printing Office, 1993), p. 16.

Why do women kill? What separates these women from the vast majority of females? Are homicidal women on the increase?

THE EXTENT AND NATURE OF FEMALE HOMICIDE

The *Uniform Crime Reports* (*UCR*) reveal that 1,899 females were arrested for murder and nonnegligent manslaughter in 1992. Of these, 1,740 or 92 percent were age 18 and over. Figure 6-1 breaks down female murder offenders by age brackets. Most female murderers fell

FIGURE 6-2

Victims in Female Perpetrated Murders, by Race and Gender, 1992

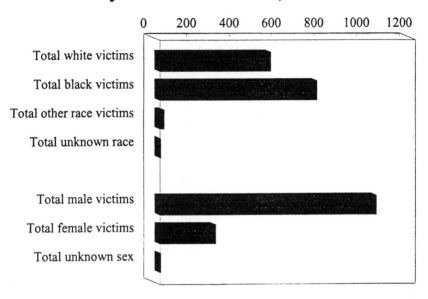

Source: Adapted from U.S. Federal Bureau of Investigation, *Crime in the United States: Uniform Crime Reports 1992* (Washington, D.C.: Government Printing Office, 1993), p. 17.

---

in the 15 to 44 age range, with the peak homicidal years of women being 20 to 24, and a gradual decline for each age bracket thereafter.

The racial and gender makeup of victims of female murderers in 1992 can be seen in Figure 6-2. In 57.6 percent of the murders the victim was black, 40.6 percent the victim was white, and in less than 2 percent of the homicides the victim's race was unknown. Males were the murder victims in 79.4 percent of the homicides, compared to females in 20.3 percent of the murders by females. Women killed their husbands or boyfriends in 623 of the female criminal homicides in 1992.[1]

Arrest trends for murder by females between 1983 and 1992 show that arrests declined by 14.2 percent. However, for females under the age of 18, arrests increased over the period by 15.5 percent.[2] Overall, male arrestees for murder and nonnegligent manslaughter outnumbered female arrestees by more than 9 to 1 in 1992.[3]

Studies show that more black women are being incarcerated for murder than women of other racial groups. In a two year study of 76 female inmates at the North Carolina Correctional Center for Women in Raleigh who were convicted of murder or manslaughter, the researchers found that 57 percent were black, 38 percent white, and 5 percent Native American.[4] Another study of women charged with murder in Los Angeles County over a seven year period, found that 60 percent of the women were black, 23 percent white, 10 percent Hispanic, and 10 percent Asian.[5]

Contrary to many stereotypes of women who kill, ranging from the "Arsenic and Old Lace" murderess to the "Stand By Her Man" or accessory female killer, most women who commit murder do so in the context of intimate relationships or family strain. In a comprehensive study of female homicides and attempted homicides in Hungary, G. Rasko found that of 125 murderesses, 40 percent of the victims were husbands, common-law husbands, or lovers, and 20 percent were their children.[6] J. Totman's study of 120 female killers revealed that husbands, common-law husbands, or lovers accounted for 40 percent of the victims, children 21 percent, and other family members 29 percent.[7] Similarly, a study of 36 accused female murderers found that 42 percent of the women were charged with killing a husband or boyfriend.[8]

There is also evidence to dispute the contention that female killers act in conjunction with male partners. A study of violent female inmates in state prisons found that 77 percent of the women incarcerated for murder were the sole offenders, and in over 50 percent of the incidents the victim was a spouse, lover, or family member.[9]

INFANTICIDE

Infanticide—or the killing of an infant usually soon after birth—is believed to be responsible for more child deaths than any single cause in history, with the possible exception of the bubonic plague.[10] The literature on infanticide is well documented. In the Bible, the New Testament speaks of the "slaughter of the innocents";[11] while the Old Testament describes the killing of countless children in Jericho by

Joshua and his nomadic warriors.[12] King Nimrod slew every first-born in his kingdom after being told by his astrologer that a boy would be born in Mesopotamia who would declare war upon the king;[13] and it is estimated that 70,000 children were killed. Children were burned at the stake during Queen Mary's reign.[14] "In rural areas of Ireland 'changeling babies' (usually babies with congenital defects—but sometimes ugly, screaming or hungry babies) were sometimes roasted alive over fires, even in the twentieth century."[15] Killing female infants was once such a common practice that in many societies the male population was 4 or 5 times greater than the female population.[16]

Infanticide has traditionally been regarded as a sex-specific offense, or one that "actually excludes the members of one sex by legal definition."[17] In describing the English legal system, one author notes that "infanticide does not apply to the British principle of equal applicability because it is an offense in which only women are considered the perpetrators."[18]

Up until the nineteenth century dead or abandoned infants were almost commonplace in the United States. In 1892, 100 dead infants and 200 foundlings were found on the streets of New York City alone.[19] It is unknown how many infant deaths are the result of infanticide today due to misdiagnosis and the sometimes difficult nature of detecting the true cause of death. Official statistics indicate that 254 children under the age of 1 were murder victims in 1992, with another 408 victims aged 1 to 4, and 126 aged 5 to 9.[20]

Infanticide has historically been a reflection of religious appeasement, collective acts of faith, Darwinian survival, and Malthusian population control. Presently, infanticide is often attributed to illegitimate births, resentment of the child, financial and personal stresses and strains, and mental illness of the mother. D. T. Lunde describes the typical mother who commits infanticide: "Women who kill their infants or young children usually are severely disturbed, suffer from extreme bouts of depression and many experience delusions. Before a woman kills her offspring, she is likely to go through a preliminary period when she thinks about how to commit the crime, visualizes the dead child, and considers suicide."[21]

Maria Piers wrote of the frightening reality of infanticide in this society:

> A doctoral candidate in the social sciences at one of the large midwestern universities, who was teaching courses in the social sciences to employees of a large city sewer system, learned from these

employees that during the previous year, four corpses of newborns had been found on the sewer screen. The newborns had been thrown directly after birth into the sewers, a preferred place for children's corpses for millennia. No identification or investigation was attempted in these cases of infant death.[22]

WOMEN WHO KILL THEIR SPOUSES

Experts believe that the most common type of female killer is the woman who kills her spouse or significant other, often after years of physical and psychological abuse. According to sociologists, spousal homicide is not "an isolated occurrence or outbreak, but rather is the culminating event in a pattern of interpersonal abuse, hatred and violence that stretches back well into the history of the parties involved."[23]

A number of recent TV programs or movies, such as "The Burning Bed," and books have dramatized the battered female victim-turned-killer. In a study of spouse killings in Kansas City, it was found that in 90 percent of the cases the police had gone to the home at least once in the 2 years prior to the killing; and in 50 percent of the cases the police had been called to the house on at least 5 occasions.[24] A study of 30 female California state prison inmates who murdered their husbands revealed that 28 had been victims of wife battering.[25]

Elissa Benedek depicts the typical pattern of an abused wife driven to kill her husband:

> Such a woman often comes from a home where she has observed and experienced parental violence and sees violence as a norm in social interaction and as a solution for conflict. Marriage is frequently seen as an escape route, but her choice of husband is not intelligently determined. Thus, the potential offender often chooses a mate with a high penchant for violence. She has been beaten repeatedly and brutally for a period of years by a spouse or lover who may be drunk, sober, tired, depressed, elated, mentally ill, or just angry. Lacking educational and financial resources, she describes a feeling of being trapped. This feeling increases proportionately with the number of young children she has. Community resources are disinterested, ineffective, or unavailable. ... The battered wife has turned to social agencies, police prosecutors, friends, ministers, and family, but they have not offered meaningful support or advice. ... Abused women who have murdered their spouses reveal that they feel that homicide was the only alternative left to them.[26]

Flowers compares the battered woman killer with the suicidal woman in that she is "so consumed with helplessness, hopelessness, despair, low self-esteem, and a distorted conception of reality, that she fails to think logically, to look beyond a horrible situation for which there seems to be no reasonable solution, and thus she seeks an unreasonable one."[27] Psychologist Lenore Walker described the before and after state of mind of the battered woman who murdered her spouse:

> Most women who killed their batterers have little memory of any cognitive processes other than an intense focus on their own survival. Although, retrospectively, it can be seen where her defenses against denial of her anger at being an abuse victim are unraveling, the women do not have any conscious awareness of those feelings. Their description of the final incident indicates that they separate those angry feelings by the psychological process of a dissociative state and thus, do not perceive them. This desperate attempt at remaining unaware of their own unacceptable feelings is a measure of just how dangerous they perceive their situation. They fear showing anger will cause their own death, and indeed it could, as batterers cannot tolerate the woman's expression of anger.[28]

FBI data indicate that 4 percent of the male homicide victims in 1992 were killed by wives or girlfriends.[29] Male spouses or lovers are far more likely than female spouses to be the perpetrators of spousal homicide than victims. Husbands or boyfriends were more than twice as likely to murder wives or girlfriends than the other way around in 1992.[30] Wives constitute about 70 percent of the murdered spouses in the United States, with husbands six to seven times more likely to have initiated the circumstances resulting in death.[31]

WHY DO WOMEN KILL?

Much of the research on criminal homicide has focused on men and been applied to women and child killers. In recent years sociologists and criminologists have studied the characteristics of homicidal women in order to attempt shedding some light on why they kill. A number of reasons and factors have been established, including self-defense, anger, jealousy, mental illness, substance abuse, exposure to domestic violence, child abuse victimization, the battered woman's syndrome, a feeling of isolation, financial gain, and the influence of another such as a male lover. Many experts agree that the primary motivating factor for the typical woman who kills is the belief that her life is threatened or compromised physically or emotionally so that her well-being is at stake.

Stress researchers John Humphrey and John Kirkpatrick coauthored a two-year study entitled, "Stress in the Lives of Female Criminal Homicide Offenders." In interviewing women incarcerated for murder or manslaughter, the researchers found common traits among them, including lives marked by loss, bereavement, and aggression. "The loss could've been a job, a person, something that gives them a real sense of grief. Aggression was behavior marked by the individual feeling some sort of attack, whether it was aggressive posturing by a mate or physical abuse. We found a high level of stress in the lives of these women."[32] Most of the women had murdered men, and their intimates tended to be "physically combative, jealous, psychologically domineering and provocateurs."[33]

Overall, Humphrey and Kirkpatrick found that female and male killers were more similar than dissimilar; although homicidal men had not experienced the stress associated with abortion or miscarriage, and while relatively few had taken on the stress and strain of child care. In homicidal women such stresses and the breakdown of support systems were often found to be contributing factors in their violent acts. The researchers differentiated women from men in general, with respect to the potential to kill, by suggesting that women seem to "have the resources to keep from murdering, the social support they give each other to put up with all manner of adversity for a longer period of time."[34]

In another study of murderous women by psychologists at the University of Southern California School of Medicine, it was found that most were typically from backgrounds characterized by family violence, child abuse, and neglect. According to the study: "Women who kill appear to have severely limited intellectual and emotional coping skills and impoverished social and economic resources."[35] The majority of the homicidal women had a history of substance abuse and suffered from various forms of mental illness.

PREMENSTRUAL SYNDROME AND HOMICIDAL WOMEN

A correlation between homicidal female criminality and the menstrual cycle has been proposed ever since the late nineteenth century.

In 1893, during the trial of Lizzie Borden, her lawyer argued that it was Lizzie's "monthly indisposition" that was responsible for the axe murder of her mother and father.[36] In a book published in 1894, Cesare Lombroso and William Ferrero reported that of 80 women arrested for resistance against public officials, 71 were menstruating at the time the offense took place.[37] Appearing in the 1945 *American Journal of Obstetrics and Gynecology* was W. R. Cooke's presidential address to the American Association of Obstetricians, Gynecologists, and Abdominal Surgeons, in which Cooke cited a Parisian prefect of police finding that 84 percent of all violent crimes committed by women occurred during the premenstrual and early phases of the menstrual cycle.[38] Other research has found that violent female criminality is more likely to occur during the 4 premenstrual days and 4 days of menstruation than during other stages of the menstrual cycle.[39]

In recent years much of the attention with respect to menstruation and female violence has centered on *premenstrual syndrome* (PMS), which refers to a series of symptoms that vary from woman to woman, and include cramps, depression, irritability, mood swings, fatigue, headaches, and nervousness. In England in the early 1980s, two homicidal women successfully used PMS as a defense for their actions. Sandie Smith, a 29-year-old barmaid, received 3 years' probation for threatening to kill a police officer with a knife after Smith's attorney argued that her crime coincided with her PMS, which turned her into a "raging bull." Smith had previously been convicted of nearly 30 other offenses, including murder, assault, and arson.[40] Similarly, Christine English, 37, pleaded guilty to "manslaughter by reason of diminished responsibility," after murdering her boyfriend by running him down with her car. Her lawyer insisted that at the time she was experiencing an "extremely aggravated form of premenstrual physical condition."[41]

Despite the association between PMS and violent or homicidal women, few criminologists, physicians, or other experts believe this to be a significant factor in female violence, primarily because most women experience some degree of premenstrual symptoms yet only relatively few engage in violent criminal acts. Furthermore, studies show that the greater influences for violent criminality tend to be reflected in the individual, social, and economic forces.[42]

7. Women and Domestic Violence

Domestic violence is one of our most serious problems with regard to victimization and family dysfunction. According to the *National Crime Victimization Survey* (*NCVS*), upward of 450,000 cases of family violence are reported annually.[1] Many believe this grossly underestimates total violence within the family, which includes child abuse, spouse abuse, and parent abuse. To a large degree, females have been perceived as being on the receiving end of abuse and violence in the home. While the available information generally supports this view, as we move closer to the year 2000 some studies have revealed that females may be at least equally represented as perpetrators of domestic violence. The magnitude and range of female-perpetrated family offenses will be examined in this chapter.

OFFICIAL DATA AND FEMALE OFFENSES AGAINST FAMILY

The FBI tracks some offenses against family and children in its arrest statistics, including abuse, neglect, and desertion. In 1992, there were 15,213 females arrested for offenses against family members.[2] Ninety-one percent of those arrested were aged 18 and over. The peak years for arrest were ages 21 to 34. Arrests of women for domestic crimes is on the rise. Between 1983 and 1992, female arrests for offenses against family and children increased 23.5 percent.[3] However, female arrests for family offenses is relatively low compared to male arrests for family crimes. Arrest figures reflect only a fraction of the domestic violence that comes to the attention of law enforcement agencies. The vast majority of offenses against family members remain hidden both to law enforcement and other social agencies.

FEMALE CHILD ABUSERS

Child abuse and neglect has reached epidemic proportions in this country. The Child Abuse Prevention and Treatment Act (CAPTA) defines child abuse and neglect as "the physical or mental injury, sexual abuse or exploitation, negligent treatment, or maltreatment of a child under the age of eighteen, by a person who is responsible for the child's welfare, under circumstances which indicate the child's health or welfare is harmed or threatened thereby."[4] The National Committee for Prevention of Child Abuse (NCPCA) estimated that 2,936,000 children were reported as being abused or neglected to child protective services and social service agencies in 1992.[5] Of these, 1,160,400 individual cases were substantiated. Long-term trends of data collected from 1976 to 1992 indicate that child abuse reporting increased by 331 percent, or from a rate of 10 reported abuse and/or neglect victims per 1,000 in 1976 to 43 children abused and/or neglected per 1,000 in 1992.[6]

Studies indicate that females or mothers are responsible for the majority of child abuse and neglect cases. Richard Gelles found that 94 percent of the mothers, compared to 65 percent of the fathers in his sample, had physically abused their children at least once during the survey years.[7] In Brandt Steele and C. Pollock's psychiatric study of abusive parents, the mother was found to be the abuser in 50 of 57 cases.[8] In his epidemiological study of abusing parents, David Gil found that mothers or mother substitutes perpetrated the abuse in 47.6 percent of the cases, compared to fathers or father substitutes in 39.2 percent of the incidents.[9] However, some studies have shown abuse and neglect to be more evenly divided among mothers and fathers.[10]

Age and Abusive Women

The majority of abusive or neglectful women fall between the ages of 20 and 40, the typical child-bearing, child-rearing years. In Blair

Justice and Rita Justice's study, 75 percent of the child abusers were between 20 and 40 years of age during the time of the reported maltreatment; while the other 25 percent were under the age of 20.[11] In Gil's study, 71.2 percent of the mothers or mother substitutes were in the 20–40 age range.[12]

Race, Ethnicity, and Abuse

Abusive women and abused and neglected children exist in every racial and ethnic group. The literature has not shown a consistent pattern with respect to incidence and racial or ethnic background of the abuser. Official data have found child maltreatment to be more prevalent among blacks than whites.[13] But other research has indicated that the rate of child abuse is lower in black families than in white families,[14] while Hispanics tend to be overrepresented in abuse cases compared to non–Hispanics.

Single Female Parent Abusers

A number of studies show a strong relationship between mothers who are single parents and abuse and/or neglect. Nearly half the children in an American Humane Association (AHA) study of abuse and neglect were living with a single, unemployed female caretaker, who received public assistance during the year of the study.[15] In Gil's sample, 29.5 percent of the maltreated children lived in single mother homes.[16] Peggy Smith and Marvin Bohnstedt found that child neglect was most often perpetrated in single female parent households.[17]

Characteristics of Abusive Women

Abusive mothers are typically characterized as immature, impulsive, self-centered, dependent, rigid, and rejecting. They generally lack coping and nurturing skills, and have a poor self-image and low tolerance level. Women who are abusive tend to be under much stress, socially isolated, distrusting of neighbors, and socially impoverished. They often find it difficult to be reliable or self-sufficient.

Most abusive or neglectful women have been the victims of child abuse, neglect, or spouse abuse, or had poor relations with their parents or spouse.[18] In studying familial correlates of child maltreatment, Michael Martin and James Walters found a relationship between child abandonment and alcoholic mothers.[19] Another study linked child abuse to tranquilizer abuse in tense young mothers, noting that "the benzodiazepine tranquilizers can have an 'alcohol-like' effect in reducing higher cortical control, thereby reducing anxiety, but increasing the risk of explosions of temper."[20] Other studies have shown a strong relationship between child maltreatment and alcohol or drug abuse by the abusive mother.[21]

FEMALE SPOUSE ABUSERS

Spouse abuse accounts for a high percentage of all domestic violence, with the typical aggressor being the male and the recipient of the abuse the female. Sociologists estimate that as many as 2 million women may be battered by their husbands in the United States each year.[22] A woman is the victim of spouse abuse every 18 seconds in this country, according to official statistics.[23] However, there is now reason to believe that perhaps as many women are battering their husbands as are being battered. Robert Langley and Richard Levy estimated that 12 million men in the United States are the victims of spouse abuse at some time during their marriage,[24] while Suzanne Steinmetz estimated that 280,000 men are battered each year in this country.[25]

According to Murray Straus, approximately 65 percent of all married couples engaged in spousal violence over the course of their relationship, with 25 percent being of a serious nature.[26] Another study estimated that 2 million husbands have been the recipients of severe marital violence, compared to 1.8 million wives.[27]

Despite these findings, most experts believe that women continue to be the victims of serious spouse abuse far more often than the perpetrators. Gelles found that 32 percent of the wives sampled had been violent at some time, compared to 47 percent of the husbands.[28] A study of college students found that 16.7 percent of their fathers and 10 percent of their mothers had physically abused the other parent during the students' senior year in high school.[29] Police data indicate that the ratio of spousal violence complaints favor the male as aggressor by around 12 to 1.[30] Similarly, victimization data suggest 13 wives are battered for every battered husband.[31]

Socioeconomics,
Education, and Spousal Violence

Studies show that spouse abusers are disproportionately represented among lower class, undereducated, under- and unemployed families. M. Bulcroft and Murray Straus found that spouse abuse perpetrated by both spouses was consistently higher in the working class than in the middle class.[32] In a national survey of family violence, it was reported that 11 percent of the households with income less than $6,000 annually reported spouse abuse, compared to only 2 percent of the households with incomes of $20,000 or more.[33] J. E. O'Brien's study of violence in divorce-prone families revealed that the wife displayed serious dissatisfaction with the husband's income in 84 percent of the violent marriages, compared to only 24 percent of the non-violent marriages.[34]

Violent marriages have been shown to be strongly related to employment and occupational status. Straus and colleagues found that the rate of severe spousal violence was two to three times greater in families where the male spouse was unemployed or employed part-time than among families where the male spouse had a full-time job.[35] Gelles found that the highest rates of marital violence occurred in couples where the husband's occupational status was lower than the wife's.[36]

Research on educational levels and spousal violence show that most violent wives tend to have some college education, while violent husbands are more likely to be without a high school diploma.[37] The rate of violence perpetrated by either spouse has been found to be greater when the husband is less educated than the wife.[38]

CAUSES OF DOMESTIC VIOLENCE

When examining the causes of family violence, most research is based in three broad categories: (1) psychiatric, (2) social-psychological, and (3) social-cultural.

Psychiatric explanations for domestic violence focus largely on the abuser's or batterer's personality characteristics — associating the violence or maltreatment with mental illness or substance abuse. Social-psychological causes of family violence point toward the external and environmental factors that affect family dynamics as well as the individual daily interactions that influence violence in the family, such as communication and stress. Finally, social-cultural or sociological reasons for domestic violence center around socially structured inequality and cultural norms in relation to abuse, violence, and family relations.

CAUSES OF CHILD MALTREATMENT

Why do women abuse or neglect their children? A number of researchers have addressed this issue. Using an environmental stress model, Gil advanced the theory that environmental and occupational stresses, such as poverty and poor education, weaken self-control and cause women to abuse their children.[39] In Gelles's social-psychological model of child abuse, frustration and stress are the main causes of child maltreatment—with the source of such stress including unemployment, marital problems, and social isolation.[40] A psychosocial systems model of abuse was developed by Justice and Justice, which related the shifting symbiosis at work in the family to that within the family environment and society.[41]

Other sociologists have established at-risk factors that predispose children to abuse and mothers to become abusers. These include the following circumstances:

- Marriage at a young age.
- Forced marriages.
- Illegitimate children.
- Unwanted children.
- Children with special needs.
- Problem children.
- Children of mothers with multiple pregnancies.
- Spousal violence.
- Emotional and/or sexual problems in the marriage.
- Social and family isolation.
- A cycle of family abuse and violence.
- Financial problems.
- The abuser's depression, neurosis, or other mental illness.
- Substance abuse.

Studies have shown that difficult children can cause some mothers to be abusive or neglectful. J. Milowe and R. Lourie related child abuse to the child's "irritable cry, the difficulty in managing, and the unappealing nature of these children."[42]

8. *Incestuous Women*

When we speak of incest today, it is almost entirely of the adult male perpetrator and the young female victim. Indeed, much of the research on incest has shown that between 90 and 97 percent of all molesters are male, while 85 percent of the victims are female. For most, it is difficult to imagine the adult female as the active aggressor in an incestuous relationship. However, in fact, women have been incestuous throughout history. Moses was the progeny of an aunt-nephew marriage.[1] Jacob was married to his two sisters; while Abraham married his paternal sister, Sarah.[2] In ancient Ireland the princess (the sister) became the wife of the prince, and occasionally the king himself married his daughter; and in Africa the queens of Gabon were known to marry their oldest sons.[3]

In spite of a near universal taboo against incest, it continues to be an act perpetrated in all societies. Though the numbers of women in the United States who molest their children are believed to be relatively low, recent studies have indicated that incestuous women may be far more prevalent than is commonly known. Why is this? What are the characteristics of female child molesters? Who are the victims?

DEFINING INCEST

The word *incest* comes from the Latin word *incestum*, which means unchaste and low. Incest is commonly defined as "sexual intercourse between relatives within the prohibited degrees of relationship defined by the law."[4] Today incest is considered a criminal offense in every state, though definitions of incest can vary from state to state. Many states and professionals have expanded the definition of incest to cover the often complex interrelationships between family members and the range of incestuous sexual contact including sexual intercourse, sodomy, oral sex, fondling, masturbation, exhibitionism, voyeurism, or any other actual or attempted sexual contact between a family member (biological or nonbiological) and a child (age 17 and under). The perpetrators can be natural parents, foster or step-parents, siblings, step-siblings, and grandparents. Incestuous women may be the birth mothers, adoptive mothers, foster mothers, stepmothers, or legal guardians.

HOW WIDESPREAD IS INCEST COMMITTED BY WOMEN?

It is estimated that between 11 and 33 million people are involved in incestuous relationships in the United States.[5] Another study suggests that as many as 1 in 3 people may be victims of incest before reaching the age of 18.[6] It is commonly believed that incest involving a mother-son or mother-daughter accounts for less than 2 percent of all incest cases. However, many believe this to be a great understatement, since accurate statistics are almost impossible to come by because incest remains largely secretive outside the family. Noted one researcher: "The family as a whole supports actively or passively their own incestuous equilibrium."[7]

Psychologist Nicholas Groth posited that the incidence "of sexual offenses against children perpetrated by adult women is much greater than would be suspected from the rare instances reported in crime statistics."[8] He attributed this to the relative ease in which incestuous women can escape detection under the guise of normal child rearing. After conducting a 450-question survey of 93 women and 9 men who were sexually abused by their mothers, therapist Kathy Evert said: "I believe that no one, including me, knows the extent of sexual abuse by females, especially mothers. About 80 percent of the women and men reported that the abuse was the most hidden aspect of their lives."[9]

THE NATURE OF FEMALE INCEST

Like male child molesters, female child molesters come from all walks of life, every social class, every educational class, and every racial, ethnic, or religious group. Most incestuous women molest their sons, though mother-daughter incest is not unheard of. Adele Mayer described the motivations associated with mother-child incest:

	Motivations
Type of Incest	**(Individual Psychopathology)**
Mother-Son	Substitute gratification for absent father
Mother-Daughter	Psychosis/infantilism[10]

In a study of more than 100 female child molesters, psychologist Ruth Mathews divided them into four major types:

- *Teacher-lover:* Often older women who have sexual relations with a young adolescent.
- *Experimenter-exploiter:* Girls from strict families where sex education is forbidden.
- *Predisposed molesters:* Women who are predisposed to molest children by their own history of severe sexual and/or physical abuse.
- *Male-coerced molesters:* Women who molest children because men make them by force.[11]

According to Mathews, the teacher-lover is the most likely to go undetected because the behavior is usually socially sanctioned. She gave examples in the movie industry, such as *Summer of 42* and *The Last Picture Show.*

Experimenter-exploiters often take advantage of babysitting jobs to "explore" young children. "Many of these girls don't even know what they are doing, have never heard of or experienced masturbation, and are terrified of sex."[12]

Predisposed female molesters victimize not only their own children but young siblings as well. Rationalizes one incestuous woman: "I was always treated as an animal when I was growing up. I didn't realize my kids were human beings."[13]

Male-coerced female sex offenders were also found by Mathews to have been victims of childhood abuse, though not as severe as predisposed molesters. Many are married to child molesters who were the first to molest their children, long before the wife became aware of it and an active participant in incest.

More than 33 percent of the incest survivors Mathews interviewed said they were molested by their mothers. Nevertheless, she found *true female pedophiles* to be rare, accounting for about 5 percent of her sample. Mathews found that incestuous women tended to take more responsibility for their behavior than incestuous men did. Seventy percent of the single female perpetrator molesters took full blame for the molestation; while 50 percent of the women acting in conjunction with a man took 100 percent of the responsibility for the incestuous relations.

MOTHER-SON INCEST

Women who are incestuous with their sons are often seriously disturbed, according to many experts, though Mathews and Evert found only a fraction of their samples to be severely psychotic.[14] In mother-son incest the father is often absent and the mother exploits her son for sexual gratification. A mother sexually active with her adolescent son, often referring to him as her "lover," may be more socially acceptable than father-daughter incest. Usually only the most blatant examples cause societal condemnation and intervention.

Even if the husband/father is present and forces the wife/mother to molest her children, she may begin to molest on her own. One such molester of her 5-year-old son admitted: "Having sex with my son was more enjoyable than with my husband."[15]

In Mathews's study of female sex offenders, she found that most of the molesters had adult male sexual partners living with them during the time the incest was taking place. In Evert's study, the incestuous women in mother-son incest often "abused their daughters violently, beat and terrorized them, and raped them with objects. But they treated their sons like substitute lovers."[16]

MOTHER-DAUGHTER INCEST

Incestuous relations between a mother and daughter is believed to be more rare than that between a mother and son. Relatively little is known about the motivating factors of mother-daughter incest. The female molester is often extremely disturbed and exhibits infantile and/or psychotic tendencies. By exploiting her daughter for emotional nurturance, she may effect a complete role reversal in the mother-daughter relationship.

R. Medlicott cited a case of mother-daughter incest where the mother slept with the daughter to avoid the husband; the mother then initiated incestuous contact with the daughter.[17] The adverse effects of a mother's homosexual attraction toward her daughter was studied by R. Lidz and T. Lidz.[18] In three such cases they found that the incestuous relationship involved molestation while the daughter was asleep, touching and anal contact, and aloofness. All three daughters became schizophrenic as adults.

In "Incest: A Chilling Report," Heidi Vanderbilt describes the nature of women molesting their daughters in which they "wash, fondle, lick, and kiss the child's breasts and genitals, penetrate vagina and anus with tongue, fingers, and other objects: dildos, buttonhooks, screwdrivers—one even forced goldfish into her daughter."[19] According to a survivor of mother-daughter incest: "My mom would play with my breasts and nipples and insert things into my vagina to see if I was normal. 'I'm your mother,' she'd say. 'I need to know you're growing properly.' She'd give me enemas and make me dance for her naked. It lasted until I was twenty. . . . I was petrified of her. Absolutely."[20]

THE FEMALE AS SILENT
INCEST COLLABORATOR

Many women who do not molest their children are guilty of being silent or passive collaborators of father-daughter incest. The wife/mother may unwittingly aid and abet in an incestuous relationship between father and daughter by allowing or arranging situations that isolate the father and daughter, or otherwise promote unnatural closeness, intimacy, or opportunities for father-daughter incestuous contact.

There are also many mothers who blame the child victim for sexual contact with the father and actually encourage circumstances for continuing the incestuous relationship. Vanderbilt speaks of one such example: "When Mariann's mother caught her husband fondling their daughter, she called Mariann a whore and accused her of trying to seduce her father. Yet when Mariann's father got a job in another state that required him to move early one spring, her mother stayed behind until summer but insisted that Mariann go with him."[21] Other mothers become silent or inactive collaborators of father-daughter incest by ignoring the signs or accusing the child victim of outright lying should she get up the nerve to tell her mother the truth about what is happening.

9. Women
and Prostitution

Our image of the adult female prostitute is largely influenced by the Hollywood portrayal of prostitutes. They are invariably either the glamorous, well-paid call girl such as Julia Roberts's *Pretty Woman*, or the drug-addicted, high-heeled, gum chewing, red-light-district streetwalker. Recently the Hollywood prostitute took on a whole new dimension with the arrest of Heidi Fleiss. Dubbed the "Hollywood Madam," Fleiss was convicted in December 1994 on three counts of pandering. She provided high priced call girls to undercover police officers.

The reality is that today's women prostitutes are both exploited and exploiters of various types and dimensions, highly visible and yet well hidden from the public eye, and predominantly in the business for financially based reasons. Then there is AIDS, which has affected the perception of female prostitutes but done little to slow down the incidence of prostitution in the United States. What all female prostitutes seem to have in common is that they are viewed as little more than sex objects by the men they service to be used, abused, and discarded. In this chapter, we will examine the definition, scope, nature, and explanations of women's prostitution.

DEFINITIONS OF PROSTITUTION

Historically, most definitions of prostitution have been sex-specific, that is, in relation to females in general and women specifically. This is reflected somewhat in the book *Howard Street*, in which it is stated that "a man is a natural pimp and a woman is a natural whore."[1] Definitions of prostitution are typically divided into two types: social definitions and legal definitions.

Social Definitions of Prostitution

Sociologists have often defined prostitution as sexual relations characterized by payment, barter, promiscuity, and emotional indifference. Prostitution was defined by one writer as "sexual intercourse on a promiscuous and mercenary basis, with emotional indifference."[2] Edwin Lemert made bartering an element of the interaction prior to sexual relations.[3] Charles Winick and Paul Kinsie defined prostitution as "the granting of nonmaterial sexual access, established by mutual agreement of the woman, her client, and/or her employer, for remuneration which provides part or all of her livelihood."[4] Paul Goldstein's definition was "nonmarital sexual service for material gain."[5]

In 1914, Abraham Flexner wrote that prostitution is characterized by

> three elements variously combined: barter, promiscuity and emotional indifference. The barter need not involve the passage of money. . . . Nor need promiscuity be utterly choiceless: a woman is not the less a prostitute because she is more or less selective in her associations. Emotional indifference may be fairly inferred from barter and promiscuity. In this sense any person is a prostitute who habitually or intermittently has sexual relations more or less promiscuously for money or other mercenary consideration. Neither notoriety, arrest nor lack of other occupation is an essential criterion.[6]

Flexner argued that the broad-based definition was based on the harm to society that prostitution brought, naming four social costs of prostitution in particular: spread of venereal disease, personal demoralization, economic waste, and the association of prostitution to crime and social disorder.

Legal Definitions of Prostitution

Early legal definitions of prostitution also focused largely on the female prostitute, immorality, and promiscuity. Near the turn of the century the U.S. Supreme Court defined prostitution as "women who for hire or without hire offer their bodies to indiscriminate intercourse with men."[7] Howard Woolston noted that prior to 1918 the only statutory definition of prostitution was Section 2372 of the Indiana Law, which read: "Any female who frequents or lives in a house of ill-fame or associates with women of bad character for chastity, either in public or at a house which men of bad character frequent or visit, or who commits adultery or fornication for hire shall be deemed a prostitute."[8]

As recently as 1968, the Oregon Supreme Court ruled with respect to identifying the prostitute from the nonprostitute: "The feature which distinguishes a prostitute from other women who engage in illicit intercourse is the indiscrimination with which she offers herself to men for hire."[9] The intrinsic legal bias toward females involved in prostitution led Kate Millett to observe: "Prostitution is really the only crime in the penal law where two people are doing a thing mutually agreed upon and yet only one, the female partner, is subject to arrest."[10]

Prostitution is a crime in every state in the country, with the exception of Nevada, where it is legal in most counties. In 38 states payment for sexual acts is expressly prohibited; solicitation laws exist in 44 states and the District of Columbia; and in other states vagrancy and loitering statutes are applied to prostitutes. Legally, prostitution is a misdemeanor, or an offense that normally carries a fine and/or 30-day jail term.

Most prostitution laws today recognize the male prostitute as well as the female; however, females continue to be subjected to more arrests and incarceration for prostitution. In 1992, there were nearly twice as many women arrested for prostitution as men.[11] Of women in jail 1 in 3 were arrested for prostitution; while 7 in 10 women imprisoned for felonies were initially arrested for prostitution.[12]

THE MAGNITUDE OF WOMEN'S PROSTITUTION

It is generally believed that well over 1 million women are actively engaged in prostitution on a full-time basis in the United States, working the streets, the massage parlors, or other avenues to earn a living. The number may double or triple when adding prostitutes who work only part-time in the sex-for-sale business, often doubling as students, housewives, or businesswomen. Only a fraction of the female prostitutes

FIGURE 9-1

Women's Prostitution
and Commercialized Vice
Arrests, by Age Groups, 1992

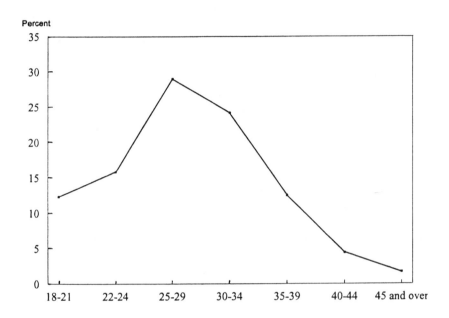

Source: Derived from U.S. Federal Bureau of Investigation, *Crime in the United States: Uniform Crime Reports 1992* (Washington, D.C.: Government Printing Office, 1993), pp. 231-232.

are ever arrested for prostitution. According to the FBI's *Uniform Crime Reports 1992*, there were 56,244 females aged 18 and over arrested in the United States in 1992 for prostitution and commercialized vice. This represented 99 percent of all prostitution-related female arrests. Figure 9-1 distributes women's 1992 arrests for prostitution and commercialized vice by age group. Over 53 percent of all arrests occurred in the 25 to 34 age category. The peak age group for prostitution arrests was ages 25 to 29, accounting for 29 percent of all arrests. Over 28 percent of the arrestees were between the ages of 18 and 24, with

12.5 percent ages 35 to 39. Arrests of women over the age of 40 for prostitution and commercialized vice accounted for just over 6 percent of the total arrests.

The vast majority of women in prostitution are white. However, among inner city, red-light-district prostitutes the percentage of racial and ethnic minorities (particularly black female prostitutes) may increase to as many as 50 percent of those walking the streets.[13] Poor black women tend to be the most penalized as prostitutes, as they are most likely to be "forced onto the streets and into blatant solicitation where the risk of arrest is highest."[14] Black women are seven times more likely to be arrested for prostitution or commercialized vice than women of other racial groups.[15] Most of such arrests occur in the inner cities where "living standards are low, the level of desperation high, and police prejudice endemic."[16]

Female prostitutes as a group appear to be victims of discriminatory law enforcement practices. For example, though 20 percent of the male population is believed to solicit prostitutes at some point in their lives, recent official statistics show that only two male customers of prostitutes are arrested for every eight prostitutes arrested.[17] Disparities are also seen in female-male prostitute statistics and incarceration data.[18]

TYPES OF WOMEN PROSTITUTES

Contrary to the young, slender, attractive white female prostitute depicted in many films and books, prostitutes come in all shapes, sizes, ages, races, and situational circumstances. Much of the research into types of prostitutes has concentrated on the motivations for entry into prostitution and the prostitute's modus operandi. Harry Benjamin and R. E. L. Masters broke down female prostitutes into two general types: *voluntary* and *compulsive*.[19] Voluntary prostitutes act rationally and freely choose prostitution. Compulsive prostitutes are, to a certain degree, acting under compulsion by "psychoneurotic" needs. The researchers found that neither type was mutually exclusive of the other.

Goldstein divided prostitutes in terms of *occupational commitment* and *occupational milieu*.[20] Occupational commitment relates to the frequency of a woman's prostitution and is subdivided into 3 types:

1. *Temporary prostitute*—a discreet act of prostitution, lasting not more than 6 months in a specific occupational milieu;

2. *Occasional prostitute*—two or more discreet acts of prostitution in a particular occupational milieu, each episode lasting no longer than 6 months; and

3. *Continual prostitute*—prostitution more than 6 months in duration in a specific occupational milieu on a regular basis.

Occupational milieu refers to the specific types of prostitution a woman is involved in. Goldstein breaks these down into 7 types:

1. *Streetwalker*—a woman who overtly solicits men on the street and offers sexual favors for payment;

2. *Call girl*—a woman who works in a residence or hotel soliciting clients or is solicited over the telephone;

3. *Massage parlor prostitute*—a woman who offers sexual services in a massage parlor, not necessarily limited to fondling of the genitals;

4. *House prostitute*—a woman who works in an establishment created specifically for prostitution where male clients are given sexual favors;

5. *Madam*—a woman who supplies other prostitutes with male customers for a percentage of the fee;

6. *Mistress*—a woman primarily supported by one man at a time, or who sees only one man at a time for money; and

7. *Barterer*—a woman who exchanges sexual favors for professional or other services, or for material goods (clothes or drugs).

Other classifications of women prostitutes include the following categories:

- *Online prostitutes*—women who sell sexual services through online computer networks and bulletin boards.

- *Bar girl*—a woman working in a bar, lounge, or other establishment not set up specifically for prostitution, where male clients are solicited or the woman is willingly solicited by males for sexual favors.

- *Referral prostitute*—a woman referred to male clients by another (often another prostitute). This differs from a madam, as the referrer often has no financial stake in the referral.

- *Sex ring-escort prostitutes*—women who are part of a large-scale phone referral operation for the purpose of selling sexual favors.

- *1–900 prostitutes*—women who sell sexual services to males by phone.
- *Middle-class prostitutes*—women who live and/or work in the middle class, including housewives and college students, who sell sexual services to men in and out of the middle class.

Most of these types of prostitutes can go from one occupational milieu to another, or engage in more than one at the same time, depending upon the prostitute's needs, circumstances, discretion, and opportunities. For example, a middle-class call girl addicted to drugs may have to resort to streetwalking to keep up her habit. (See also chapter 14 on girl prostitutes.)

STREETWALKERS

Streetwalkers, or curbside prostitutes, represent the lower level of the women's prostitution hierarchy. It is estimated that only 10 to 15 percent of all female prostitutes are streetwalkers.[21] However, they are disproportionately likely to have pimps, be victims of violence, substance abusers, or arrested. Jennifer James, an anthropologist, has done extensive research on streetwalkers: their relationship to pimps and their motivations for hustling.[22] She divided prostitutes into two classes: *true prostitutes* and *part-timers*. From these James established 13 roles played by prostitutes. True prostitutes included *outlaws, rip-off artists, hypes, ladies, old-timers*, and *thoroughbreds*. Part-timers included women *who had no style* and *amateurs* or "hos." James described true prostitutes as follows:

- *Outlaws* are prostitutes independent of pimps.
- *Rip-off artists* are thieves disguised as prostitutes; prostitution is not their main source of income.
- *Hype* refers to the prostitute who works to support her drug habit.
- *The Lady* prostitute is identified by her carriage, class, finesse, and professionalism.
- *Old-timers* are seasoned pros who lack the class of the lady.
- *Thoroughbred* refers to young, professional prostitutes.

None of the roles are deemed as mutually exclusive of each other since they "describe different dimensions of streetwalker behavior rather than complete behavioral sets, each containing elements from all relevant streetwalker behavioral dimensions."[23]

James contradicted the stereotypical view of the pimp-prostitute relationship in her findings, concluding that "it is not true that pimps force women to work against their will, seduce young girls, turn women into drug addicts for the purpose of control, give no sexual satisfaction to their women, keep them from ever leaving their stable, and are never married to prostitutes who work for them."[24] Beyond the expected advantages and disadvantages a prostitute has in having a pimp, it appears that the "severe social isolation that pre-prostitutes feel predisposes them to join up with someone who 'plugs' them into the world, giving them a set of social relations, a place to call their own, and an ideology to make the world intelligible."[25] The streetwalking prostitute's entry into the pimp's world is seen in not so much as a reflection of the pimp's charm, coercion, or violence but rather in the social environment that the prostitute came from.

James identified three groups of motivations for streetwalkers:

1. *Conscious*—economics, working conditions, adventure, and a persuasive pimp;
2. *Situational*—early experiences in life, child abuse and/or neglect, and occupation; and
3. *Psychoanalytic*—general factors, oedipal fixation, latent homosexuality, and retardation.[26]

Although James's work has made a significant contribution to understanding the dynamics of streetwalking prostitutes, there is much evidence that supports the physical or psychological captive perspective of the prostitute-pimp relationship, irrespective of the streetwalker's history.[27] An indication of the manipulative powers of the pimp can be seen in this ex-streetwalker's reflections: "My pimp took all my money. If I needed a new coat or pantyhose, I had to ask him. The illusion was that he was taking care of me. I thought this arrangement was okay till I got arrested and sent to a treatment center for alcoholics. That stopped me long enough to get a look at what was really happening."[28]

MIDDLE-CLASS PROSTITUTES

A growing number of women from the middle class are turning to prostitution to pay for college, the mortgage, to supplement other income, or to support their or their husband's drug habits. No one knows for certain just how many middle-class women are turning tricks, but the indication is that they may represent the largest group of prostitutes by class.

Middle-class prostitutes can work for pimps, escort services, massage parlors, madams, or on their own. They include women from all backgrounds and circumstances, such as "nursing students, housewives in the process of getting a divorce, a teacher with a sick husband who is trying to raise money to bring a relative to the United States."[29] Many college students, college graduates, would-be artists, struggling actresses, single mothers, and unemployed or part-time employed middle-class women have entered the prostitution business on the side. "For women who are short on money and unconventional, hooking has become like waitressing—a means of getting by."[30]

Unlike most streetwalkers, middle-class prostitutes tend to be more educated, sophisticated, self-respecting, and careful about to whom they sell their sexual favors and where they perform these favors. Many cater to the convention center and expensive hotel crowds, charging their male clients—often men 30 to 40 years their senior—anywhere from $50 to $200 an hour. Others use the escort service route to find tricks and make money. These services often advertise the escorts as "gorgeous," or "models" selected for their "beauty, personality, and charm." A New York Police Department official estimated that in New York City there were several hundred escort services, or prostitution services, that can call on anywhere from 50 to 150 women "from as far away as Rhode Island."[31]

A typical example of a middle-class woman turned middle-class prostitute can be seen in the following account of a young woman who began working for a massage parlor after months of struggling to become a singer: "It was so simple, so natural, I got right into it. ... I'd always been promiscuous, ever since I first got started sexually as a teenager. I had a need for security—you know, problems with self-hatred, lack of confidence, and all that stuff—and sex made me feel worthwhile. ... I decided, if I'm going to be obsessive about sex, I might as well get paid for it. You know, why give it away?"[32] Another part-time prostitute, working for an escort service, admitted: "In a way, it was good for my ego. These men were telling me that my presence was worth money, that I was a desirable person to be with."[33]

Though middle-class prostitutes are less likely to encounter some of the dangers and risks often associated with streetwalking, they still face possible hazards including drug addiction, rape, and sexually transmitted diseases. Emotional stress has been found to be high among all prostitutes. One ex-middle-class prostitute in describing how she dealt with the stress of turning tricks noted: "You have to do something to deal with it. I did a lot of drugs, mostly cocaine, during the period I was working. And I drank a lot too."[34]

CALL GIRLS

Call girls represent the highest tier of prostitutes and least visible. Because they can afford to ply their trade in four-star hotels and expensive apartments where detection or arrest is difficult, if not impossible, the number of women working as high-class call girls may never be known. However, it is generally believed that there are at least as many call girls in the prostitution business as streetwalkers. According to Linda Lee, "what distinguishes call girls from streetwalkers is appearance, money, and class (and the possession of a telephone). An appropriately dressed call girl can walk into a good hotel or drive into a residential neighborhood without attracting police attention. The gear of street prostitution—revealing clothes, excessive makeup, a garish hairstyle—is not for her."[35]

Unlike streetwalkers, where the racial and ethnic distribution can be evenly divided between white, black, and Hispanic women, most call girls tend to be white. They are also more likely to be college educated than their streetwalking counterparts. Sydney Barrows, who ran an escort service, declared of her employees: "Most of my girls were college grads . . . good, nice people with serious goals in life—the kind mothers would be proud to have as daughters."[36] Another operator of a New York escort service noted, "Some of our escorts are married women. Their husbands think they're working as hostesses. One of our girls is the daughter of a diplomat. She has two art galleries, but she's bored with her life, and she wants to meet executives."[37]

The image of the call girl as beautiful, intelligent, articulate, financially secure, and marriage material but who's in the business for fun, profit, and to escape boredom, allows its participants to maximize the benefits of prostitution (money, sex, travel, and fun) while minimizing the downside (labeling, discovery, danger, and arrest). The money, undoubtedly, is the biggest lure for women who become call girls, with potential yearly incomes of six figures or more.

It has been found in some studies that upper-class prostitutes have few, if any, pathologies in relation to their profession, compared to lower-class prostitutes who have been found to have many pathologies:

At the upper level, among the full-time call girls and part-time housewives who appear to lead economically secure, stable, arrest-free lives, there is no evidence of special pathology. At the lower levels, inhabited by streetwalkers, drug addicts, juvenile runaways, and deviants of many different stripes, the population is so prone to psychological pathology that it is difficult to know what part, if any, prostitution contributes to their many difficulties.[38]

In a study of white-collar prostitution, Coramae Mann found no evidence of pathology among these prostitutes or hostility toward males.[39] The women interviewed reported that the primary factor in their prostitution was money or something else of value (such as luxury items, rent, or money for medical bills). However, James found in her study of call girls and streetwalkers that 42 percent had been victims of sexual abuse and a high percentage came from broken homes.[40]

Other studies have found a relationship between call girl prostitution and psychological and sociological factors. Harold Greenwald examined upper-class prostitution in relation to differential association and economic and environmental variables.[41] He found severe personality disorders in his call girl patients, but was uncertain if these disorders had come before entry into prostitution or were as a result of it. Greenwald suggested that prostitution "was not necessarily more degrading than working at a job one hated or being married to a man one found physically repulsive."[42] Despite its complex etiology, he believed there was an easy means to prevent women from becoming high-class prostitutes, for he had "never known a call girl who had strong bonds of love and affection with her family."[43] In her study of call girls, Karen Rosenblum found that they were motivated by the desire to be independent of men and make as much money as possible.[44]

James Bryan examined call girls in terms of apprenticeship and individual attitudes.[45] He found that call girls basically learned their trade by serving as an apprentice to an established call girl, an arrangement that ended once the apprentice had developed her own book of clients or ran into problems or disagreements with the trainer. The apprenticeship included two areas: *verbal behavior* and *attitude*. "The verbal behavior was difficult for many apprentices to master because it was more contrary to traditional sex roles than the overt sexual activity that was sold. Call girls had to learn to be verbally aggressive on the phone and to ask directly for dates."[46] Bryan found that with regard to attitude, call girls saw themselves as social workers, counselors, and sex therapists whose services were desperately needed.[47] Such is the example of Delores French: "I'm from a very middle-class background. I wasn't raped, I'm not a victim of incest. I do this because I choose to do it, and I plan to do it for the rest of my life. I love it. There aren't many careers where your job is to renew people's self-esteem. That's really what this job is all about—renewing people's self-esteem."[48]

Call girl prostitutes have the lowest risk for victimization of every type, yet they still have a relatively high incidence of substance abuse and sexually transmitted diseases. As long as there is much money to be made and many men willing to spend it, women who otherwise have little incentive to become prostitutes will continue to be lured into the upper echelons of the business.

MONEY AND WOMEN'S PROSTITUTION

Whether a streetwalker, middle-class prostitute, high-class call girl, or other type of prostitute, the primary motivation for women entering prostitution and continuing in it is the money to be made. The reasons for needing or wanting the money may vary from prostitute to prostitute and include supporting children or a drug habit, buying clothes, saving money, or maintaining a lifestyle. James described five aspects of our social and economic structure that draws women into prostitution:

1. There are virtually no other occupations available to unskilled or low-skilled women with an income comparable to prostitution.
2. There are virtually no other jobs available to unskilled or low-skilled women that provide the adventure and independent lifestyle of the prostitute.
3. The traditional "woman's role" is almost synonymous with the culturally defined female sex role, which focuses on service, physical appearance, and sexuality.
4. The discrepancy between accepted male and female sex roles creates the "madonna-whore" notion of female sexuality, such that women who are sexually active outside the parameters of their normal sex role expectations are labeled deviant and lose social status.
5. The cultural importance of wealth and material items leads some women to desire advantages they are normally not afforded by their socioeconomic position in society.[49]

How much money can prostitutes hope to make? It varies with the type and class of prostitute, as well as the service or services offered. A National Task Force on Prostitution put the average "full-time gross between $15,000 and $25,000; $200 to $500 weekly for solicitors on the streets; $500 for sauna workers, $300 to $1,200 for brothel hostesses."[50] Call girls make the most in the business on average, with anywhere from $1,000 to $2,500 a week at an escort service to more than $1,000 a day for some women operating independently. One high-priced call girl claimed to have made $2,000 an hour and up, "loved all her clients, and was proud of being told she had magic fingers."[51] Being a madam is potentially even more profitable. Barrows reportedly grossed more than $1 million a year by renting out attractive escorts to men by the hour.

VICTIMIZATION AND WOMEN AS PROSTITUTES

Many adult female prostitutes began as runaways-turned-girl prostitutes, and were victims of child abuse and/or neglect, sexual abuse, and other family and background dysfunction. Substance abuse is a common theme among women prostitutes, as are sexual assaults. Rates of victimization tend to be higher for lower-class prostitutes than middle- or upper-class prostitutes; however, all women prostitutes risk assaults, robberies, and other crimes of violence with each trick they turn.[52]

Aside from the range of venereal diseases to which prostitutes expose themselves, the risk of AIDS (Acquired Immune Deficiency Syndrome) is ever present. According to the Centers for Disease Control (CDC), the rate of AIDS among female prostitutes is higher than that of the general public.[53] The incidence of AIDS among prostitutes does appear to vary depending on the type of prostitution and whether or not the prostitute is an IV drug user. Typically, street prostitutes face the highest risk of contracting AIDS, while high-priced call girls face the lowest. A study at the University of Miami of escort service prostitutes and streetwalkers found that none of the 25 female escorts sampled tested positive for the virus, but of the 90 streetwalkers tested there was a 41 percent rate of infection.[54] Another study found that 37 percent of the women street prostitutes who admitted being IV drug users tested positive for the Human Immunodeficiency Virus (HIV).[55]

In a study of high-class call girls, only one woman with a history of drug abuse tested HIV-positive.[56]

In one of the few studies of customers of prostitutes, it was found that approximately 2 percent of the men sampled carried the AIDS virus.[57] Half of the men had additional risk factors such as IV drug use and homosexual relationships; the other half had no apparent risk factors aside from that of engaging the services of female prostitutes.

10. Women
and Drug Abuse

Historically, women have been abusing drugs. During the last part of the nineteenth century and early into the twentieth century, female addicts outnumbered male addicts two to one.[1] Opiates, the "little pink pills," were used as "nerve medicine" by millions of American women "who were quite literally drug addicts without anyone especially noting the nature of their dependence."[2] Today, women are far less likely to be involved in drug use, abuse, or dealing than men. However, women *offenders* are equally likely to be using or abusing drugs as men offenders.[3] Overall, the number of adult female drug addicts has risen steadily in recent years. A strong correlation has been shown between female drug use and other crimes such as child abuse, drug dealing, prostitution, and violent crimes.[4] There is also a significant relationship between female IV drug abusers and AIDS.[5] This chapter will examine women and drug involvement.

THE SCOPE OF
WOMEN'S DRUG USE/ABUSE

Because of the range of drugs women use and abuse—including illicit drugs, prescription drugs, and alcohol—it is impossible to guess just how many women are involved in abusive or illegal drug use. It is generally believed that millions of women in the United States today are abusing drugs and/or are addicted to drugs.

Alcohol abuse among women is a serious problem. In 1992 there were 292,784 women arrested for alcohol-related offenses in the United States.[6] Listed below are recent statistics on women and alcohol:

- Sixty percent of adult females are drinkers; 5 percent heavy drinkers.
- One in 3 members of Alcoholics Anonymous is female.
- Thirty to 40 percent of the patients in alcohol treatment centers are women.
- Women frequently combine alcohol abuse with the abuse of other drugs.
- Female alcoholics drink on average 11 times as often as nonalcoholic drinkers.[7]

According to the liquor industry newsletter, *Impact*, women were projected to spend $30 billion on alcoholic beverages in 1994, compared to $20 billion they spent in 1984.[8]

Illicit drug use among women is increasing at a faster rate than alcohol-related abuse. There were 143,183 females aged 18 and over arrested for drug abuse violations in the United States in 1992.[9] As shown in Figure 10-1, women's arrests for drug abuse violations (including unlawful possession, use, sale, growing, and manufacturing of narcotics), rose nearly 85 percent between 1983 and 1992. In a national household survey on drug abuse, 34 percent of the women surveyed admitted using illicit drugs.[10] In addition, 5 percent of the female respondents said they had used illegal drugs within the past month.

One-third of the women inmates in state prisons in 1991 were convicted of drug offenses such as possessing and trafficking. This represented a 21 percent increase in the proportion of women prisoners sentenced for drug offenses in 1986.[11] Over half the women in prison in 1991 had used drugs in the month prior to the offense for which they were convicted. Furthermore, 65 percent of the female inmates had used drugs regularly, of these 41 percent used them daily and 36 percent were under the influence of drugs during the commission of the crime that put them in prison.[12]

ILLEGAL DRUG
USE/ABUSE AMONG WOMEN

Women are using and abusing every illegal or nonprescription drug available in the United States, including marijuana, cocaine,

FIGURE 10-1

Trends in Women's Arrests for Drug Abuse Violations, 1983–92

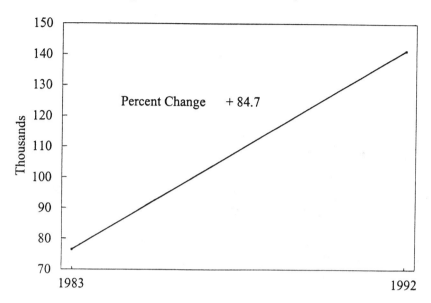

Source: Adapted from U.S. Federal Bureau of Investigation, *Crime in the United States: Uniform Crime Reports 1992* (Washington, D.C.: Government Printing Office, 1993), p. 222.

---

crack cocaine, heroin, LSD, PCP, and Darvon. The National Institute on Drug Abuse (NIDA) recently illustrated the percentage of men and women who use four of the more popular illicit drugs: heroin, cocaine, crack cocaine, and marijuana (see Figure 10-2). Among heroin users, 57.3 percent of the users are women, compared to 42.7 percent men. Nearly 30 percent of the cocaine users are women, and more than 80 percent of crack cocaine users are men. Over 33 percent of the marijuana users are women.

Studies on women drug addicts have established the following characteristics:

• Adult female addicts are older than adult male addicts, usually beginning drug use in their mid-twenties.

FIGURE 10-2

Percentage of Men and Women Illicit Drug Users, by Drug Type, 1991

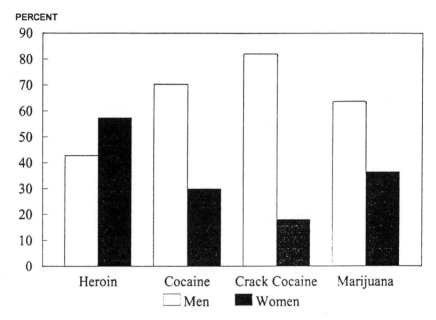

PERCENT

Note: Based on persons interviewed in 1991 who used drugs within the past year.

Source: Adapted from U.S. Department of Justice, *Drugs, Crime, and the Justice System* (Washington, D.C.: Government Printing Office, 1992), p. 28.

- Black women addicts and female addicts of other racial minorities are younger than white women addicts.
- Hispanic women are disproportionately more likely to be drug addicts compared to non–Hispanic women.
- White and Hispanic women are about twice as likely to inject drugs as black women.
- Native American women have a higher rate of drug abuse than non–Native American women.
- Most women prisoners have used drugs; about 40 percent were daily users.

- Women addicts are more likely to be divorced, separated, widowed, or have children than the men who are addicts.
- Female drug addicts often are high school dropouts and have unsuccessful work histories.
- Female drug abuse is more indicative of some pathology than male drug abuse.
- Women addicts tend to have more family related and financial problems than male addicts.
- Female drug abusers tend to have a lower self-esteem and self-image than female nonaddicts and male addicts.[13]

Women and Cocaine

Cocaine is believed to be the most highly used and abused illicit drug by women. Sold on the street "as a fine, white powder," cocaine or coke "can be snorted, smoked, or injected intravenously. The effects, which last for about 30 minutes, include a feeling of euphoria, heightened self-confidence, a rush of energy, and intensified sensuality."[14] Approximately 30 million men and women have tried cocaine, with 5 million regular users.[15] About 1 in every 3 cocaine addicts in the United States is a woman,[16] and it is estimated that 53 percent of the women cocaine addicts in drug treatment centers are under 30 years of age.[17] A high percentage of these women have also been found to be addicted to alcohol and amphetamines, often spending as much as $500 a week to support their habits. "They are usually in middle- or upper-income brackets, well-educated, in competitive demanding jobs or dissatisfied with their lives."[18]

Now in its second wave of epidemic in the United States, cocaine use by women is on the rise. For example, the percentage of women inmates who had used cocaine in the month prior to their incarceration went from 23 percent in 1986 to 36 percent in 1991 for a 13 percent increase.[19] A number of reasons are given for this surge in women's cocaine use. One is the gradual decline of Valium prescriptions—the most abused prescription drug by women. The senior vice president of a drug treatment center suggested, "Since two out of three Valium prescriptions are written for women, presumably many females who cannot get Valium have switched to coke."[20]

Another reason women are believed to be lured to cocaine is the drug's image. Notes one writer: "Heroin is a grubby street product, and PCP, an animal tranquilizer known as angel dust, is the 'unemployment drug' because it relieves depression. . . . Cocaine is thought of as the champagne of drugs."[21] According to some experts, many women see cocaine as an aphrodisiac. Ronald Siegel, a psychopharmacologist, found that "women respond more euphorically and ecstatically than males to sex with coke and rate their sexual experiences with cocaine much higher than males do."[22]

Crack cocaine is blamed by some on the rising number of female cocaine addicts. Crack, an inexpensive, smokable, more potent version of cocaine, is seen as "rapidly taking over and increasing the number of cocaine addicts."[23] Finally, another reason attributed to women's use and abuse of cocaine is a follow-the-leader syndrome — that is, "whatever substance men abuse is often later taken up by women."[24]

WOMEN OFFENDERS AND DRUG ABUSE

The relationship between women who abuse drugs and commit other crimes is strong. One-third of the women drug addicts are prostitutes, while a high percentage of the women abusing or addicted to drugs commit thefts, often to support their habit.[25] Violence by women is also linked to drug use or addiction. In a National Institute of Justice (NIJ) study of violent crime arrestees in New York City and Washington, D.C., more than 50 percent of the women arrested for violent crimes had been using one or more illicit drugs prior to their arrest.[26] A Baltimore study of street addicts found that 96 percent of the addicts who were daily users committed crimes to support their addiction, including shoplifting, prostitution, con games, and robbery.[27]

Table 10-1 shows the most serious offenses of women in state prisons by their drug use history in 1991. In 39 percent of the drug offenses, 30 percent of the property offenses, and 25 percent of the violent offenses committed, the women inmates reported using drugs in the month prior to the offense that resulted in their incarceration. Women prisoners who were under the influence of a drug at the time the offense was perpetrated accounted for 24.3 percent of the violent crimes, 30.6 percent of the property crimes, and 39.6 percent of the drug crimes. In 42.6 percent of the property offenses, 36.0 percent of the drug offenses, and 17.1 percent of the violent offenses, the women in prison said they committed the crime to get money or purchase drugs.

Researchers have found the following characteristics of women caught in the cycle of drug addiction and other crimes:

- A high number of drug-involved female offenders have children.
- Many pregnant IV drug users have infants born addicted.
- A relatively high proportion of women drug addicts test seropositive for the AIDS virus.
- There is a significant relationship between women's prostitution and drug addiction.
- Many women child abusers are also drug abusers.
- Most female drug dealers are female drug users.
- For drug-involved offenders who come into contact with the criminal justice system, women are less likely than men to receive adequate drug treatment.[28]

Many women who use drugs also sell drugs. Though the number of female drug user-dealers is very small compared to male drug user-dealers, and even smaller among top-level or mid-level dealers, more than half the women who use and deal drugs "play an active role in the lowest levels of the drug trade and facilitate as many sales as men who are also involved at the lowest levels."[29] According to the NIJ, women drug dealers are categorized as part of the "lesser predatory" type, and have the following typical characteristics:

- Their drug use tends to be moderate to heavy, with some addiction.
- Heroin and cocaine are often their drugs of choice.
- Many are also into prostitution and/or theft.
- Many have addicted or AIDS babies.
- Their children are at high risk for becoming involved in drugs and other crimes.
- They tend to have only low to moderate contact with the criminal justice system.[30]

WOMEN'S PRESCRIPTION DRUG MISUSE/ABUSE

It is believed that millions of women in the United States are abusing or addicted to prescription or legal drugs, including tranquilizers, sleeping pills, amphetamines, and pain killers. There are 3.7 billion such drugs consumed in the country each year.[31] Many women have become "Valium 'junkies' by collecting prescriptions from as many doctors as they could manipulate into writing them."[32] In addition,

TABLE 10-1

Most Serious Offenses of Women
Inmates in Prison, by Drug Use History, 1991

Most serious offense	Percent who used drugs in the month before current offense		Percent under the influence of drugs at the time of the offense		Percent who committed offense to get money to buy drugs	
	Yes	No	Yes	No	Yes	No
Violent offenses	25.0	40.8	24.3	37.0	17.1	37.0
Homicide[a]	8.8	22.5	8.5	19.0	2.2	19.3
Sexual assault[b]	0.4	3.0	0.3	2.4	0.0	2.2
Robbery	9.6	5.7	10.7	6.1	13.2	6.0
Assault	5.2	7.3	3.7	7.6	1.5	7.7
Other violent	0.9	2.2	1.0	1.8	0.3	1.9
Property offenses	30.0	27.1	30.6	27.6	42.6	24.4
Burglary	5.7	3.2	5.4	4.1	7.2	3.7
Larceny/theft	12.9	8.9	13.9	9.5	21.9	7.8
Fraud	8.8	12.0	9.0	11.0	11.9	9.6
Other property	2.6	3.1	2.4	3.1	1.5	3.3
Drug offenses	39.0	25.7	39.6	28.8	36.0	31.8
Possession	15.4	7.5	15.8	9.3	11.2	11.9
Trafficking	21.9	17.4	21.7	18.7	23.3	18.7
Other drug	1.7	0.7	2.1	0.8	1.4	1.2

Public-order offenses	5.5	5.8	5.2	5.9	3.9	6.1
Weapons	0.6	0.4	0.5	0.4	0.3	0.5
Other public-order	4.9	5.4	4.7	5.5	3.7	5.6
Other offenses	0.5	0.7	0.3	0.8	0.4	0.7
Number of inmates	20,758	17,639	13,827	24,220	9,098	28,812

Note: Percentages may not add to total due to rounding.

[a]Includes murder, negligent manslaughter, and nonnegligent manslaughter.
[b]Includes rape and other sexual assault.

Source: U.S. Department of Justice, *Survey of State Prison Inmates, 1991: Women in Prison* (Washington, D.C.: Government Printing Office, 1994), p. 8.

recent surveys have shown a high rate of psychotherapeutic drug use (a combination of medical and nonmedical drug use) among women. Prescription or "psychotropic" drugs—such as Demerol, Seconal, Valium, and Librium—are mood altering, potentially addictive drugs that "are easily misused . . . that is, using them in greater amounts, or for purposes other than those for which they were prescribed and thereby developing a psychological and/or physical dependency."[33]

Studies have found that women are far more likely to receive hospital emergency room treatment for psychotherapeutic drug abuse than males, with the number doubling in drug overdose situations.[34] Women who die as a result of drug abuse are twice as likely as men to be over the age of 36, a figure attributed to women's greater use and abuse of psychotherapeutic drugs during these years.[35] In conclusion, females who enter drug treatment programs are more likely to be abusing psychotherapeutic or prescription drugs than cocaine, heroin, methadone, or alcohol;[36] and the typical woman who chronically abuses prescription drugs is a middle- or upper-class housewife.[37]

11. Female
White-Collar Criminals

The involvement of women in white-collar crimes is increasing at a faster rate than any other type of crime. What was once considered almost entirely a male crime has gradually become *both* a male and female crime in recent decades. What is white-collar crime? The term refers to offenses such as forgery and counterfeiting, fraud, and embezzlement, which are generally committed by persons working in white-collar professions—such as bank employees and office workers—and differentiates from other crime categories including violent crimes, property crimes, and public-order crimes. Who are the female white-collar criminals? Why are more and more women entering the arena of white-collar crimes?

THE DIMENSIONS OF
FEMALE WHITE-COLLAR CRIME

By every measurement the incidence of male perpetrated white-collar crime exceeds female perpetrated white-collar crime by a wide margin. However, females are gaining ground on males in committing white-collar offenses. The rate of women's arrests for white-collar crimes is increasing at a faster rate than men's arrests, though men continue to account for the majority of white-collar crime offenders and arrestees. The ratio of male–female white-collar crimes is much smaller than other types of traditionally male dominated crimes, including

FIGURE 11-1

Trends in Women's Arrests
for White-Collar Crimes, 1977–92[a]

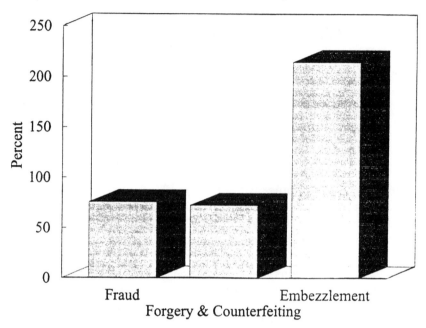

[a] Based on contributing police agencies and estimated population figures for 1977 and 1992.

Source: Adapted from U.S. Federal Bureau of Investigation, *Crime in the United States: Uniform Crime Reports 1986, 1992* (Washington, D.C.: Government Printing Office, 1987, 1993), pp. 169, 222.

---

the Crime Index offenses of violent and property crimes, and crimes involving alcohol, drugs, and weapons.[1]

The growth in women's participation in white-collar offenses is reflected in arrest data. As shown in Figure 11-1, between 1977 and 1992, women's arrests for embezzlement increased 214.5 percent, fraud by 75.7 percent, and forgery and counterfeiting by 72.5 percent. A National Institute for Mental Health report noted that it was "larceny, embezzlement, fraud, and forgery that [were] proving attractive to women and not homicide, assault and armed robbery."[2]

FIGURE 11-2

The Distribution of Female Arrests for White-Collar Offenses, 1992

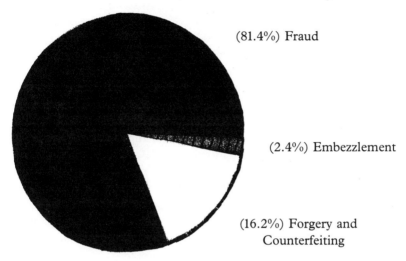

(81.4%) Fraud

(2.4%) Embezzlement

(16.2%) Forgery and
Counterfeiting

Source: Derived from U.S. Federal Bureau of Investigation, *Crime in the United States: Uniform Crime Reports 1992* (Washington, D.C.: Government Printing Office, 1993), p. 231.

The distribution of female arrests for white-collar crimes in 1992 can be seen in Figure 11-2. The majority of arrests were for fraud. More than 81 percent of the female arrestees were charged with fraud. Forgery and counterfeiting accounted for the second most arrests with over 16 percent of all female arrests for white-collar crimes. Embezzlement ranked a distant third, making up less than 3 percent of the women's arrests for white-collar offenses.

THE NATURE AND TYPES OF FEMALE WHITE-COLLAR CRIMINALS

The women committing white-collar crimes fall anywhere between secretaries and top executives, with jobs in small businesses,

large corporations, and the government. What follows is a number of
recent examples of convicted female white-collar criminals that gives
some indication of their range, occupations, and crimes:

- Sandra Brown, feminist and author, was convicted of stealing
  federal and other funds that were supposed to be used for start-
  ing women's businesses, totaling $10 million. She was sentenced
  to 2⅓–14 years in prison.
- Frances Cox pleaded guilty to embezzling $48,000 from the Fair-
  fax, Virginia, government, where she was serving as treasurer.
- Adela Holzer, a producer, was convicted of defrauding investors of
  their savings by claiming to invest in nonexistent land deals in
  Spain and an automobile distributorship in Indonesia. She was
  sentenced to 2–6 years in prison.
- Lillian Markson, bookkeeper for the Spartacus spa, was sentenced
  to 3 years' probation and 100 hours of community service for
  aiding and abetting in the filing of a fake tax return.
- Mary Hudson, board chairman of Hudson Oil Company, pleaded
  no contest to the charge that she fixed gas pumps to shortchange
  customers.
- Barbara Bowman was convicted of embezzling more than $12,000
  from the Senate Post Office, where she was chief clerk. She was
  sentenced to 3 years' probation and 100 hours of community
  service.
- Frances Penn, an applications clerk for the Immigration and Nat-
  uralization Service, was convicted of taking bribes to tamper
  with the records of aliens.
- Mary Treadwell was convicted of defrauding tenants of thousands
  of dollars in rent money at a Washington, D.C., housing project
  she managed.[3]

Experts point out that female white-collar criminals are not merely
a reflection of salaried or professional women, but can also be found
in significant numbers among poor, less educated, drug addicted,
nonwhite-collar females. For example, Phyllis Baunach of the U.S.
Bureau of Justice Statistics reports that many women "use stolen credit
cards or forge checks to support their kids or buy drugs."[4]

EXPLANATIONS FOR WOMEN'S WHITE-COLLAR CRIMES

What are the reasons for the explosion in female white-collar crime? There has been much debate on this. Many criminologists blame the increase on greater employment opportunities for women, suggesting "this trend was to be expected as more women moved into high level jobs that have always tempted males and females alike to cheat employers or consumers."[5] Or as white-collar offender Sandra Brown advanced: "Since you now have more women in business, more women are naturally going to be accused. If you had more zebras in business, you would have more white-collar crimes committed by zebras."[6]

There are other experts who reject the opportunity theory and instead blame the rise in women's white-collar criminality on "economic distress and inflation," or "frayed-collar" crimes.[7] Further explanations include the increased pressures of single female parent families, the low risk of detection and potentially high rate of return, and the committing of white-collar offenses in cooperation and/or partnership with a male partner or lover.

Many believe female white-collar criminals are the beneficiaries of a double standard when it comes to committing certain kinds of nontraditional crimes such as fraud and embezzlement—a view largely based on the traditional role of women in society as childbearers, child raisers, and housewives supported by men. As more and more women gain entry into the white-collar world, many are abandoning popular mores in favor of white-collar theft and fraud, while perpetrating their crimes unsuspectingly. A typical example of a computer operator employed with a large firm, while committing fraud and larceny on the side, can be seen below:

> Men *still* think of women as sweet and innocent, timid, moral and decent—and above temptation. Well I think this is just great because it helps protect me. I used to have a great deal with one of our suppliers. ... I'd generate a phony invoice from him in the computer, and after it was paid, we'd split the take. I felt that even if the company found out this was going on, they'd never suspect nice little sweet hardworking Amy.[8]

CHIVALRY, PATERNALISM,
AND FEMALE WHITE-COLLAR CRIMINALS

When women are caught committing white-collar crimes, there is evidence that they are treated more leniently by a chivalrous and paternalistic criminal justice system than male white-collar criminals. In a study of 10 federal district courts, it was found that women nearly always received more lenient treatment than men for white-collar offenses.[9] Said one of the authors of the study, "In talking with judges, we found that they thought imprisonment would impose a greater hardship on women, and they showed concern and compassion over that possibility."[10] Another study, conducted by Rita Simon, reached the same conclusion. Upon interviewing 30 Midwestern criminal court judges, she found that the majority indicated they planned to continue to give women convicted of white-collar crimes preferential treatment when it came to sentencing, noting that many of these women "are often responsible for children, and many of them are first-time offenders."[11] Other studies have found that female white-collar offenders are less likely than male white-collar offenders to be arrested, prosecuted, or incarcerated.[12] Relatively few women convicted of white-collar crimes end up serving time. Most are given fines, community service, and/or probation.[13]

Unlike more traditional property crimes such as larceny-theft and violent offenses, the biggest problem facing law enforcement officials in tracking white-collar criminals of both sexes is recognizing that a crime has been committed, let alone identifying the white-collar criminal. This point is illustrated in the following case of a female commodities dealer who managed to avoid paying taxes on nearly a million dollars by creating false losses on her tax return. In her own words:

> It's the perfect scam. My friends and I set up prearranged trades in soybeans, pork bellies, and other futures to create "losses" to use on our tax returns. In just the past three years, I've been able to avoid paying taxes on over a million dollars in real profits. . . . And I can not imagine how they would ever catch us . . . the scheme is so complicated, you'd have to be a commodities trader yourself to even begin to understand how it operates. . . . Even if the exchange or the regulators got suspicious, nothing could really be proved. I'm really not concerned about going to jail since I can see practically no likelihood that I'll ever get caught.[14]

12. Female Rapists and Con Artists

By and large, women's crime statistics today continue to reflect those crimes traditionally committed by adult females, such as larceny-theft, prostitution and commercialized vice, offenses against family and children, and drug- and alcohol-related offenses. However, there is some indication that more women are becoming involved in nontraditional crimes or criminality generally considered male crimes, such as white-collar crimes as discussed in chapter 11, *forcible rape*, and *confidence games*. The latter two female perpetrated offenses and possible causes will be examined in this chapter.

FEMALE RAPISTS

Though females commit relatively few violent crimes, they are not altogether *nonviolent*. Between 1983 and 1992, female arrests for crimes of violence increased by 73 percent. Among individual violent crimes, female arrests for forcible rape rose 46.5 percent, the second highest increase for violent crime arrests next to aggravated assault, where arrests climbed more than 88 percent.[1] Even so, only 359 women were arrested for forcible rape in 1992. This was far less than the 3,867 male arrests for the same crime. Some experts believe that considerably more women may be involved in rape and other sexual assaults than the statistics indicate.

There are a number of problems in recognizing female rape and rapists. Foremost is the notion of a female rapist goes entirely against the traditional definition of rape as male perpetrated sexual intercourse, usually with a female, by force or threat of force, or sexual "penetration of a woman not married to the offender that was nonconsensual because the victim was unconscious or in some other way physically helpless."[2] In many states only in recent years has male rape of other males been recognized as rape or criminal sexual assault. For women who rape, the nature of the rape is even less certain and more controversial. What constitutes female rape? How is this possible? What woman would rape and why? Who are the victims of female rape?

Female rape or attempted rape by force or threat of force is not a new phenomenon. For instance, "during a certain time in our country's history, a white woman in the South could force a black man to have sexual intercourse with her by threatening to scream 'rape.' Since the mere accusation could cost the black man his life, this incident would certainly qualify as rape by the very real threat of bodily harm."[3] Although there have been case histories of men sexually assaulted by women, very few have been reported in the scientific literature.

Most women charged with rape are accomplices to male rapists, but may not actually have physically raped the person. An example is a recent case in California in which a woman assisted her husband, who regularly raped and battered her, in finding other potential rape victims.[4] Females *can rape* other females, children, and even males— often using objects to rape and physically overpowering the victim into compliance. Many incest victims, female and male, were in fact the victims of rape by their mothers.[5]

FEMALE RAPE OF MALES

Sex researchers William Masters and Philip Sarrel, who presented clinical evidence of the actual rape of four men on separate occasions by one or more women under the threat of violence or death, rejected the "sexual myth" that it would be virtually impossible for a man to achieve or maintain an erection if he was physically assaulted by a woman, insisting:

> like most other sexual myths . . . its general acceptance has exerted an unfortunate influence on medicine, psychology and the law. Consequently, men who have been sexually assaulted by women have

been extremely loath to admit this experience to anyone. They have feared that either they will be disbelieved or that they would be degraded socially and made the object of lewd jokes, not only by their peers but by representatives of the law and the health care professions.[6]

While Masters and Sarrel acknowledge that female rape of males is rare, they do suggest that many of these rapes go unreported by the victims unless they seek professional help. Said Masters of female perpetrated rape: "Many of us have been taught that nothing of the kind could happen. Nothing is further from the truth."[7]

Few men who are the victims of female rape or other sexual assaults talk to therapists about their experience. Those who do, exhibit responses similar to female rape victims—loss of self-esteem, depression, and rejection of intimacy. In many cases the law offers little, if any, protection. In seven states women are excluded from the rape statutes; thus, "even those few men with the courage to report rape may find they have no legal recourse against their attackers."[8] Even in states where male rape laws exist, the chance that a female rapist will be prosecuted is very small. The reality of the uphill battle male victims of female rape and sexual aggression face was summed up by rape expert Nicholas Groth, who noted: "We've seen these guys forcibly assaulted by women, but they get in front of the police or courts, and who's going to believe them?"[9] Groth found that 60 percent of the imprisoned rapists and child molesters were victims of child sexual abuse, and 20 percent of the perpetrators were female.[10]

FEMALE RAPE OF FEMALES

Lesbian rape of women also occurs, though this is rarely documented or researched. Sociologist Stuart Miller argued that when speaking candidly about rape, the truth is that "young rape old, blacks rape whites, whites rape women and girls, juveniles rape juveniles, and women rape women and girls."[11] In a survey on rape and child sexual abuse, Diana Russell found that five of her female respondents reported being raped by another female.[12] Rape was defined in the survey as the victim of being forced to engage in oral or anal sex, or sexual relations without consent because the victim was unconscious, drugged, or otherwise physically incapacitated.

Women inmates may be at particularly high risk of being raped by other female prisoners. In a personal narrative, a female inmate noted that during the course of being assaulted and burned by eight women inmates, she was raped, though she gave no specifics of the rape.[13] There is no evidence that rape in female prisons is as widespread as in male prisons. However, the fact that it exists at all is cause for concern. And the same is true for the growing incidence of female rapists and sexual assaultists outside the prison gates.

WHY WOMEN RAPE

What motivates a woman to rape? Women who commit sexual assaults are largely driven by the same forces as male rapists—power, hostility, hatred, sadism, violence, alcohol and/or drugs, mental illness, and/or opportunity.[14] Some female rapists are controlled and coerced by male rapists or batterers. Many female rapists were themselves victims of rape or child sexual abuse, domestic violence, or other physical or mental trauma.[15]

WOMEN CON ARTISTS

The number of women con artists (women who defraud people through a dishonest scheme or swindle) has grown sharply from the 1960s to the early 1990s, if arrest statistics are any indication. Female arrests for fraud, including confidence games, has risen more than 550 percent between 1960 and 1992.[16] Although men are arrested more often for fraud than women, the differential has shrunk in recent years. In fact, the number of women arrested for fraud is much closer to the number of men arrested for fraud than for most of the other crimes dominated by men. Nationwide, tens of thousands of people are taken in by con games and con artists annually, costing them millions. Many victims are embarrassed, ashamed, and humiliated, and therefore do not report the crime. Police estimate that only one in three confidence games is ever reported.[17]

Most women's con games are perpetrated on other women—not particularly surprising when we consider that con women "can approach other women without arousing suspicion the way a strange man might."[18] In many scams, women and men pair up and the victims can be women, men, or children—depending upon the nature of the con.

The three most common women-conning-women confidence games are the *pocketbook drop*, the *boujoo*, and the *handkerchief switch*.

The Pocketbook Drop

The pocketbook drop, the most prevalent of the three, is also referred to as "the *pigeon* (slang for 'victim', also termed *mom, lame, chump, vic) drop, dropping the leather, drag playing* (from playing the main drag in town)."[19] According to some historians on confidence games, women have been perpetrating some form of the pocketbook drop for at least 1,000 years, it having originated in China.[20] This con usually involves two women con artists — the *roper* (the person who ropes the pigeon into the game) and the *capper* (the person who caps the game by producing "found" money or other valuables). The con women, each "adept in the art of deceit, obfuscation, and disguise," often scout their locations and potential pigeons well in advance.

The typical con victim is elderly, a window shopper, "indicating she had the time to spare required to develop the successive stages of the con," lives alone, has enough money to make the scam worthwhile, and talks a lot about herself and circumstances.[21] The con woman's conversation is often "glib, fast, mesmerizing," aimed at keeping the pigeon off guard and unable to think clearly and rationally. At the end of a successful con game the victim is usually bilked out of anywhere from hundreds to thousands of dollars before she realizes what has occurred.

Most drag teams are made up of current or ex-prostitutes. They tend to work for or with a pimp, with whom they normally split the take. The pimp "takes care of them" by providing clothes, shelter, and bail if they are taken into custody. He is sometimes the lover of one or more of his con women. Some pimps may have a dozen drag teams operating, with profits into the thousands per week. The relationship between prostitutes and pocketbook drop con games can be seen as follows: "A veteran pocketbook dropper, meeting a hooker with the requisite looks, personality, and slickness of speech, will introduce her to her pimp. The novice then learns the game by playing it in tandem with her discoverer. If she proves adept, she never goes back to streetwalking. The drag money is too good, the life infinitely more pleasant."[22]

The Boujoo

A second classic women's con game is the *boujoo*, a Romany term, which means "big lie." As with the pocketbook drop, this scam robs victims of their life savings, with long-term emotional effects as well. The *boujoo* is "an age old swindle involving magic and the supernatural," often beginning "in the standard fortune-telling parlor and typically ends with its pigeons in penury and shame."[23]

Gypsy queens can usually be found perpetrating the *boujoo* in major cities. Relying largely on observation and savvy, the gypsy can often discover much about a potential victim by her facial expressions, gestures, clothing, posture, and style. An even greater knowledge of a pigeon's psychological makeup is often uncovered with the aid of common parlor devices such as palm readings, tarot cards, and tea leaves.

Inevitably the victim—usually beset by romantic failures and real or imagined health woes—is deceived into believing she is being possessed by evil spirits. Only the gypsy can rid her of these with the help of magic, a serpent, sleight of hand, and of course, the pigeon's money which appears to be torn to shreds before her very eyes. Successful *boujoo* scores in excess of $200,000 have been reported by police con squads.

The Handkerchief Switch

The handkerchief switch is yet another typical flimflam, often perpetrated on women by women. Generally, both the con artists and the conned victim are black or Hispanic. The success of this confidence game "depends on the players' ability to arouse in their victim the desire to aid a fellow countryman in trouble far from home."[24] Basically, the con revolves around a sad tale as told by the roper—often involving a large sum of cash—the pigeon or chump producing money as an act of good faith to match the duper's money roll, which is then put into a large handkerchief, and soon substituted by the con artist with a handkerchief filled with paper or something similarly worthless.

When women con artists are arrested and convicted, they rarely receive stiff sentences, often plea bargaining for lesser sentences. Notes an expert on fraud crimes: "Con games look pretty mild to a criminal court judge compared to the murderers and rapists who pass before his bench, so he tends to impose lighter sentences on the players."[25]

WHY DO WOMEN
PLAY CONFIDENCE GAMES?

Some wonder why con women, with their "guts, smarts, and skills," embark on a life of fraudulent crime when it would seem that their abilities could just as productively be applied to acceptable occupations. Experts suggest that, like other skilled professional criminals, many women con artists are the victims of a criminal subculture—poverty, broken homes, child abuse and/or substance abuse—any or all which may play an influential role in their criminality. Psychiatrist William Frosch suggested that women "playing con games may be a conscious occupational choice that represents some abusive relationship within the family."[26]

For many con women it is the thrill of the game that motivates them to be repeat offenders. Frosch notes: "It takes bravura. In a twisted way, she resembles the skier or the mountain climber. One imagines her asking, 'Will I make it again this time?' She is a risk taker."[27]

PART IV

Girls, Crime,
and Delinquency

13. *Runaway Girls*

Runaway youth is perhaps the most serious type of status offense (applicable only to juveniles, and includes such other offenses as truancy and incorrigibility), with the gravest potential implications such as involvement in criminal activities (including prostitution, drug abuse, and violent crimes) and victimization (including AIDS, rape, and murder). Most runaways are female, many of whom left physically, sexually, or emotionally abusive homes only to find that life on the streets is equally harmful and often far worse. Not all runaways are forced to leave home. Some prefer independence from parental control and discipline, with varying results. In this chapter we will explore the growing problem of runaway girls.

THE EXTENT OF FEMALE RUNAWAYS

How many girls run away from home annually? Estimates vary from source to source, but it is believed that overall in the United States anywhere from hundreds of thousands to over 1 million children run away each year. Of these, as many as 60 percent may be female.[1] More than 50 percent of the runaways are recidivists, having run away from home at least three times. Approximately 300,000 runaway teens are described as hard-core street kids who run away repeatedly.[2]

An indication of increasing female participation in running away can be seen in arrest trends (see Figure 13-1). Between 1983 and 1992 arrests of female runaways rose by nearly 29 percent. This compares to a 65.5 percent decline in juvenile female arrests for prostitution and

141

FIGURE 13-1

Female Arrest Trends for Running Away and Juvenile Prostitution, 1983 and 1992

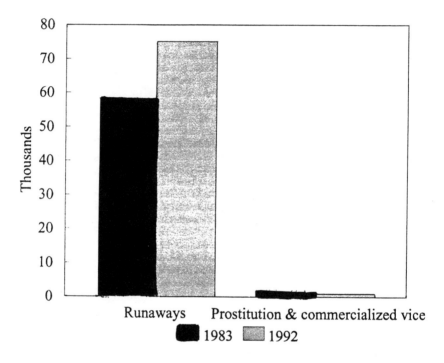

Source: Adapted from U.S. Federal Bureau of Investigation, *Crime in the United States: Uniform Crime Reports 1992* (Washington, D.C.: Government Printing Office, 1993), p. 222.

commercialized vice. Given the correlation between running way and child prostitution, the latter figure may reflect more girl prostitutes being arrested as runaways or charged with other offenses, such as curfew and loitering law violations.

AGE AND THE FEMALE RUNAWAY

Most girl runaways fall between the ages of 13 and 16, with the median age being 15. In J. A. Bechtel's study of runaways, 81.6 percent

FIGURE 13-2

Female Runaways, by Age, 1992

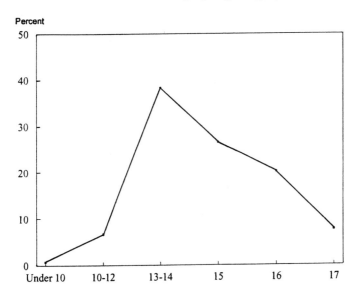

Source: Adapted from U.S. Federal Bureau of Investigation, *Crime in the United States: Uniform Crime Reports 1992* (Washington, D.C.: Government Printing Office, 1993), p. 231.

---

of the girl runaways were between age 13 and 16, and 26.8 percent were age 15.[3] Arrest data show a similar pattern. As seen in Figure 13-2, 26.5 percent of the females arrested as runaways in 1992 were age 15, with 85 percent of those arrested being 13 to 16 years of age.

CHARACTERISTICS
OF GIRLS WHO RUN AWAY

The majority of runaway girls are white and from middle class families. Nearly 80 percent of the runaways arrested in 1992 were white and about 17 percent were black. However, Hispanic and black runaways tend to be overrepresented as runaways relative to their population figures.

Most girls run away from the cities and suburbs. The rate of arrests for city runaways was more than twice as high as that for rural county runaways in 1992; and the arrest rate for suburban area runaways was 52 percent higher than in rural counties.[4]

A relationship between class and running away has been established in a number of studies. James Hildebrand found that most of the runaways from his sample were from the middle class.[5] Similarly, 57 percent of the runaways studied by Robert Shellow came from middle- and working-class families.[6] In a study of runaway girls Louise Homer found that the majority were from lower- and lower-middle-class homes, with 70 percent coming from families on welfare.[7] Some research suggests that the rate of runaways is equally distributed across social classes.[8]

In studies of runaway and homeless children, the following characteristics were revealed:

- Seventy percent are white, 1 in 5 black.
- The majority are between 13 and 15 years of age.
- They come from white-collar and blue-collar families.
- Twenty-five percent were born to mothers under 17 years of age.
- Fifty percent were victims of physical or sexual abuse.
- Most come from dysfunctional families.
- Sixty percent of runaways have parents who abuse drugs or alcohol.
- Seventy percent of runaways use/abuse drugs.
- Twenty-five percent of female runaways had been raped.
- Thirty-six percent had been pregnant.
- Eighty percent have serious psychological or behavioral problems.[9]

Many runaways are beset by a range of emotional disorders. According to a study of runaways in youth shelters by David Shaffer and Carol Canton of the New York State Psychiatric Institute, 41 percent were identified as depressed and antisocial, 30 percent depressed, 18 percent antisocial, and 50 percent had attempted or seriously considered suicide[10]. In a comparison study of runaways and nonrunaways conducted by the Division of Adolescent Medicine at the Children's Hospital of Los Angeles, 85 percent of the runaways were characterized as clinically depressed and 21 percent as having serious mental illness.[11] The runaways were four times as likely as nonrunaways to develop emotional problems and to have been sexually abused.

TYPES OF GIRL RUNAWAYS

Runaway girls can generally be divided into two types: *preteen* and *early teen runaways* and *later teen runaways*. Preteen and early teen runaways are often seen as "junior adventurers seeking some form of action," whereas later teen runaways are girls that seek to "establish themselves as adults."[12] In both instances running away is often also a reflection of precipitating factors such as sexual abuse. C. J. English established a typology of girl runaways based on the commitment to remain a runaway and the reasons for leaving home, as follows:

1. *Floaters*—girls who run away for a short period of time, usually just until things "cool off."
2. *Runaways*—girls who are away from home for weeks or months, often due to a destructive family crisis or a problem the runaway is unable to share.
3. *Splitters*—girls who are pleasure seekers. They run away to gain status among their peers.
4. *Hard-road freaks*—girls who leave home permanently. They reject conformity for life on the streets, usually due to serious family problems.[13]

Many runaway girls are in fact *throwaway* girls. Throwaways, also referred to as "pushouts," are literally forced out of the house by parents or guardians for reasons ranging from incorrigibility to molestation to substance abuse by the throwaway. It is estimated that 40 percent of the homeless children in the United States are throwaways.[14]

Other girl runaways become *rat packers*, or teenagers that band together and against parental or school authority. These youths often leave home for weeks, months, or longer, supported by friends, neighbors, and even other family members. Many rat packers have been sexually or physically abused, others are abusive or violent. It is estimated that upward of 30,000 children, primarily from the middle, upper-middle, and upper classes, become rat packers annually, where they "glory in anarchy and destruction," engage in larceny-theft, drugs, alcohol, and vandalism.[15]

MOTIVATING FACTORS
FOR RUNAWAY GIRLS

Runaway girls decide to leave home for a number of reasons. Child maltreatment is often at the core of this motivation. The National Network of Runaway and Youth Services estimated that 70 percent of the runaways in youth shelters have been victims of sexual molestation or physical abuse.[16] Other factors in running away include the following:

- Broken or dysfunctional home environment.
- Disciplinary problems.
- School problems.
- Substance abuse.
- Pregnancy.
- Sexual identity problems.
- Promiscuity.
- Mental illness.
- Boredom.

According to one writer, "The children who run look for companionship, friendship, and approval from those they meet. Many such youths are easy marks for gangs, drug pushers and pimps. Runaways often sell drugs or their bodies, and steal to support themselves."[17]

Some runaway girl adventurers court the imagined thrills of the runaway, independent youth—combining promiscuity, precocity, immaturity, and rebellion to survive on the streets. One sociologist suggested that "the rule for runaway girls everywhere is often 'ball for bed'—meaning that implicit in an offer of lodging is the expectation of sexual intercourse."[18] In a study of runaway girls it was found that the girls' initial objectives were to "acquire a place to sleep and then look for adventure—get a crash pad and some kicks."[19]

THE REALITIES OF LIFE
FOR THE GIRL RUNAWAY

Few runaway girls can escape the dark, frightening realities of life as a runaway. Most girl runaways end up on the streets and often must find themselves turning to prostitution within days, if not hours.

"Runaway girls, scared and alone, are welcomed by pimps who watch for them as they arrive at bus and train stations. They offer them a roof over their heads, a 'caring adult,' clothes, makeup and promises of love and belonging."[20] What follows is often an unstable, dangerous path from status offender to juvenile delinquent to, in many instances, adult criminal. These girl runaways typically engage in petty crimes and substance abuse, are sexually and physically assaulted, incarcerated, and sometimes their tragic journey ends in death. June Bucy, of the National Network of Runaway and Youth Services, noted the high mortality rate for runaway girls and, further, that they "suffer from malnutrition, venereal disease, a high incidence of suicide, and are frequently sexually exploited."[21]

RUNAWAY GIRLS AND AIDS

The biggest threat to runaway girls' long-term health and survival may be the risk of contracting AIDS. Patricia Hersch writes of the relationship between AIDS and the runaway:

> If geography is destiny, runaway and homeless kids gravitate to the very locations around the country where the risk is greatest. . . . Often their immune systems are already compromised by repeated exposure to infections. . . . The risk-related behavior of runaway and homeless adolescents puts them directly in the path of the disease. . . . Sex more than anything puts runaway kids at risk for AIDS. . . . Their bodies usually become the currency of exchange. . . . There is . . . an epidemic of exposure, and many runaway kids, years hence, may pay horribly for the events of their troubled youth.[22]

It is estimated that tens, maybe hundreds, of thousands of runaways are actively involved in high-risk behavior for contracting AIDS, such as prostitution and intravenous drug use. At New York City's largest shelter for runaways, Covenant House, an AIDS specialist estimated that 40 percent of the runaway, homeless youth may carry the AIDS virus.[23] Runaway girls, who already face a high rate of sexually transmitted diseases, violent johns and pimps, juvenile detention, and a bleak outlook on life, must now deal with the reality and unpredictability of AIDS.

14. Girl Prostitutes

The prostitution and exploitation of young females has flourished throughout history. In ancient Egypt, for example, the "most beautiful and highest born Egyptian maidens were forced into prostitution as a religious practice, and they continued as prostitutes until their first menstruation."[1] Child prostitution in the United States did not really become a staple of American society until the early nineteenth century as men "demanded more esoteric forms of sexual titillation."[2] Girl prostitutes today reflect a more broad set of dynamics than their predecessors. They are more sophisticated, street smart, opportunistic — and more susceptible to drug addiction, violence, arrest, and contracting AIDS. In this chapter we will examine the girl prostitute, her characteristics, the role of the pimp, and other factors that figure into the adolescent female prostitute's life.

DEFINING GIRL PROSTITUTION

What constitutes a girl prostitute? Girl or child prostitution can be defined as the use of or participation for pay by girls or minors (usually persons under the age of 18) in sexual acts with adults or other minors where no force is present. This includes sexual intercourse, anal sex, oral sex, multiple partner sex, sadomasochism, urination or defecation, and pornographic sexual performances. What differentiates child prostitution from incest or statutory rape is that it involves some form of payment — usually money, but often drugs, shelter, clothing, food, and other items. In some cases parents have been known to initiate their children into prostitution to support the parents' drug habit, lifestyle, or own prostitution.

Girl prostitutes can be found actively plying their trade in any big or small city or town in the country. Many adolescent female prostitutes can be identified simply by "working the streets" in high heels, heavy makeup, and tight, scant clothing. Others are less visible, performing in massage parlors, alleyways, hotels, and the back seats of cars.

HOW MANY GIRL PROSTITUTES ARE THERE?

Because of the complex tripartite relationship between girl runaways, girl prostitutes, and nonuniform tracking of either, accurate statistics are hard to come by. Police sources place the number of child prostitutes on the streets at any given time at anywhere between 100,000 and 200,000.[3] Other nonofficial but likely more accurate data have estimated that as many as half a million children under the age of 16 are involved in prostitution, with that number doubling when including 16- and 17-year-old prostitutes.[4] Experts generally agree that the majority of child prostitutes are female, with some estimates as high as two-thirds of the juvenile prostitutes being female.[5]

In a recent 50-state survey of child prostitutes, it was found that child prostitution increased in 37 percent of the "affected" cities.[6] This growth has been blamed on greater numbers of teens leaving or escaping troubled homes. According to the survey, the majority of child prostitutes are:

1. Runaways with alcohol and/or drug problems;
2. Ages 13 to 17, though many were found to be much younger; and
3. Plying their trade in central business districts, arcade game rooms, and bus and train stations.

The study called for tougher teenage curfew and loitering laws, more runaway centers, and stiffer penalties for pimps and johns.

The correlation between girl prostitution and runaway girls is well documented.[7] More than 1 million girls run away from home each year—often coming from Midwestern cities and rural areas—due to sexual or physical abuse, neglect, loneliness, rebellion, or a need for adventure. Within a month, many of these runaways have become prostitutes, petty criminals, drug users, inmates, and/or carriers of the AIDS virus. The people they service are almost exclusively men, from all walks of life. Many are married, educated, and powerful. Virtually all feel inadequate and are unable to relate to peer sexual partners.

The girl prostitute typically finds life on the streets to be fraught with violence, disease, risk, uncertainty, insincerity, and hopelessness. Yet many remain in the business for years, having nowhere to go or no safe place to which they could return.

GIRL PROSTITUTES BY AGE

Most girl prostitutes tend to fall between the ages of 15 to 17. Figure 14-1 distributes girls arrested for prostitution in 1992 by age. Over 50 percent of the arrestees were age 17, with nearly 23 percent 16, and 12.6 percent 15 years old. Jennifer James found the mean age for girl prostitutes to be 16.9 years.[8] However, the majority of girl prostitutes entered the business prior to becoming 16, with the average age of first experience found to be 14.[9]

GIRL PROSTITUTES BY SOCIAL CLASS

It is commonly believed that female juvenile prostitutes are primarily a product of the lower classes. In fact, all classes of society are represented, with most girl prostitutes coming from the middle and upper-middle classes. In a study of juvenile prostitutes in Minnesota, nearly 1 in 4 prostitutes had parents with some college education and many had fathers who were in professional or skilled occupations.[10] Mimi Silbert found that 70 percent of her sample came from families of average or higher incomes.[11] A similar finding emerged from James's study. She also noted a "phenomenal" increase in the number of "affluent and overindulged" girl prostitutes."[12]

RACE AND ETHNIC COMPOSITE
OF GIRL PROSTITUTES

Girls entering prostitution are of every racial and ethnic persuasion. Studies show that white girls constitute the vast majority of

FIGURE 14-1

Girl Prostitutes, by Age, 1992 [a]

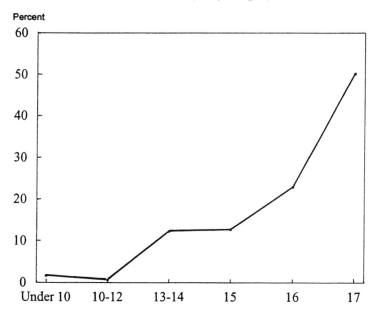

[a] Based on female juvenile arrest figures for prostitution and commercialized vice.

Source: Derived from U.S. Federal Bureau of Investigation, *Crime in the United States: Uniform Crime Reports 1992* (Washington, D.C.: Government Printing Office, 1993), p. 222.

---

juvenile female prostitutes. Studies in Minneapolis[13] and San Francisco[14] found that 80 percent of the girl prostitutes were white; and James's study revealed that 62 percent were white teenagers.[15]

Black girls make up the second highest percentage of juvenile female prostitutes, with estimates ranging from just over 10 percent to nearly 50 percent of those sampled.[16] The larger the sample, the lower the percentage of black prostitutes tended to be. The numbers of girl prostitutes from other racial and ethnic groups is believed to be much lower than for white or black prostitutes. Different studies have shown Hispanic and Native American girls to represent between 2 and 11 percent of the girl prostitutes.[17]

FAMILY CIRCUMSTANCES
OF GIRL PROSTITUTES

Studies show that most girl prostitutes come from broken homes. In Maura Crowley's study, 85 percent of the female juvenile prostitutes reported the absence of at least one parent during their upbringing.[18] In the Huckleberry House Project, 70 percent of the sample reflected homes with the absence of one or both parents.[19] A similar percentage of girl prostitutes from broken homes was found in James's study.[20]

Other research has focused on the correlation between adolescent female prostitutes and a parental relationship characterized by stress and conflict. The Huckleberry House research found that few girl prostitutes had positive, caring relationships with their parents.[21] In Diana Gray's study, 75 percent of the sample described the relationship with their parents as "poor" or "very bad."[22] Crowley's study found that mothers were more likely than fathers to be the source of the child-parent dysfunction: she cited evidence that 45 percent of the mothers, compared to 25 percent of the fathers, were reported to be responsible for the girl prostitutes' poor relationship with parents.[23]

One other factor is worth noting: the mother's prostitution or promiscuity has also been linked to girl prostitutes and their stressful family situations.[24]

CHILD SEXUAL
AND PHYSICAL ABUSE

Most girl prostitutes have been sexually and physically abused prior to entry into prostitution. The Huckleberry House study found that 90 percent of the girls has been sexually molested.[25] Nearly 66 percent of the sample in Silbert's study were victims of incest and child abuse.[26] Other research has found many girl prostitutes to be rape victims, participants in child pornography, or otherwise sexually exploited.[27]

A strong relationship has been documented between female teenage prostitutes and a background of physical abuse and violence. More than two of every three girl prostitutes in the Crowley study and Huckleberry House Project reported being physically abused at home.[28]

SUBSTANCE ABUSE
AND GIRL PROSTITUTION

Drug and alcohol use and abuse is high among girl prostitutes. The majority of all adolescent prostitutes have tried at least one drug and/or alcoholic beverage before or after entry into prostitution. It is estimated that between 20 and 50 percent of all juvenile prostitutes use drugs regularly;[29] while at least 70 percent of all female minors consume some form of alcohol.[30] Marijuana is the most commonly used drug by girl prostitutes, though psychedelic drugs and narcotics are also popular.[31]

Many juvenile female prostitutes have abused alcohol or drugs before becoming prostitutes, often in order to "deaden memories" associated with sexual or physical abuse. Girl prostitutes also tend to become substance abusers to "desensitize present experiences" in the often vicious, dehumanizing world of child prostitution.[32]

VIOLENT GIRL PROSTITUTES

Although most girl prostitutes engage in nonviolent crimes such as drug use and petty theft, an increasing number are resorting to violence to support drug habits or reach a money quota established by their pimps. One study found that half the girl prostitutes admitted robbing customers regularly.[33] Some female prostitutes use knives or guns in the course of a robbery or in self-defense from violent johns.

GIRL PROSTITUTES AND PIMPS

The role of the pimp in a girl prostitute's life has been depicted in numerous movies and books as one of physical and emotional abuse, coercion, and intimidation, with him sometimes even killing the prostitute as a lesson to other girls in his stable. A classic example of this type of sexual slavery pimp–girl prostitute relationship with nearly tragic results can be seen in the following example:

> In New York City, a girl's pimp kept her on the street six nights a week. She hated being a prostitute, but the pimp was the only person who had shown her any kindness. When she could stand it no longer and told him she had to quit, he broke her jaw. At the hospital where

her jaw was wired shut, she was given pain pills and told to rest. But
her pimp put her on the street the next night.

Later, she tried to commit suicide using the pills, but she
vomited, breaking the wires in her jaw. Her pimp would not allow
her to return to the hospital and sent her back on the street.[34]

Though the scenario is all too real for many girl prostitutes, is it
an accurate reflection of the life and circumstances that binds most
girls to their pimps? In James's study of the pimp-prostitute relationship, she found that most pimps do not force or seduce girls into prostitution or keep them from ever leaving their stable.[35] Other studies,
such as Dorothy Bracey's, have noted the pimp's charm, flattery, and
emotional exploitation in enticing the girl into entering prostitution.[36]
Freda Adler described a successful urban pimp who bragged of robbing a young girl of her values and morality and creating a new environment for her. Adler rejected the notion, suggesting that the pimp
could not cut girl prostitutes' previous ties, for "if the ties were at all
viable, he would have few attractive inducements to tempt them into
his stable. It is the very absence of those ties and the vulnerability in-
herent to the nonadapted state that ensures his success."[37]

One study found that only 5 percent of the girl prostitutes entered
into prostitution because of physical threats or intimidation by a
pimp.[38] The indication that few girls are physically forced into prostitution was furthered by Bracey, who noted: "Although we have heard
stories of kidnapping and of totally innocent girls being raped and then
'turned out,' none of the girls interviewed claimed to know anyone
who had started in prostitution in these ways."[39]

Despite the apparent voluntary entry into prostitution for most
girls, few other choices may seem to exist for them short of starving or
freezing to death. Upon entry into the pimp's world, the majority of
girl prostitutes find themselves subject to his control, rules, orders,
drugs, violence, and manipulation.

GIRL PROSTITUTES,
ADVENTURE, AND PROMISCUITY

Not all girls who sell their bodies are victims of abuse, broken
homes, running away, or violent, dominant pimps. There are a growing number of girl prostitutes who are motivated primarily by fun, excitement, adventure, perception, money, and sex. Bracey found that

many girls entered prostitution because they knew other girls in the profession.[40] One article noted that "a lot of kids take to prostitution as an 'on and off job'—when you need a few bucks."[41] A San Francisco social worker who counseled girl prostitutes sadly observed: "Sex is no longer for love and procreation, but solely for enjoyment. But this leads to fleeting sexual contacts which turn out to be meaningless. What gives them meaning is the profit."[42]

For many young girls the relative ease of entering into prostitution, combined with the money that can be made and the joy that can be derived from sex, makes prostitution a tempting choice of engagement. This is made all too clear in the following commentary by a person who worked with girl prostitutes: "There are more younger hookers, thirteen and fourteen year olds. They just don't care. It's a way they can have all the clothes they want, all the blue jeans and shoes they want. . . . Girls sell their bodies to get money. If it was legal and had a tax on it, they would find something else."[43]

The rise in prostitution among affluent girls is seen as a way for excitement and adventure as opposed to other motivations often associated with girl prostitutes, such as running away or being thrown out of the house. According to James, for affluent girl prostitutes "it is basically entertaining to dress up with your friends and go down on the street and con, cajole, and be the aggressor. The extravagant sensations from the illegality, projected immorality, and danger of prostitution [are] a relief from the neutrality of suburbia."[44]

WHY DO GIRLS BECOME PROSTITUTES?

The study of why girls enter into prostitution generally falls into three categories: *psychoanalytic, situational,* and *economic* motivations. Psychoanalytical research has linked adolescent female prostitution with such mental disorders as depression, schizophrenia, and emotional deprivation.[45] Situational studies have found girl prostitution to be associated with such situational factors as child abuse and neglect, incest, rape, and early sexual experiences.[46]

The economically motivated explanation for girls becoming prostitutes has been given the most attention. Based on her research, James posited that "the apparent reason for prostitution among adolescents is for economic survival and to meet other needs."[47] Most girl prostitutes have admitted in surveys that money and material items top the list of motivating factors for entering into prostitution.[48] Furthermore, since most girl prostitutes tend to be runaways or throwaways, prostitution becomes and stays the primary means for economic survival out on the streets. This is underscored by a former girl prostitute and street kid, who argues: "There's no doors open to us. . . . How are you going to be able to hold down a job if you have no high school diploma, if you're not able to take a shower every day, if you don't have clean clothes to wear to work?"[49]

EXPLOITATION, DISEASE, AND VICTIMIZATION

Girl prostitutes place themselves at risk the moment they enter the business. They are exploited and victimized by pimps, johns, cops, robbers, muggers, drug addicts, drug dealers, and more. There is a high rate of rape among girl prostitutes, as most ply their trade in high-risk crime areas.[50] Even in the most upscale neighborhoods, girl prostitutes still face serious hazards to their health and well-being. They are at risk for pregnancy, abortion, and a variety of sexually transmitted diseases, including syphillis, gonorrhea, crabs, chlamydia, and AIDS. They also face going to jail or juvenile hall at a higher rate than boy prostitutes or the male customers that the girls service.[51]

It is the risk of contracting AIDS that most compromises the girl prostitute's future. Jim Kennedy, a physician at Covenant House, New York's largest shelter for runaway children, estimated that 15 percent of the 11,000 juveniles that pass through the house each year would test positive for the HIV virus, the precursor to AIDS. For girls turning tricks each night, he estimated that over 50 percent would test HIV-positive.[52] In an article on runaways and teen prostitutes, Patricia Hersch writes: "AIDS has a potentially disastrous effect on what is going on in the streets, particularly in the inner cities where sex, drugs and poverty cross paths that often lead out to the suburbs and all across the country."[53]

For young female prostitutes, many of whom have unprotected sex with their customers, there is no such thing as *safe* sex. AIDS has only compounded what for most girl prostitutes has always been an uphill battle of survival on and off the streets.

15. Girls, Alcohol, and Drugs

Alcohol and drug use among girls appears to be on the decline, yet the number of girls who are using and abusing alcohol and/or drugs continues to reflect a high percentage of females in the United States under the age of 18. The association between girls, alcohol, and drugs manifests itself in two important ways with respect to crime and delinquency. First is the fact that the purchase, possession, and use of illicit (and illegally used prescription) drugs and alcoholic beverages by minors is prohibited by status offense and/or criminal laws. Second, female juvenile and/or drug use/abuse has been shown to be a factor in many other female crimes and delinquencies, including violent, property, and drug-related crimes and such offenses as running away and prostitution. Most experts agree that girls who regularly use alcohol and drugs face higher risks for involvement in other self-destructive behavior such as delinquency, crime, and suicide than girls who abstain from or have never used alcohol or drugs.

GIRLS' ALCOHOL AND DRUG-RELATED OFFENSES AND ARREST STATISTICS

An indication of adolescent female involvement with alcohol and/or drugs can be seen through arrest data. In 1992, there were 40,224 arrests of females under the age of 18 in the United States for drug- and alcohol-related offenses.[1] As shown in Figure 15-1, the vast majority of

FIGURE 15-1

Girls and Alcohol-Related Offenses, 1992[a]

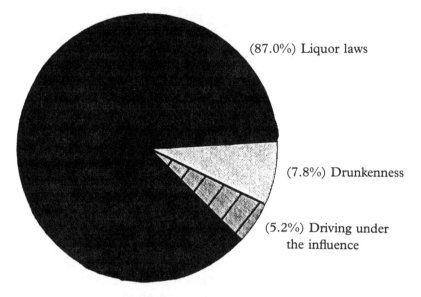

(87.0%) Liquor laws

(7.8%) Drunkenness

(5.2%) Driving under the influence

[a] Based on female juvenile arrest figures for alcohol-related offenses.

Source: Derived from U.S. Federal Bureau of Investigation, *Crime in the United States: Uniform Crime Reports 1992* (Washington, D.C.: Government Printing Office, 1993), p. 222.

girls' alcohol-related arrests were for liquor law violations. Eighty-seven percent of all alcohol-related offenses in which girls were arrested in 1992 were violations of liquor laws. Drunkenness, at just under 8 percent, of the arrests, accounted for the second most common alcohol-related offense, followed by driving under the influence at just over 5 percent of the female juvenile arrests.

The distribution of girls' substance abuse offenses in which arrests occurred in 1992 can be seen in Figure 15-2. More than 69 percent of substance abuse offenses leading to arrests were liquor law violations. Girls' drug abuse violations accounted for more than 20 percent of the substance abuse offenses, while drunkenness and driving under the influence constituted under 11 percent of the total substance abuse offenses for which girls were arrested.

FIGURE 15-2

Girls and Substance Abuse Offenses, 1992[a]

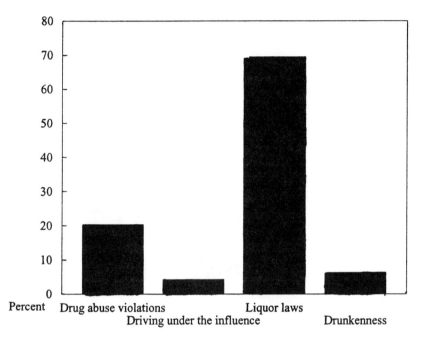

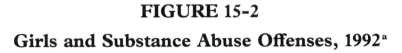

[a]Based on arrest figures for juvenile females for drug- and alcohol-related offenses.

Source: Adapted from U.S. Federal Bureau of Investigation, *Crime in the United States: Uniform Crime Reports 1992* (Washington, D.C.: Government Printing Office, 1993), p. 222.

Most girls arrested for drug- or alcohol-related offenses are ages 16 to 17 (see Figure 15-3). Over 38 percent of the female juvenile arrests for substance abuse violations in 1992 were age 17, while nearly 28 percent were age 16. Arrests declined with age. Almost 18 percent of the girl arrestees were 15, and 14.5 percent were ages 13 to 14. Less than 2 percent of the girls arrested were age 12 and under.

As we see in Figure 15-4, long-term arrest trends show that fewer girls are being arrested for alcohol- and drug-related offenses. Between 1983 and 1992, arrests of females under the age of 17 decreased for

FIGURE 15-3

Girl Arrests for Substance
Abuse Violations, by Age, 1992

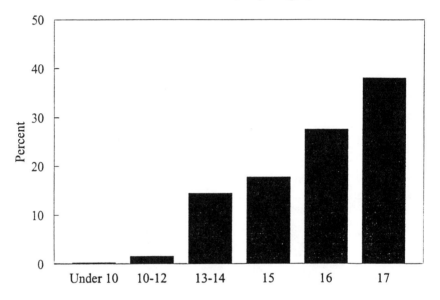

Source: Adapted from U.S. Federal Bureau of Investigation, *Crime in the United States: Uniform Crime Reports 1992* (Washington, D.C.: Government Printing Office, 1993), p. 231.

every drug- and alcohol-related offense. The greatest declines were for driving under the influence and drunkenness arrests, at −48.3 and −44.3 percent, respectively. Arrests for drug abuse violations decreased by 28.2 percent, while arrests for liquor law violations dropped 3.1 percent. Though short-term arrest trends for alcohol-related offenses also show a decline in female juvenile arrests, they indicate a rise in the number of girls arrested for drug abuse violations. Between 1991 and 1992, arrests of females under 18 for drug abuse violations rose by more than 18 percent.[2]

    White girls comprise the majority of female juveniles arrested for drug- and alcohol-related offenses. However, black and Native American females under the age of 18 and girls of Hispanic origin are disproportionately likely to be arrested for drug- and alcohol-related crimes.[3]

FIGURE 15-4

Female Juvenile Arrest Trends for Alcohol- and Drug-Related Offenses, 1983–92

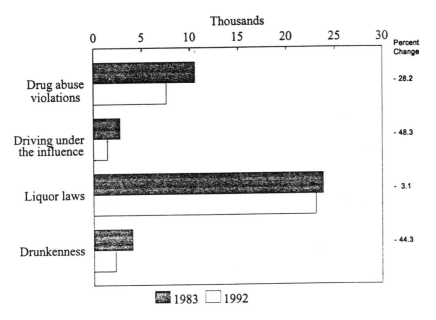

1983   1992

Source: Adapted from U.S. Federal Bureau of Investigation, *Crime in the United States: Uniform Crime Reports 1992* (Washington, D.C.: Government Printing Office, 1993), p. 222.

GIRLS AND ALCOHOL USE/ABUSE

The magnitude of girls drinking and abusing alcohol can be seen in several studies and self-report surveys. One survey found that 70 percent of the girls sampled were drinkers, while 15 percent were classified as problem drinkers.[4] A government report on alcohol and health found that by the time they reached their senior year in high school, 83.2 percent of the females will have tried an alcoholic beverage at least once.[5] In a study of changing patterns of delinquent behavior, Peter Kratcoski and John Kratcoski found that 90 percent of the girls sampled had purchased or drunk beer, wine, or liquor.[6] The prevalence of

FIGURE 15-5

Most Recent Alcohol Use
by Female High School Seniors, 1992

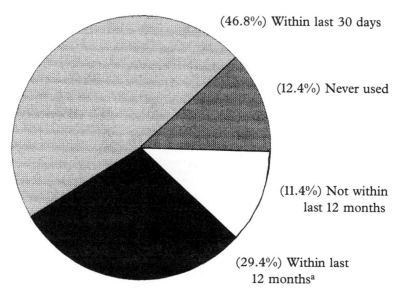

(46.8%) Within last 30 days

(12.4%) Never used

(11.4%) Not within
last 12 months

(29.4%) Within last
12 months[a]

[a]Not within the past 30 days.

Source: Derived from U.S. Department of Justice, *Sourcebook of Criminal Justice Statistics—1992* (Washington, D.C.: Government Printing Office, 1993), p. 326.

---

alcohol use by female high school seniors can be seen in Figure 15-5. According to the National Institution on Drug Abuse survey, nearly 88 percent of the female high school seniors surveyed in 1992 had consumed alcoholic beverages in their lifetime, compared to only 12.4 percent who had not. Of those who had ever used alcohol, nearly 50 percent had done so within the last 30 days, while more than 29 percent had consumed alcohol within the last 12 months.

The purchase and consumption of alcoholic beverages by female juveniles is a status offense in many states, or applicable only to minors.[7] However, the criminal laws also apply to girl drinkers when they are arrested for drunkenness, driving under the influence, and liquor law violations. Despite the complexities of the double standard with regard to juveniles and alcohol use, most minors find little difficulty in obtaining and consuming alcoholic beverages. One study reported that 7 in 10 high school students felt that they could easily purchase or acquire alcohol with few, if any, obstacles.[8]

In addition to the relationship between female and male juvenile alcohol use and involvement in criminal activities, studies show a significant correlation between teenage drinking and traffic fatalities. Twenty percent of automobile fatalities in the United States involve drivers under the age of 20, and in 60 percent of such fatalities the drivers were found to have been drinking.[9]

Many girl alcohol users have also been found to be drug users or addicts.[10] The danger in teens mixing alcohol and other drugs was pointed out by one researcher: "Teenagers typically take the sedative and tranquilizing drugs in combination with alcohol or other drugs. When depressants are taken with alcohol, the intensity of intoxication increases, and the combination is potentially lethal."[11]

GIRLS AND DRUG USE/ABUSE

Girls' most serious violations of substance abuse laws are for drug abuse offenses. In Kratcoski and Kratcoski's study, 40 percent of the girls had used or dealt drugs.[12] Comparatively, 40 percent of the female adolescents in Nechama Tec's study of suburban juvenile drug use were marijuana users, of whom 11 percent were regular users.[13] The results of a 1992 survey on the most recent use of marijuana, cocaine, and heroin by female high school seniors can be seen in Table 15-1. Of the three illicit drugs, marijuana was the one most likely to be used by female high school seniors. Nearly 29 percent admitted to using marijuana at some point in their lifetime, and more than 10 percent had used marijuana within the last 30 days. Cocaine was used at some point by 5.1 percent of the female seniors, with 1.5 percent having used cocaine within the last 12 months, and almost 1 percent within the past 30 days. Heroin was the least likely of the three drugs used at any time, with less than 1 percent of the female respondents reporting ever using the drug.

Girls are less likely to be drug users or addicts than boys, though the differential has lessened in recent years.[14] Girls are more likely than boys to use such drugs as amphetamines for weight control, but not as likely to use PCP or cocaine.[15] Female teens are almost equally likely as male teens to report having a drug problem.[16]

TABLE 15-1

Most Recent Drug Use by Female
High School Seniors, by Drug Type, 1992

Drug Type	Never used	Ever used	Most Recent Use		
			Within last 30 days	Within last 12 months[a]	Not within last 12 months
Marijuana	71.4	28.6	10.2	8.7	9.7
Cocaine	94.9	5.1	0.9	1.5	2.7
Heroin	99.2	0.8	0.2	0.1	0.5

[a]Not within the last 30 days.

Source: Derived from U.S. Department of Justice, *Sourcebook of Criminal Justice Statistics—1992* (Washington, D.C.: Government Printing Office, 1993), p. 327.

In general, surveys of girls and boys have produced the following findings on adolescent drug use:

- Adolescent drug use in this country often starts between the ages of 13 and 15.
- Marijuana is the most popular drug among adolescents.
- Cocaine use among juveniles is on the rise.
- Nearly 20 percent of high school seniors have tried cocaine or crack cocaine.
- Juvenile use of stimulants and inhalants is increasing.
- The number of teenagers using sedatives and hallucinogens is on the decline.
- One in 3 juvenile substance abusers abuses both alcohol *and* drugs.
- One in 10 teenage drug abusers uses multiple drugs.
- Girls and boys in the United States have a higher rate of alcohol and drug use than any other industrialized country.[17]

The increasing use of crack cocaine—a smokable, highly addictive, inexpensive form of cocaine—among teenagers is cause for concern. The National Cocaine Hotline, which estimates that over 1 million Americans have tried cocaine, reports that children using crack as young as 12 have called the hotline for help. A recent article in *Time* illustrated a typical girl crack addict:

> "Eva" is a 16-year-old patient at New York City's Phoenix House drug rehabilitation center who got hooked on crack two years ago. The product of a troubled middle-class family, she was already a heavy drinker and pot smoker when she was introduced to coke by her older brother, a young dope pusher. "When you take the first toke on a crack pipe, you get on top of the world," she says.
>
> She started stealing from family and friends to support her habit. She soon turned to prostitution and went through two abortions before she was 16. "I didn't give a damn about protecting myself," she said. "I just wanted to get high. Fear of pregnancy didn't even cross my mind when I hit the sack with someone for drugs."[18]

GIRL DRUG USERS AS DRUG DEALERS

Although relatively few girls are involved in the drug dealing business, studies show that girls who use drugs are often likely to also be low-level drug dealers.[19] In a study of teens, drugs, and crime, Cheryl

Carpenter and colleagues found that the majority of teenagers who sold a drug used the same drug, and many were regular users of alcohol and marijuana.[20] Most juvenile drug dealers sell marijuana, crack, amphetamines, and tranquilizers to support drug habits and make money. A 16-year-old female drug addict described the nature and ease in which she sold drugs:

> It is really easy to make money off of drugs. It has got to be the easiest job anyone could do. All you have to do is sit on your butt and wait for people to call. My boyfriend was dealing in drugs, and he was making nearly $200 a day. The money is nice, but when you get caught, it is another story. But I have never been caught. I've broken into houses, too, but I have never been caught doing that either.[21]

The customers of adolescent drug dealers are nearly always people they know and usually other teenagers, including siblings, friends, and acquaintances. Drug sales by juvenile dealers are typically arranged by phone, at school, or other places frequented by teenagers. The drugs themselves are often distributed in cars or homes, rather than in public places. Few girls or boys who sell small amounts of drugs view their activity as drug dealing, per se. Such is the example of a girl addict and dealer, who says of her drug selling, "I don't consider it dealing. I'll sell hits of speed to my friends and joints and nickel bags [of marijuana] to my friends, but that's not dealing."[22] Indeed, relatively few low-level juvenile drug dealers, particularly females, are targeted by law enforcement. Adolescent females who are involved in drug use and selling are more likely to be in contact with the criminal or juvenile justice systems for nondrug offenses such as prostitution or theft.[23]

GIRLS' SUBSTANCE ABUSE
AND JUVENILE DELINQUENCY

Girls who use and abuse alcohol and drugs are often involved in other delinquent activities, including violent crimes, sex crimes, and property crimes. There is a strong relationship between girl drug addicts and property crimes, such as petty theft and shoplifting, though studies show that half the girl drug abusers were perpetrating property offenses before they began using drugs.[24] A significant association also exists between adolescent female substance abuse, runaways, and prostitution. Many girl runaways become drug and/or alcohol abusers and turn to prostitution to support their habit.[25] Others abuse alcohol or drugs as an escape from the reality of a life of prostitution or being homeless.[26] There is also evidence that girls' substance abuse is linked to family offenses such as sibling abuse, child abuse, and incest.[27] These girl substance abusers furthermore have a high risk of becoming adult female substance abusers, in addition to being involved in other criminal activities in adulthood.[28]

WHY DO GIRLS USE/ ABUSE ALCOHOL AND DRUGS?

Girls generally become involved with alcohol and/or drugs for the same reasons as boys, including:

- Having family members who use alcohol or drugs.
- Peer group pressure.
- The easy accessibility of alcohol and drugs.
- A rite of passage into adulthood.
- The glamorizing of alcohol and drug use through television shows, motion pictures, and fiction books.
- Family problems.
- Sexual abuse.
- Running away from home.
- Prostitution.
- Depression.
- Addiction to other substances.
- Boredom.

The pressure to fit in with peers or attract boys may be the strongest influence in girls' use of alcohol and/or drugs. Girls also tend to use and abuse substances as a way to reduce inhibitions, gain respect, and enjoy the highs and sensations of alcohol and/or drugs. Girl involvement in drug use and dealing often leads to multiple drug use and alcohol abuse, as well as other high-risk activities such as promiscuity, drunk driving, and suicide.[29]

16. *Girl Thieves*

Girl offenders are involved in theft crimes more than any other type of offense. Nearly one-third (32 percent) of all arrests of females under 18 are for crimes of theft (see Figure 16-1), and over 35 percent of the arrests of girls under 15 are for theft crimes. Girls are arrested for larceny-theft more than any other type of theft crime. Most girls' thievery tends to be petty theft, and is often associated with other forms of nonviolent crime or delinquency, such as alcohol or drug use/abuse, running away, and prostitution. The biggest cost of juvenile female theft crimes may be in economic terms. It is estimated that billions of dollars are lost each year as a result of theft crimes, and statistics indicate that the proportion of thieves who are girls or women is on the rise.[1]

LARCENY-THEFT

Larceny-theft crimes (which include such offenses as shoplifting, purse-snatching, and bicycle theft) are committed by girls more than any other type of offense and are most likely to come to the attention of law enforcement authorities more than any other girls' offense. According to *Uniform Crime Reports 1992* information, 77 percent of the females under the age of 18 arrested for Crime Index offenses in 1992 were charged with larceny-theft (see Table 16-1). More than 26 percent of all arrests of girls under 18 in 1992 were for larceny-theft. Younger girls, under 15 years of age, were even more likely to be arrested for larceny-theft than other crimes. Seventy-eight percent of the

FIGURE 16-1

Girls and Theft Crimes, 1992[a]

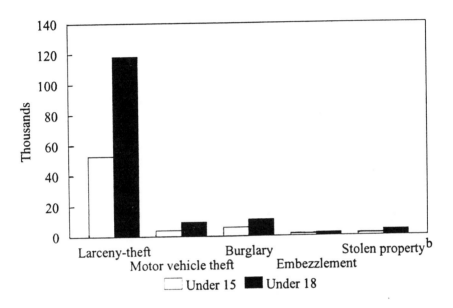

[a] Based on arrest figures for females under 18 in 1992.
[b] Buying, receiving and/or possessing.

Source: Adapted from U.S. Federal Bureau of Investigation, *Crime in the United States: Uniform Crime Reports 1992* (Washington, D.C.: Government Printing Office, 1993), p. 231.

---

arrests of girls younger than 15 for Crime Index offenses and nearly 30 percent of their total arrests were for larceny-theft. Of the 118,404 arrests of females under 18 for larceny-theft in 1992, 52,862, or just over 44.6 percent, were arrests of girls under the age of 15. Slightly more than 75 percent of the females age 18 and over arrested for Crime Index offenses and 16.4 percent of those arrested for all crimes were charged with larceny-theft.

Most girls arrested for larceny-theft are between the ages of 15 and 17, with the peak age of arrests being 15 (see Figure 16-2). In 1992, more than 55 percent of the girls arrested for larceny-theft were 15 to 17 years

TABLE 16-1

Percent of Female Arrests for Larceny-Theft,
of Crime Index and Total Offense Arrests, by Age, 1992

Larceny-Theft	Total females	Ages		
		Under 15	Under 18	18 and over
Total arrests	415,248	52,862	118,404	296,844
Percent of Crime Index arrests	75.6	78.0	77.0	75.1
Percent of Total arrests	18.4	29.7	26.5	16.4

Source: Derived from U.S. Federal Bureau of Investigation, *Crime in the United States: Uniform Crime Reports 1992* (Washington, D.C.: Government Printing Office, 1993), p. 231.

FIGURE 16-2

Girls Arrested for
Larceny-Theft, by Age, 1992

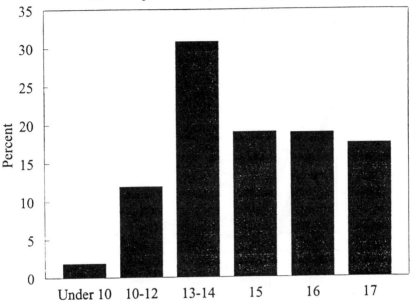

Source: Adapted from U.S. Federal Bureau of Investigation, *Crime in the United States: Uniform Crime Reports 1992* (Washington, D.C.: Government Printing Office, 1993), p. 231.

of age. Girls aged 13 to 14 were responsible for about 31 percent of the larceny-theft arrests, with girls age 12 and under accounting for less than 14 percent.

In comparing long-term trends in girl arrests for larceny-theft with other theft crimes, we can see in Figure 16-3 that between 1983 and 1992, girls arrested for larceny-theft increased more than 24 percent. By comparison, arrests for motor vehicle theft rose by 148.5 percent; embezzlement, 114.8 percent; and stolen property offenses, 59.8 percent. The arrest figures for these crimes remained relatively low during the 10-year period compared to larceny-theft, making the climb in larceny-theft arrests far more significant. Girl arrests for burglary increased the least, at 4.2 percent from 1983 to 1992. Despite this, girl arrests for burglary in 1992 were second among theft crimes only to larceny-theft.

FIGURE 16-3

Trends in Girl Arrests for Larceny-Theft and Other Theft Crimes, 1983–92

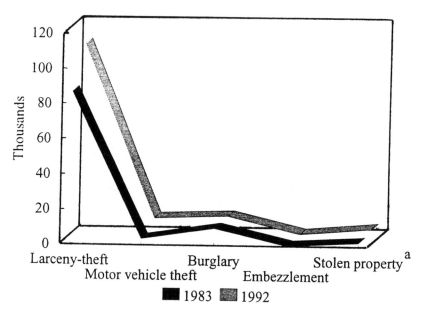

a Buying, receiving and/or possessing.

Source: Adapted from U.S. Federal Bureau of Investigation, *Crime in the United States: Uniform Crime Reports 1992* (Washington, D.C.: Government Printing Office, 1993), p. 222.

Shoplifting

The most common form of girl thieves are shoplifters. One study found that over 60 percent of all shoplifters apprehended in the United States were females under the age of 17.[2] Girl shoplifters cross all racial, ethnic, income, and class levels and come from every kind of background. A typical example of the girl shoplifter—a 16-year-old who began shoplifting at age 10 and has been a chronic shoplifter ever since—can be seen in the following exchange with a researcher:

GIRL: After I stole those records, I didn't do it for a long time. Then my friends started doing it, so I started doing it. Only little things mostly . . . just like necklaces.
INTERVIEWER: Do you think that's a pretty common thing?
GIRL: To steal?
INTERVIEWER: Shoplifting.
GIRL: Uh-huh. 'Cause it is. Everybody does it.[3]

Why do girls shoplift, and why is this crime perpetrated more frequently than any other type of female delinquency? Experts have attributed girls' tendency to shoplift to a number of reasons, including:

1. Opportunity and accessibility of items to steal;
2. Low detection rate;
3. Appearance has been shown to be very important to girls, thus the desire to obtain (or steal) such things as accessories or clothing to enhance one's appearance;
4. Peer pressure;
5. Impulsive behavior;
6. Substance abuse;
7. Habitual shoplifting; and
8. Involvement in multiple delinquent or criminal activities.[4]

Some girl shoplifters steal for the adventure in risk or the thrill of being bad without being caught or discovered. One former girl shoplifter explains this pattern:

I began shoplifting when I was 13 years old and living in the Valley in Los Angeles. Not occasionally, but with a vengeance, and ritualistically: the same day each week, the same stores, the same partner. At 13, my best friend, Paula, and I had already discovered the seductions of a secret life—the good girls that we were depended increasingly on the release offered by the secret "bad girl."[5]

Anne Campbell offers a perspective on the pressures that girls feel to shoplift:

With so many demands on incomes that are often quite low, it is hardly surprising that girls are heavily involved in shoplifting. The pressures—material, psychological, social, romantic—assault from every side. The shops invite them to touch, smell, feel, and wear everything that they need for instant success in all these spheres.

When the temptations are all weighed up and the chances of detection calculated, it is remarkable that so few girls do it.[6]

GIRLS' THEFT CRIMES AND SUBSTANCE ABUSE

Many studies show a strong relationship between girls' thieving and use/abuse of alcohol and/or drugs. This relationship is generally a reflection of two needs: (1) the need or desire for alcohol and/or drugs, and (2) the need for money or property that can be converted into money to purchase alcohol and/or drugs, or to support an addiction.[7] Cheryl Carpenter and colleagues described juvenile theft by juvenile substance users/abusers as "partly a product of a consumeristic mentality," which they referred to as the desire by young thieves to acquire what they wanted or needed as the primary reason for stealing—involving direct acquisition of valued items, property stolen for resale, and larceny-theft as a direct source of money.[8] Carpenter and associates found that adolescent thieves–substance users were less motivated to steal to buy alcohol or drugs than to acquire consumer goods such as stereo equipment, which was considered important for peer group popularity.

Girl alcohol abusers or drug addicts are more likely to engage in property crimes such as shoplifting and petty theft to support habits than violent crimes.[9] Girl thieves who are drug-involved have also been found to resort to drug dealing and stealing of drugs to support their habits and/or lifestyle.[10]

GIRL THIEVES AND RUNAWAYS

Girls who run away from home almost inevitably must turn to stealing to feed, shelter, and support themselves.[11] The girl runaway thief often ends up stealing not only food or clothing but drugs for habits or soon-to-be habits, and anything else that can help pay for survival on the streets. Once runaway thieves turn to prostitution, thefts can include a john's property and be on behalf of their pimp for profit or to support a drug habit.[12] Many runaway girls were already involved in theft crimes before leaving home. Others return home as thieves and continue to commit larcenies and other forms of theft acquired from living on the streets.

FIGURE 16-4
Women and Theft Crimes, 1992^a

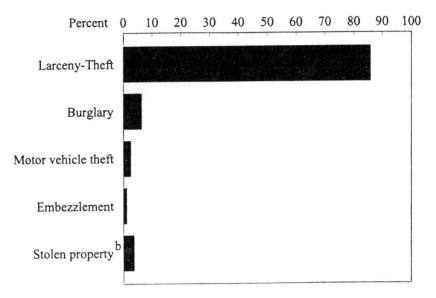

^aBased on arrest figures for females aged 18 and over in 1992.
^bIncludes buying, receiving and/or possessing.

Source: Calculated from U.S. Federal Bureau of Investigation, *Crime in the United States: Uniform Crime Reports 1992* (Washington, D.C.: Government Printing Office, 1993), p. 231.

WOMEN THIEVES

Adult female offenders are also more likely to be involved in theft crimes than any other type of criminal offenses.[13] The vast majority of these crimes are larceny-thefts (see Figure 16-4). There were 296,844 arrests of females ages 18 and over for larceny-theft in 1992, representing nearly 86 percent of all women's arrests for crimes of theft. Long-term arrest trends indicate that more women are becoming thieves. As seen in Figure 16-5, from 1983 to 1992 women's arrests increased for every type of theft. Arrests for larceny-theft rose nearly 27 percent, while burglary arrests increased 20.5 percent, and arrests for stolen

FIGURE 16-5

Trends in Women's Arrests
for Theft Crimes, 1983 and 1992

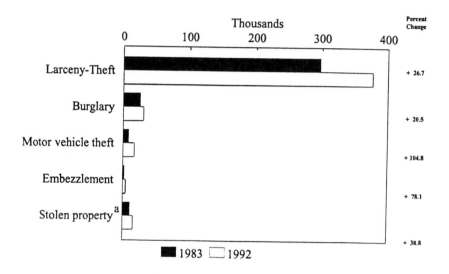

ᵃIncludes buying, receiving and possessing.

Source: Adapted from U.S. Federal Bureau of Investigation, *Crime in the United States: Uniform Crime Reports 1992* (Washington, D.C.: Government Printing Office, 1993), p. 222.

property offenses (including buying, receiving, and/or possessing) grew by nearly 39 percent. Motor vehicle theft arrests showed the greatest increase over the 10-year period at 104.8 percent. A 78.1 percent increase was recorded for women's arrests for embezzlement. The most alarming of these is the rise in arrests of women for larceny-theft.

Similar to girls, women thieves stretch across racial and ethnic lines and the socioeconomic strata. They are largely involved in traditional female thievery, such as shoplifting. A recent report estimated that 59 percent of all shoplifters are women.[14] Another study found that 51 percent of the apprehended female shoplifters were employed.[15] Women shoplifters most commonly steal cosmetics, clothing, and jewelry.[16] Many girl shoplifters become women shoplifters who steal for many of the same reasons: opportunity, the challenge, boredom, impulsiveness, the risk of getting caught, and the rush achieved from stealing. Said one former female shoplifter of her compulsion to steal: "It's all I thought about. Even when I wasn't stealing, I was thinking about what I was going to steal. When I was home alone, I'd try on my stolen things, one after another. I always feel more beautiful in something I've stolen."[17]

Women's thievery, like that of girls, is often associated with other forms of deviance or abnormal behavior—including involvement with drugs and/or alcohol, prostitution, and family dysfunction, such as wife battering, child abuse and neglect, and sexual abuse—and is also linked to economic impoverishment.[18]

17. Girls in Gangs

Juvenile gangs have been associated almost solely with males. However, studies show that females have been in gangs for more than a century. "During periods of high gang activity, such as the '50s, women form their own gangs. At other times, they can be found only as members of male gangs."[1] Criminologists have found that females generally join gangs for two reasons. One is to "fight, steal, and spy with the same gusto as some of the roughest men on the streets," and the other reflects the female's "traditional desires to find a husband and build a family."[2] Who are the girls in gangs today? How many girl gang members are there in the United States? Are girls' activities in gangs similar to activities in boys' gangs? What makes a girl join a gang?

THE EXTENT OF GIRLS IN GANGS

Juvenile gang activity is one of the nation's most serious crises. What once was thought of as an inner-city problem has now spread out into the suburbs and countryside across America—and with it an epidemic of gang-related drive-by shootings, violence, drug abuse, and drug dealing. It is estimated that there are over 2,200 gangs in the United States, consisting of more than 96,000 members who are believed to be responsible for "one-third of all crimes of violence, terrorizing entire communities, and maintaining a state of siege" in many urban and nonurban schools.[3]

How many of these gang members are female? Most experts believe that girls represent only a very small portion of total gang members.

178

From his study of youth gangs, Walter Miller estimated that 90 percent or more of the gang members were male.[4] However, that leaves as many as 10 percent that may be female. According to law enforcement officials, the relatively low percentage of females involved with male gangs still numbers in the hundreds or even thousands.[5] There is also evidence that many females belong to independent female juvenile gangs and prison inmate gangs "as a measure of stabilizing and legitimizing roles."[6]

Female gang members are believed to reflect male gang members with respect to race, ethnicity, and social status. They are disproportionately likely to be racial or ethnic minorities (black, Hispanic, or Asian).[7] Serious gang activity is most often associated with urban, underclass gangs, but gang violence has erupted in every size community in the country. Some studies have found that white gangs are emerging in the suburbs and small towns.[8] The average age of a female gang member is 17.[9]

THE NATURE OF
GIRL GANG MEMBERS

Girls belong to both independent female gangs and male gangs, where their roles appear to depend largely on the nature and location of the gang. In Peggy Giordano's study of institutionalized delinquent girls, she found that more than half of the 108 girl inmates sampled reported being part of a gang with a name.[10] Based on a study of girl gang members in Philadelphia, Waln Brown found girls generally to be involved in sexually integrated gangs rather than autonomous female gangs, with their roles being limited to such duties as spying on other gangs.[11] In Dale Hardman's study of small-town juvenile gangs, he found that girls tended to be included as full-fledged members of male gangs and all that entailed, as opposed to an auxiliary status.[12]

There is evidence that girl gang members of the 1990s are becoming increasingly more violent and dangerous than their counterparts of earlier decades. Indeed, since the 1970s researchers have noted an evolution in the nature of girl gang activity. Freda Adler contended that girls were becoming "more highly integrated in male gang activity and were moving closer to parallel but independent, violence-oriented, exclusively female gangs."[13] Even in male gangs the role of females is changing. According to gang expert Kurt Kumli: "Feminism ... has come to gang life. It used to be that girls provided support for boys' gangs while the boys did the real work. Today, girls are committing criminal acts for themselves, sometimes against the boys' orders."[14]

Sociologist Anne Campbell described the role of the girl gang member as similar to the male gang member with respect to violence and protecting one's turf, noting that:

> a cardinal gang rule is that men fight men and women fight women. Many of the same things that trigger brawls among men—invasion of turf or harm to a fellow gang member, for instance—do so among women, gang members say. But, they add, when women are involved, the violence tends to erupt faster and end more quickly. The weapons used are more likely to be fingernails, teeth and knives rather than crowbars and guns.[15]

However, many girl members of gangs have resorted to guns in the course of gang violence, chasing "down rivals with .22-caliber handguns" as well as going to school armed with "X-acto knives (wrapped in cardboard to elude the metal detector)."[16]

Despite this greater penchant for violence by girls in gangs, most gang experts believe that girl gang members continue to be typically less violent and aggressive than their male counterparts. In Miller's study, he found little evidence of independent female gangs and concluded that female gang members were far less likely to be involved in violent gang activity than male gang members.[17]

Sheila Weller noted that the biggest change in the evolution of girl gang members is the "apparent devaluation of human life—including their own. Gang girls recite virtual suicide codes with a stunning matter-of-factness."[18] With such gang names as "Lowlifes" and "*MGSs*—Mean Gangsta Bitches," some girl gang members "etch their boyfriends' initials in their skin with razors."[19] Most females in gangs are surrounded by violence and alliances in one respect or another, and are ruled by the new three R's: "Readin', Ritin', and Retaliation."[20]

Girls' initiation into male gangs is often fraught with abuse, degradation, sexual acts, and danger. This is particularly true in the Southwest, where "their initiation consists of having sex with a string of gang boys, one after another—like cars on a train. . . . Some prefer ritual sex to being 'jumped' in (unmercifully kicked, pummeled, and beaten). Other girls even view dangerous sex as a badge of courage."[21] For many girls, leaving a gang comes only by way of "face" out, or saving face—by getting pregnant. Estimates are that about 50 percent of the females in gangs quit as a result of pregnancy.[22]

WHY DO GIRLS JOIN GANGS?

In general, girls tend to gravitate toward gangs for the same reasons that boys do—for a sense of belonging, community, and identity. Said one female member of a gang in explaining the lure of the gang, "We're one big family pulling together to survive in this world."[23] Kumli found that "girls join gangs for all the things their families haven't given them: devotion, support, acceptance—love."[24] Sociologists believe that for many lower-class girls "gangs are the singles bars of the street set, reservoirs of some of the brightest, toughest, and most sociable youths from urban ghettos."[25] Many girls join gangs to escape abusive, violent, or traumatic childhoods where trust was severely violated. According to Claudette Faison of the New York Youth at Risk, such psychologically or physically damaged girls are attracted to gangs as a "tough haven where [they'll] find safety, power, and belonging."[26]

Several theories have been advanced in explaining why lower-class female and male juveniles join gangs and participate in crime, delinquency, and violence. The most prominent of these are the reaction-formation, opportunity, and lower-class culture theories.

Reaction-Formation Theory

The reaction-formation theory of juvenile gangs and gang delinquency was first proposed by Albert Cohen in 1955.[27] This theory postulated that lower-class youths turn to gang delinquency as a necessary group response to their failure to acquire status as determined by middle-class values and norms. Cohen argued that middle-class goals and values (such as ambition and success through hard work) are desired by lower-class adolescents, but they are generally at a disadvantage in institutional settings (such as school), where they are measured in terms of middle-class standards, and are further deprived of approved opportunities to reach culturally prescribed goals.

Because of these blocked opportunities and conflicts with middle-class institutions, Cohen advanced that lower-class youth undergo a delinquent behavioral response to their limitations, which he called a "status frustration" or a "reaction-formation against a middle class organized status dilemma in which the lower class boy suffers status frustrations in competition with middle status boys."[28] This often leads many juveniles to band together in juvenile gangs or a delinquent subculture—where they engage in behavior that is "nonutilitarian, malicious, negativistic, and hedonistic."[29] According to Cohen, the values of this delinquent subculture are the opposite of middle-class values. Because of an emotional attachment to "middle class goals that are unachievable, these youths must reject such goals and develop their own standards by which success can come and with it status, self-esteem, and solidarity."[30] Girls who join lower-class juvenile delinquent gangs are seen as being driven by the same status frustration as boys.

Cohen's reaction-formation theory has been criticized for not being empirically validated, being too broad in its generalizations in describing gang members (such as malicious and nonutilitarian), and placing too much value on the rejection of middle-class standards in explaining juvenile gang formation and delinquency. In response to this criticism, Cohen, in conjunction with James Short, Jr., later expanded on his original theory by advancing that more than one kind of lower-class delinquent gang subculture existed. They proposed that a *parent subculture* was the primary type of juvenile gang subculture, with other gang orientations specialized offshoots of it, such as a middle-class subculture and a drug addict subculture.[31]

Opportunity Theory

Delinquent subcultures were also studied by Richard Cloward and Lloyd Ohlin. In 1960, they proposed an opportunity theory or differential opportunity theory to explain the existence of delinquent juvenile gangs.[32] The theory maintained that access to both legitimate and illegitimate means is greatly influenced by the social structure; that is, although differential opportunity "exists in reaching culturally prescribed goals through legitimate means so too does differential opportunity operate in the use of illegitimate means for attaining socially approved goals."[33]

Opportunity theory explains juvenile gang delinquency as a reflection of the discrepancy between lower-class youth aspirations and what they have access to, assuming that "discrepancies between aspirations and legitimate chances of achievement increase as one descends in the class structure."[34] Since lower-class youths are unable to lower their aspirations, which come from middle class standards, their lack of access to legitimate means to attain culturally defined goals leads to deep frustrations and turning to illegitimate means to achieve these cultural goals.

Cloward and Ohlin found two types of opportunities that are distributed unequally: access to "learning structures," or the "appropriate environments for the acquisition of the values and skills associated with the performance of a particular role"; and access to "performance structures," or the opportunity to organize with those who share a related problem of adjustment and the opportunity to receive approval from one's peers for one's behavior.[35] Opportunity structure holds that it is the social structure in a community that determines the access juveniles have to learning and performance structures. Thus, the type of gang and delinquent subcultures in a given area is determined in large part by the community's social structure or environment.

According to Cloward and Ohlin, there are three main types of lower class youth gangs, or subcultural responses to blocked legitimate or illegitimate avenues for success—each or all depending upon the available means: criminal gangs, conflict gangs, and retreatist gangs.

1. *Criminal Gangs:* youth gangs which take on criminal values and skills as learned from adult gangs and organized crime gangs. These gangs operate primarily through illegitimate means, such as extortion and drug dealing, in acquiring money, power, and prestige.
2. *Conflict Gangs:* youth gangs established when both legitimate and illegitimate opportunities for success are blocked. These gangs allow members to achieve prestige and status among peers, often through violence, fighting, and intergang conflict.
3. *Retreatist Gangs:* juvenile gangs formed when youths are denied or reject success through illegitimate and legitimate means. Retreatist teens often sink into a world of substance abuse and get involved in secondary criminal activities, such as prostitution and theft, to support their habit.

Opportunity theory has been criticized primarily for its focus on lower-class gang delinquency, while not adequately accounting for delinquent gangs of the middle class. Cloward and Ohlin also failed to explain why some communities have different types of delinquent juvenile gangs simultaneously. Many critics also contend that there is insufficient evidence that lower-class juveniles reflect middle-class values.

Lower-Class Culture Theory

A lower-class culture theory of gang delinquency was advanced by Walter Miller.[36] Unlike Cohen's belief that delinquent gangs were formed as a rejection of middle-class values, Miller theorized that lower-class gang delinquency is the result of "positive attempts by youths to attain goals as determined by the values or focal concerns of the lower class culture."[37] Miller identified six lower class focal concerns for lower class youths: trouble, toughness, smartness, excitement, fate, and autonomy.

1. *Trouble* refers to circumstances resulting in undesired involvement with the criminal justice system. Staying out of or getting into trouble are seen as daily concerns of lower-class juveniles.
2. *Toughness* relates to masculinity, physical superiority, bravery, and daring.
3. *Smartness* is the ability to outsmart, outwit, or con others while avoiding being deceived or duped.
4. *Excitement* means the desire for thrills, risks, and avoiding boredom.
5. *Fate* concerns interests or beliefs related to luck, fortune, superstitions, and jinxes.
6. *Autonomy* is the desire to be in control of one's own destiny or life.

According to lower-class culture theory, the juvenile delinquent gang acts as a social setting through which youths can gain prestige through actions relative to lower-class focal concerns.

Critics of Miller's lower-class culture theory reject the argument that lower-class youths do not aspire to middle-class values. Further, the theory fails to explain how these focal concerns originated, or differentiate the focal concerns of delinquent youth gangs from those of nondelinquent lower-class occupants who appear to embrace middle-class norms and values.

PART V

Females Behind Bars

18. Girls in Custody

With the rise in arrests of females under 18 years of age in recent years, more girls are being taken into custody and put in jails, prisons, and juvenile detention facilities. Most girl offenders are held for delinquent offenses rather than status offenses or other nondelinquent reasons.[1] Drug and alcohol use/abuse play a major role in female minors' crimes and confinement in adult and juvenile correctional facilities. Many girl inmates are recidivists and a number will become adult female criminals and jail and prison inmates.

GIRLS IN JAILS AND PRISONS

Less than 1 percent of the girls in custody are held in adult correctional facilities. The vast majority tend to be detained in jails.[2] Girls are 7 times more likely to be put in jail than prisons.[3] However, even jail detention has decreased for girl offenders in recent years. From mid–1983 to mid–1991, total jail admission of female juveniles dropped from 18,516 in 1983 to 6,924 in 1991—or a decline of 62.6 percent (see Figure 18-1). Girl jail or prison inmates constitute a smaller proportion of the jail or prison inmates than the girls held in juvenile detention facilities.[4] The fact that girls are held at all in adult jails or police lock-ups is a reflection of inadequate facilities for detaining juvenile offenders. It is estimated that in 93 percent of the juvenile court jurisdictions, including some 2,800 cities and counties nationwide, jails are being used to hold juvenile offenders.[5]

Although most girls in jail are older teenagers, many are younger

FIGURE 18-1

Girl Admissions to Local Jails, 1983–91

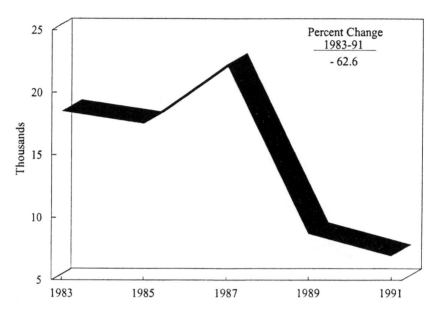

Source: Adapted from U.S. Department of Justice, *Sourcebook of Criminal Justice Statistics—1992* (Washington, D.C.: Government Printing Office, 1993), p. 594.

teens, and some are even younger than 10 years of age.[6] Most girl jail inmates are held for minor or status offenses. A study of juvenile jail inmates in 18 states found that over 40 percent were arrested for status offenses.[7] A study on the nature of delinquency committed by jailed juveniles found that only 20 percent of girls and boys in jail were being held for violent or property crimes.[8] The less serious nature of crimes perpetrated by most girls in jail is reflected in their short jail confinement on average. One study found that 70 percent of the female and male juvenile inmates were in jail for 2 days or less, and 80 percent were returned home or placed within the community when released.[9] In a study of girls and boys held in Minnesota jails, it was found that the average length of stay was 1.9 days, but 50 percent of the juvenile inmates were confined for no more than 14 hours.[10] The study also found a wide variation in jail time depending upon the county—with jail detainment of juveniles ranging from 8 hours to 6.9 days.

Girls placed in adult jails face an increased risk for physical or sexual assaults, as well as suicide. The rate of suicide for jailed juveniles is seven times greater than that of juveniles held in juvenile correctional institutions.[11] Abuse of girls can sometimes take place even before they reach jail. Sexual abuse in vans transporting juveniles to jails and prison has been found to occur at a high rate.[12] Once in jail, even a short stay can be a traumatic experience for even the most precocious or streetwise girl as "the conditions in which [girls] are kept are often like something out of Dickens. . . . Small, dark cells. Little human contact. Hours of boredom and depression. And in the worst cases, physical abuse by jail staff and other inmates."[13]

GIRLS HELD IN PUBLIC AND PRIVATE JUVENILE FACILITIES

In 1989, there were a total of 3,267 public and private juvenile detention, correctional, and shelter facilities that confined girls. These facilities are divided into short- and long-term institutions and are further broken down as institutional and open environment settings. Short-term facilities include juvenile detention centers, reception and diagnostic centers, and shelter homes. Long-term facilities include training schools, forestry camps, ranches, farms, halfway houses, and group homes. The following list describes the key characteristics of institution types:

- *Detention centers* or *juvenile halls* are secure custody facilities that detain delinquent juveniles temporarily, usually ranging from a few hours up to 90 days. These include jails, police lockups, and juvenile detention centers.
- *Shelter care facilities* are short-term facilities that house mostly status offenders, dependent children, or neglected children.
- *Reception and diagnostic centers* are where many juvenile offenders who receive a disposition of confinement go to be evaluated through psychological, medical, and aptitude testing to determine their treatment and institutional placement. Evaluation is generally from 4 to 6 weeks.
- *Training schools* are the most secure long-term juvenile facilities,

FIGURE 18-2

Juveniles Held in Private Facilities, by Sex, 1991

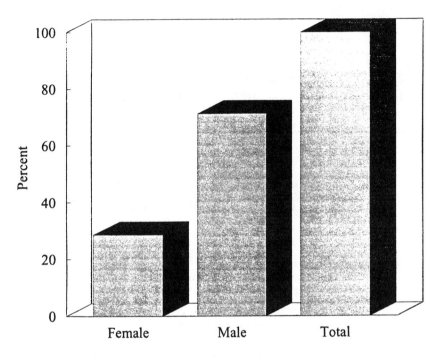

Source: Adapted from U.S. Department of Justice, *Sourcebook of Criminal Justice Statistics—1992* (Washington, D.C.: Government Printing Office, 1993), p. 579.

confining the most violent, serious, and habitual juvenile offenders.

- *Ranches, forestry camps,* and *farms* generally serve as minimum security facilities for nonviolent juvenile offenders and first-time delinquents.
- *Halfway houses* and *group homes* are small, often privately run juvenile facilities mostly for minimum risk juvenile detainees. They offer an alternative to the more secure detention facilities and a short-term community placement for juvenile offenders to ease their way back into society.

FIGURE 18-3

Juveniles Held in
Public Facilities, by Sex, 1989

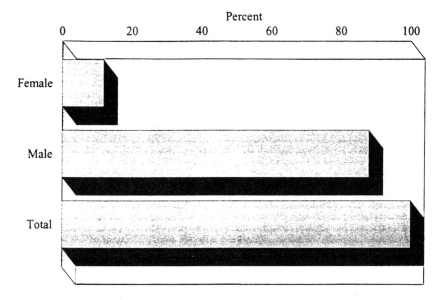

Source: Derived from U.S. Department of Justice, *Public Juvenile Facilities: Children in Custody 1989* (Washington, D.C.: Government Printing Office, 1991), p. 4.

The percentage of girls held in private juvenile facilities is higher than those confined to public juvenile facilities. In 1991, nearly 29 percent of the 36,190 juveniles held in private juvenile correctional facilities were female, compared to over 71 percent male (see Figure 18-2). In the latest figures for public juvenile facilities, counted on the 1989 census date, females accounted for just under 12 percent of the 56,123 juveniles in detention, while more than 88 percent of those being held in public facilities were male (see Figure 18-3).

There were 17,900 total admissions of female juveniles to public and private juvenile facilities in 1989. This represented an increase in total admissions of 17.5 percent since 1979 (see Figure 18-4). In the one day counts from 1979 to 1989, the number of girls being held in

FIGURE 18-4

Girls Held in Public and
Private Juvenile Facilities, 1979–89

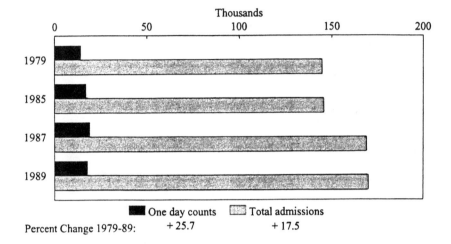

Source: Adapted from U.S. Department of Justice, *National Juvenile Custody Trends 1978–1989* (Washington, D.C.: Government Printing Office, 1992), p. 7.

public and private facilities rose nearly 26 percent, totaling 17,900 in 1989. The majority of girls in juvenile custody are held in halfway houses, followed by shelters, training schools, and ranches or camps (see Figure 18-5).

CHARACTERISTICS
OF GIRLS IN CUSTODY

Girls held in juvenile facilities closely mirror boys with respect to certain characteristics such as race, ethnicity, and age range. Minority youths of both sexes make up about 60 percent of the juveniles in custody. More than 8 in 10 juvenile detainees are black or white, with about 15 percent of Hispanic origin.[14] Most girls in juvenile detention

FIGURE 18-5

Girls in Private Juvenile Facilities, by Type of Facility, 1991

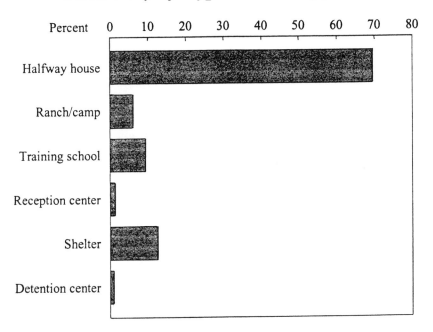

Source: Adapted from U.S. Department of Justice, *Sourcebook of Criminal Justice Statistics—1992* (Washington, D.C.: Government Printing Office, 1993), p. 579.

are between the ages of 15 and 17, with the average age of girl detainees at 15.[15]

The types of offenses committed by girl residents of juvenile facilities and other reasons for girls' confinement can be seen in Table 18-1. Nearly 80 percent of girl detainees in public juvenile facilities in 1989 were being held for delinquent or criminal offenses. Most involved property offenses or offenses against persons. Almost 80 percent of confined girls were in for property offenses, such as larceny-theft, vandalism, and unauthorized use of a motor vehicle. More than 20 percent of institutionalized female juveniles had committed offenses against persons, including murder, aggravated assault, and simple

TABLE 18-1
Girls Held in Public Juvenile Facilities, by Type of Offenses and Reasons for Detention, 1989

Total juveniles	Total juvenile detainees	Females
	56,123	6,680
Delinquent offenses[a]	53,037	5,194
Offenses against persons	14,327	1,117
Violent[b]	8,566	590
Other[c]	5,761	527
Property Offenses	22,780	1,931
Serious[d]	15,181	1,069
Other[e]	7,599	862
Alcohol/drug offenses	6,586	519
Public order offenses	2,788	382
Probation violations	4,920	978
Other delinquent offenses[f]	1,636	267
Nondelinquent reasons	**3,086**	**1,486**
Status offenses[g]	2,245	1,117
Abuse/neglect[h]	426	221
Other[i]	113	35
Voluntarily admitted	302	113

[a] Offenses that would be criminal if committed by adults.
[b] Includes murder, forcible rape, robbery, and aggravated assault.
[c] Includes manslaughter, simple assault, and sexual assault.
[d] Includes burglary, arson, larceny-theft, and motor vehicle theft.
[e] Includes vandalism, forgery, counterfeiting, fraud, stolen property, and unauthorized use of a motor vehicle.
[f] Includes unknown and unspecified delinquent offenses.
[g] Offenses that would not be criminal for adults, such as running away, truancy, and incorrigibility.
[h] Also includes those held for emotional disturbance or mental retardation.
[i] Includes all other unspecified reasons for detention or commitment.

Source: Adapted from U.S. Department of Justice, *Public Juvenile Facilities: Children in Custody 1989* (Washington, D.C.: Government Printing Office, 1991), p. 4.

assault. Ten percent of girls in public juvenile facilities were in for alcohol- and drug-related offenses, while nearly 20 percent had violated probation.

Nondelinquent reasons accounted for 20 percent of girls being held in juvenile detention facilities in 1989. The most common nondelinquent reason for confinement was a status offense. More than 75 percent of female juveniles in public facilities for nondelinquent reasons had committed status offenses such as running away, truancy, and incorrigibility.

BACKGROUND FACTORS OF GIRL INMATES

Research shows that a high percentage of girl delinquents in long-term juvenile detention facilities grew up in homes where one or both parents were absent, had family members who were incarcerated at some time, knew friends who were involved in delinquent activities, and were with others at the time they committed the offense that resulted in their placement in a juvenile institution.[16] Other common features among female juveniles in custody include the following:

- A relatively high rate of recidivism.
- A high rate of substance abuse prior to confinement.
- The use of alcohol and/or drugs in relation to other delinquent activities.
- Parents who abused alcohol and/or drugs.
- Mental and emotional problems.
- Physically and/or sexually abused.
- A background high in domestic violence or other family pathology.[17]

Studies indicate that girls whose backgrounds are fraught with family dissention, violence, abuse, a cycle of crime and delinquency, and other severe problems are at greater risk for delinquent behavior and subsequent placement in juvenile correctional facilities than girls who have relatively stable, normal backgrounds and family life.[18]

LIFE FOR GIRLS
IN JUVENILE CUSTODY

Girls who enter juvenile detention facilities must immediately face the loss of freedom. This includes being subjected to strict rules and regulations, restricted movement, strip searches, and solitary confinement. Discrimination, racism, exploitation, and physical or sexual abuse are common in many juvenile facilities. Many female juvenile detainees find it difficult to deal with the realities of confinement and thus experience depression, stress, frustration, low self-esteem, and other emotional or physical problems. Some respond through rebellion; others learn to control their emotions while doing their time. Other modes of adaptation include conformists, retreatists, innovators, con artists, and scapegoats.[19] For most girls placed in juvenile custody, life is what they make of it. For many it is the life afterward that will never be quite the same.

One Girl's Path to Juvenile Hall

Rachel, 15, was recently put in Los Angeles's Central Juvenile Hall, one of the largest juvenile detention facilities in the country. She was placed there by the juvenile court for two months prior to being transferred to a long-term facility—a group home for delinquent girls—for a stay of up to three years. She had robbed a small clothing store. Also figuring in her confinement was a history of delinquent behavior, including drug abuse.

Rachel's journey to juvenile hall began when she and her 18-year-old sister robbed a clothing store of $118. Within 15 minutes the sisters were questioned at their home by police, eventually identified by the store owner and two witnesses, and placed under arrest. In handcuffs, Rachel was brought to the police station and held in a cell while her mother was contacted and her arrest record investigated (her sister was referred to criminal court jurisdiction). "I sat alone in a jail cell for about five hours," Rachel recalled. "I was glad to finally have the handcuffs off because my wrists hurt."[20]

Hours later, a probation officer showed up. This person's disposition of Rachel's case would be based on her history, the nature of the offense, her family situation, and other factors. Noted the probation officer: "It became clear she was living in a home essentially without supervision. .... It was very clear that [Rachel] did not understand the seriousness of her crime."[21] Eventually, the probation officer decided she was to be placed in juvenile hall while her case went through the juvenile justice process.

A detention hearing was the next step, where the merits of the detention decision would be reviewed, thereby establishing whether or not the accused should be detained until her case came to trial. Due to the serious nature of Rachel's crime and her recidivism in violating the law, following the detention and juvenile court hearings the judge determined that she would spend two months in juvenile hall before her confinement to the group home.

Los Angeles's Central Juvenile Hall is coed, spread over 20 acres. The girl residents

> live in groups of 20. Each living unit has 16 individual rooms, each with a bed, small sink, and toilet. The toilet has no seat. The narrow institutional bed with its steel frame is purely functional— there is no decoration. The walls are blank and the single window is enclosed with a thick metal screen. .... Each group of 20 girls will stay together all day, at school, meals, and during recreation time.[22]

Rachel's day as a juvenile delinquent detainee begins at 6:30 A.M. with a shower, followed by cleaning her room, and a silent, straight-line march to breakfast. At 8:30 A.M., the march resumes, this time to school, where there are five periods with classes ranging from math to art to a recreational period. Wearing their prison "uniform" of sweat-shirts, jeans, and tennis shoes, the girl inmates are watched each minute of the day by guards.[23]

NONINSTITUTIONAL
DISPOSITIONS FOR GIRL OFFENDERS

The majority of girls who are adjudicated delinquent receive dispositions other than institutionalization. Probation is the most common disposition of female juvenile cases disposed by the juvenile court. The length of probation varies from state to state. It may be anywhere from six months up until the time the girl reaches adulthood.[24] The often conflicting goals in probation of rehabilitation and control were described by R. M. Emerson:

> The formal goal of probation is to improve the delinquent's behavior
> ... to "rehabilitate." ... This goal is short-circuited, however, by a
> pervading preoccupation with control. Reflecting insistent demands
> that the court "do something" about recurrent misconduct, proba-
> tion is organized to keep the delinquent "in line," to prevent any fur-
> ther disturbing and inconveniencing "trouble." The ultimate goal of
> permanently "reforming" the delinquent's personality and conduct
> becomes subordinated to the exigencies of maintaining immediate
> control. Probationary supervision consequently takes on a decidedly
> short-term and negative character; probation becomes an essentially
> disciplinary regime directed toward deterring and inhibiting trouble-
> some conduct.[25]

Diversionary programs reflect another common means for dealing
with girl offenders outside the formal juvenile justice system. A study
of over 1 million juveniles taken into custody found that more than 33
percent of their cases were handled informally.[26] Police diversionary
referrals of girl delinquents are generally to such social agencies as
child welfare services, youth service bureaus, and mental health agencies. Informal probation is the form of diversion most employed by the
juvenile court. In a recent study of juvenile offenders referred to intake
units, 14 percent were placed on informal probation and 64 percent
were released.[27] The courts further divert girl offenders to diversionary
alternatives to the juvenile justice system such as shoplifter's programs,
substance abuse clinics, and crisis intervention programs.

Other noninstitutional approaches to treating girl delinquents include the following:

- *Residential treatment programs* such as foster care placement and 24
  hours a day group homes.
- *Nonresidential day treatment programs* are informal correctional programs that girl delinquents or status offenders attend during
  standard school hours and then they return home in the evenings
  or on weekends.
- *Aftercare*, or the aftercare program, is the juvenile justice system's
  parole of juvenile offenders and the support and supervisory services accompanying the juvenile's release into society.[28]

19. Women
as Jail Inmates

As women's involvement in criminal activity rises, so too does their rate of incarceration in jails and prisons. The average daily population of female jail inmates increased nearly 3 percent from 1991 to 1992. It is estimated that 1 in every 2,417 women in the United States was in a local jail on June 30, 1992.[1] Many of these women were convicted of drug-related offenses or were substance abusers prior to incarceration. Most jailed women are racial or ethnic minorities, mothers, and have experienced physical or sexual abuse or other family dysfunction prior to incarceration. Women in jail often find intolerable conditions that include strip searches and sexual assaults.

THE EXTENT OF WOMEN IN JAIL

Women make up approximately 9 percent of the inmate population in jails in the United States. According to the annual survey of jails, there were 40,674 females being held in local jails on June 30, 1992.[2] This represents a significant increase from just 10 years earlier. As we see in Figure 19-1, between 1983 and 1992, the number of women jail inmates rose almost 160 percent. The female percentage of the total jail population increased from 7.1 to 9.2 during this period. In 1991, there were 1.2 million female jail admissions compared to 1.1 million female jail admissions in 1990. Regionally, most female jail inmates are in Southern jails, followed by jails in the West, North Central, and Northeast.[3]

FIGURE 19-1

Women Held in Local Jails, 1983 and 1992[a]

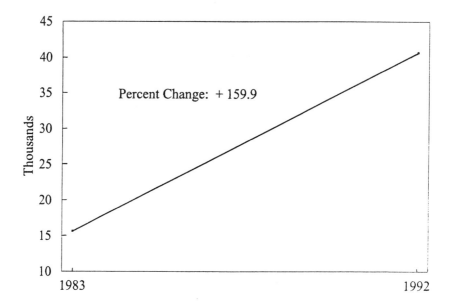

[a] Figures are for females in jail on June 30, 1983 and June 30, 1992.

Source: Calculated from U.S. Department of Justice, *Women in Jail 1989* (Washington, D.C.: Government Printing Office, 1992), p. 2; U.S. Department of Justice, *Jail Inmates 1992* (Washington, D.C.: Government Printing Office, 1993), p. 2.

More than 60 percent of jailed women were convicted of an offense (see Table 19-1). Over 50 percent of the women in jail have been sentenced to jail or prison, while nearly 40 percent of female jail inmates await arraignment and/or trial. About 50 percent of the women inmates in jail have been sentenced, with nearly 80 percent sentenced to jail terms and more than 15 percent to prison terms. The median sentence length for women sentenced to jail is 6 months; the mean jail sentence, 16 months. For women jail inmates sentenced to prison, the median length of sentence is 60 months; the mean is 72 months.

TABLE 19-1

Detention Status and Sentence Length of Female Jail Inmates, 1989

	Percent of Female Jail Inmates
DETENTION STATUS	
Convicted	61.4
Sentenced	52.2
Awaiting sentence	9.2
Unconvicted	38.6
Arraigned and awaiting trial or on trial	22.6
Not yet arraigned	16.0

	Percent of Sentenced Female Jail Inmates
LOCATON WHERE SENTENCE WAS TO BE SERVED	
Jail	77.0
Prison	15.4
Unknown	7.6
MAXIMUM SENTENCE LENGTH	
Sentenced to jail	
Median	6 months
Mean	16 months
AWAITING TRANSFER TO STATE OR FEDERAL PRISON	
Median	60 months
Mean	72 months

Source: Adapted from U.S. Department of Justice, *Women in Jail 1989* (Washington, D.C.: Government Printing Office, 1992), pp. 4-5.

FIGURE 19-2

The Distribution of Female Jail Inmates, by Race and Ethnic Origin, 1989

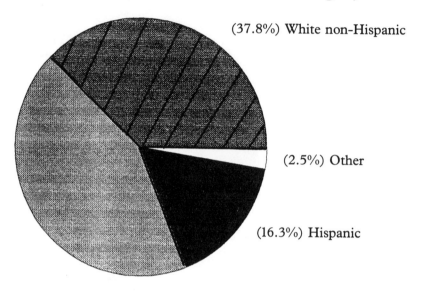

(37.8%) White non-Hispanic

(2.5%) Other

(16.3%) Hispanic

(43.4%) Black non-Hispanic

Source: Adapted from U.S. Department of Justice, *Women in Jail 1989* (Washington, D.C.: Government Printing Office, 1992), p. 3; U.S. Department of Justice, *Jail Inmates 1992* (Washington, D.C.: Government Printing Office, 1993), p. 3.

CHARACTERISTICS OF FEMALE JAIL INMATES

Women in jail are largely black and Hispanic. In 1989, more than 43 percent of the female jail inmates were black and over 16 percent Hispanic (see Figure 19-2). White non–Hispanic women made up nearly 38 percent of the jail inmates, while racial minorities such as Asians and American Indians constituted less than 3 percent of all women in U.S. jails.

The majority of females in jail fall between the ages of 25 and 34, with the median age 28.[4] Other characteristics of women jail inmates are as follows:

- More than 80 percent of women in prison are single, divorced, or widowed.
- Thirty-three percent are high school graduates.
- About thirty-three percent have some high school education.
- The majority of inmates were unemployed prior to arrest.
- Of the women reporting income, more than 50 percent earned less than $500 per month.
- Welfare was the main source of income for approximately 33 percent of female jail inmates before incarceration.[5]

Nearly 75 percent of women in jail in this country have children (see Table 19-2), as is shown in a 1989 survey. Of the 25,173 women interviewed, they had approximately 52,267 total children under the age of 18. Black inmates were more likely to have young children who lived with them before they entered jail than white inmates or female inmates of other racial groups. White women were more likely to have up to 2 children younger than age 18, whereas black women were more likely to have 3 to 5 children under that age. Relatives were most likely to be responsible for the care of children of female jail inmates. The majority of inmates indicated they planned to live with their children younger than 18 once released from jail.

CRIMINAL HISTORY
OF JAILED WOMEN

The types of crimes for which women are most often being held in jail vary depending upon the conviction status. We can see in Table 19-3 that in 1989 women who were convicted of a crime were most likely to be in jail for property offenses, followed by drug offenses, public-order offenses, and violent offenses. Female inmates unconvicted—awaiting trial or arraignment—were most likely to be held for drug offenses, followed by property offenses, violent offenses, and public-order offenses. The differences were greatest for violent offenses, where unconvicted female inmates were more than twice as likely to be in jail than convicted female inmates.

TABLE 19-2

Children of Female Jail Inmates, by Race, 1989

Characteristic	Percent of Female Inmates		
	All[a]	White	Black
Have children			
No	26.2	28.6	23.3
Yes	73.8	71.5	76.7
Any under age of 18	67.9	64.9	71.3
Adult only	5.9	6.6	5.4
Number of inmates	37,071	19,306	16,513
Number of children under age 18[b]			
1	37.8	38.9	35.5
2	33.4	37.0	31.3
3	17.9	14.9	21.1
4	6.4	5.3	7.9
5 or more	4.4	3.9	4.2
Lived with child(ren) under 18 before entering jail[b]			
No	32.8	35.9	27.7
Yes	67.2	64.1	72.3

Where child(ren) under 18 live(s) now[b, c]

Child's father	23.5	30.1	15.8
Maternal grandparents	41.6	34.9	50.0
Paternal grandparents	8.7	9.3	7.1
Other relative	22.9	18.6	27.0
Friends	4.3	4.2	4.5
Foster home	6.5	7.2	6.1
Agency/institution	1.6	2.2	0.9
Other	4.0	5.0	1.9

Plan to live with child(ren) under 18 after release from jail[b]

Yes	84.5	77.7	91.7
No	12.4	18.1	6.3
Don't know	3.1	4.3	1.9

[a]Includes Asians, Pacific Islanders, American Indians, Alaska Natives, and other racial groups.
[b]Percents are based on those inmates with children under age 18.
[c]Percents add to more than 100 because inmates with more than one child may have provided multiple responses.

Source: Adapted from U.S. Department of Justice, *Women in Jail 1989* (Washington, D.C.: Government Printing Office, 1992), p. 9.

TABLE 19-3

Type of Offense Female Jail Inmates
Held For, by Conviction Status[a] and Race, 1989

Most Serious Offense	Percent of convicted female inmates[b]			Percent of unconvicted female inmates[b]		
	All[c]	White	Black	All[c]	White	Black
All offenses	100.0	100.0	100.0	100.0	100.0	100.0
Violent offenses	9.2	6.4	12.6	19.6	16.7	20.0
Homicide	1.1	0.8	1.7	3.9	3.7	4.4
Robbery	3.5	2.0	5.3	4.6	3.1	6.6
Assault	3.6	2.9	4.4	7.7	7.4	8.4
Other violent	0.9	0.7	1.1	3.4	2.5	0.6
Property offenses	34.5	31.8	38.8	27.9	26.3	30.1
Burglary	2.9	3.5	2.4	5.7	5.6	5.6
Larceny–theft	15.4	13.7	17.9	9.0	7.5	11.4
Fraud	13.3	11.5	15.6	8.9	9.3	8.2
Other property	2.9	3.1	2.9	4.2	3.9	4.9
Drug offenses	32.7	32.2	33.8	35.1	36.2	36.5
Possession	16.5	15.1	17.7	12.3	11.4	14.5

Trafficking	15.4	16.1	15.3	19.3	21.5	18.2
Other drug	0.8	0.9	0.8	3.6	3.3	3.8
Public-order offense	21.4	27.9	11.9	15.3	18.2	11.7
Obstruction of justice	2.8	3.8	1.7	5.0	5.5	4.8
Driving while intoxicated	5.3	9.4	0.4	1.0	2.0	0.0
Commercialized vice	5.7	5.5	5.0	2.2	1.5	2.5
Violation of parole/probation	4.1	4.4	3.1	2.8	3.1	2.0
Other public-order	3.5	4.9	1.7	4.4	6.1	2.3
Other offenses	2.3	1.7	2.9	2.1	2.6	1.8
Number of inmates	21,854	11,596	9,637	13,771	6,703	6,457

[a]Excludes an estimated 1,758 jail inmates whose conviction status or offense was unknown.
[b]Detail may not add to totals because of rounding.
[c]Includes Asians, Pacific Islanders, American Indians, Alaska Natives, and other racial groups.

Source: Adapted from U.S. Department of Justice, *Women in Jail 1989* (Washington, D.C.: Government Printing Office, 1992), p. 5.

TABLE 19-4

Criminal History of Female Jail Inmates,[a] by Most Serious Current Offense, 1989

Criminal History	Total	Most Serious Current Offense			
		Violent	Property	Drug	Public-order
Total	100.0	100.0	100.0	100.0	100.0
First offense	31.5	45.4	23.3	36.6	26.0
Previous offenses	68.5	54.6	76.7	63.4	74.0
Violent offenses	10.0	15.5	9.7	7.9	10.8
Property offenses	40.2	27.1	64.1	30.3	30.3
Drug offenses	20.6	12.9	11.4	32.9	19.4
Public-order offenses	30.5	21.4	23.5	27.1	55.9
Number of inmates	35,087	4,656	11,233	11,771	6,642

[a]Excludes an estimated 2,296 inmates for whom data on present or prior offenses were unknown. Subtotals may add to more than total because inmates may have been sentenced more than once or for more than one type of offense.

Source: U.S. Department of Justice, *Women in Jail 1989* (Washington, D.C.: Government Printing Office, 1992), p. 7.

For both convicted and unconvicted women in jail, more than 60 percent of the crimes they were charged with were property or drug offenses. Convicted and unconvicted female property offenders were most likely to be in jail for larceny-theft and fraud; while convicted female drug offenders were most likely to be incarcerated for possession, compared to trafficking for most unconvicted female inmates.

Black female convicted inmates were nearly twice as likely to be in jail for a violent offense as white female convicted inmates, and had a higher percentage of convictions for property offenses than white or other race inmates. Convictions for drug offenses were roughly equal among black and white inmates; however more than 25 percent of white women were in jail for public-order offenses, compared to about 12.5 percent of black women. Unconvicted black women inmates were slightly more likely to be in jail for violent, property, and drug offenses than unconvicted white women inmates; whereas more unconvicted white inmates were being held for public-order offenses than black inmates.

Nearly 1 in 3 female jail inmates are first-time offenders, while most women in jail with previous offenses tend to be currently incarcerated for similar type offenses. As shown in Table 19-4, 31.5 percent of the female jail inmates in 1989 were in for a first offense. Over 45 percent of the women being held for violent offenses were first-timers. Female inmates in jail for property, drug, or public-order offenses were most likely to have previously committed crimes in the same categories than other types of crimes; while women jailed for violent offenses were more likely to have previously been convicted of a violent crime than inmates in jail for other offenses.

DRUG AND ALCOHOL ABUSE
HISTORY OF WOMEN IN JAIL

The vast majority of women in jail have a history of drug use/abuse, as shown in Table 19-5. Nearly 84 percent of the convicted female jail inmates in 1989 had used drugs at some point in their lifetime, including 70 percent on a regular basis. Almost 40 percent of the inmates reported being under the influence of drugs at the time they committed the offense for which they were in jail. Over 70 percent of the women had used major drugs such as cocaine, crack cocaine, and/or heroin, with nearly 33 percent under the influence of one or

TABLE 19-5

Drug Use History of Convicted Female Inmates, 1989

Drug Use	Percent of Convicted Female Inmates
Any Drug	
Ever used	83.6
Ever used on a regular basis	70.0
Used in the month before current offense	55.1
Used daily in month before current offense	40.1
Under the influence at the time of current offense	37.5
Major Drug	
Ever used	70.7
Ever used on a regular basis	56.7
Used in the month before current offense	43.9
Used daily in month before current offense	31.8
Under the influence at the time of current offense	31.3

Drug Use

	Percent of Convicted Female Inmates	
	In the month before the offense	At the time of the offense
Any Drug[a]	55.1	37.5
Major Drug	43.8	31.3
Cocaine or crack	39.3	24.9
Heroin	15.0	12.0
LSD	0.8	0.1
PCP	2.1	0.8
Methadone	1.1	0.7
Other Drug	27.4	9.9
Marijuana	23.4	5.0
Amphetamines	6.6	4.1
Barbiturates	3.0	1.4
Methaqualone	1.0	0.2

[a] Detail may add to more than total because an inmate may have been using more than one drug.

Source: Constructed from U.S. Department of Justice, *Women in Jail 1989* (Washington, D.C.: Government Printing Office, 1992), pp. 7–8.

more major drugs when they committed the offense that resulted in incarceration.

Of the convicted women who had used drugs in the month prior to the offense, most had used cocaine, crack, or marijuana. For those using drugs at the time of the offense they were currently serving time for, almost 25 percent were using cocaine or crack. One-third of the female jail inmates in 1989 were in jail for drug offenses, including possession.

A strong relationship exists between alcohol use and women in jail. Twenty percent of female inmates in 1989 were under the influence of alcohol when they committed their offense, more than 13 percent said they were alcoholics, and over 8 percent reported being drunk or very drunk at the time of the offense that sent them to jail.[6]

Less than 10 percent of the female jail inmates had ever participated in an alcohol abuse treatment program, compared to nearly 37 percent in a drug abuse treatment program.[7]

BACKGROUND DYSFUNCTION
AND ABUSE OF FEMALE JAIL INMATES

Most women in jail grew up in broken homes and a high percentage were victims of physical and/or sexual abuse. According to the Bureau of Justice Statistics (BJS), nearly 6 in 10 female jail inmates were raised in homes in which one or both parents were absent.[8] For black female inmates, 7 in 10 came from homes absent of one or both parents. More than 4 in 10 jailed women had been physically or sexually abused at some point prior to incarceration, and of these, more than one-third had been abused before reaching the age of 18. Females in jail were slightly more likely to have been sexually abused than physically abused before entering jail. There are far more violent female jail inmate recidivists who have been found to be victims of abuse than have been shown as never being abused.[9]

A correlation has also been shown between female jail inmates and family members who were ever incarcerated and/or substance abusers. The BJS found that more than 44 percent of the women in jail surveyed had family members who were incarcerated at some time. Nearly 49 percent of the black female inmates had an immediate family member who had been in prison or jail, and white female inmates were more than twice as likely as black female inmates to have had a father who had been in jail or prison.[10]

One-third of jailed women had parents or guardians who had abused drugs or alcohol when the inmate was growing up, with about 25 percent of the abuse being of alcohol, and almost 6 percent being of both alcohol and drugs. White women in jail were nearly twice as likely as black women to have had parents who abused alcohol and/or drugs.[11]

WOMEN SERVING TIME IN JAIL

Women entering local jails face a variety of indignities and abuses, with little productive use of their time. "It starts the moment she is brought to jail in handcuffs or waist chains. After paperwork and a 'pat search,' she is made to strip and is thoroughly searched for narcotics, including vagina, buttocks, and under the breasts."[12] Following a shower or bath and "stinging spray for body lice," the female jail inmate is fingerprinted and photographed.[13]

The vast majority of women in jail are held in facilities that include male inmates. One study found that there were only 18 local jails nationwide that incarcerated only females.[14] The lack of adequate, separate facilities for female inmates means that many women end up being put in solitary confinement in jails that contain both sexes. In addition, many jails fail to differentiate between female offenders who are violent, mentally ill, or nonviolent—such inmates are often "thrown in together." In some metropolitan jails as many as 10 or 15 women can be found "packed like sardines in cells with no air conditioning," meant to hold half the number of inmates, sleeping 2 to a bed, and with some inmates forced to sleep on the floor.[15]

Unsanitary conditions are prevalent in many jails across the country. Journalist Patsy Sims wrote about the conditions she observed in Southern jails: "I heard and saw a lot that made me understand why ... the sex [among consenting female prisoners] is more a matter of self-survival than immorality. I heard about filth, about going weeks— even 10 months—without a bath or shower, without towels or sheets, or even hot water. I heard about these conditions and then I saw them."[16] Health care, or lack of, is a serious problem for female inmates. Studies have found health care in jails to be inadequate in addressing women's gynecological and obstetrical problems.[17]

Most women in jail spend their time in their cells or rooms— on average 17 hours a day, with only about 1 hour a day outside the cell for exercise.[18] For the minority of jailed women who have work assignments, the most common jobs are janitorial work, food preparation, and other service jobs such as stockroom duty.[19]

WOMEN'S SEXUAL AND
PHYSICAL ABUSE IN JAIL

Sexual and physical abuse of women in jail has been found to be a common practice in some parts of the country. The case of Joanne Little, a black female inmate in a North Carolina county jail, focused greater attention on this reality when she killed her white jailer after he tried to sexually assault her. In Sims's investigation of sexual and physical abuse of women in Southern jails, she revealed:

> In my interviews with more than 50 women serving time in Southern jails or work-release programs, inmate after inmate repeated virtually the same stories of what happened to them, or to the woman in the next cell: the oral sex through bars; the constant intrusion of male trustees who slither in and out of the women's cells as unrestricted as the rats and roaches; the threats of "you do, or else;" the promises of "Girl, you got thirty days, we'll knock off ten if you take care of my friend here."[20]

Though there are few statistics to document the prevalence of sexual and physical abuse in jails, Sims's findings have been substantiated by many attorneys, correctional officers, and police agencies.[21] Most cases of sexual or physical assaults on female jail inmates undoubtedly go unreported, due "partly because of fear, partly because the jailer is considered more believable than a woman already accused of another crime. . . . Much of the abuse—sexual and otherwise—is due to an attitude that women prisoners, especially black ones, are little better than animals."[22]

20. Women Prisoners

Much like women in jail, the incidence of women sent to prison in the United States has risen dramatically in recent decades. This appears to be a reflection of greater numbers of women committing crimes for which they are arrested and convicted, and more women becoming involved in drug- and alcohol-related lifestyles and criminal activities. Minority women tend to be overrepresented in correctional facilities, along with women who grew up in dysfunctional or abusive homes. Most female prison inmates are single mothers, younger than age 34, serving sentences of five years or less, and repeat offenders who had previously been sentenced to jail or prison or given probation.

THE EXTENT OF WOMEN IN PRISON

According to the Department of Justice, there were 55,365 females under the jurisdiction of state or federal correctional authorities as of December 31, 1993. The rate of incarceration for sentenced females was 38 per 100,000 female residents in the United States.[1] This represented a significant increase in imprisoned women since 1981. In the period between 1981 and 1993, the female prison population soared more than 256 percent (see Figure 20-1). Female prisoners in state and federal institutions increased nearly 10 percent from 1992 to 1993, compared to an increase in male prisoners of just over 7 percent.

Women accounted for 5.8 percent of total prisoners in the United States at the end of 1993. However, among federal prisoners the

FIGURE 20-1

Female State and Federal Prisoners, 1981–93

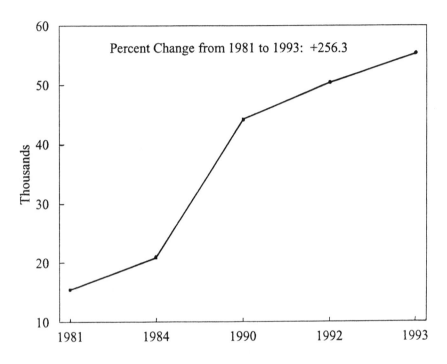

Source: Constructed from U.S. Department of Justice, *Prisoners in State and Federal Institutions on December 31, 1982, 1984* (Washington, D.C.: Government Printing Office, 1984, 1987), pp. 13, 17; U.S. Department of Justice, *Correctional Populations in the United States, 1990* (Washington, D.C.: Government Printing Office, 1992), p. 80; U.S. Department of Justice, *Prisoners in 1993* (Washington, D.C.: Government Printing Office, 1994), p. 5.

---

percentage of female inmates was 7.7 percent. As seen in Table 20-1, the bulk of female inmates are in state prisons, representing nearly 88 percent of all women in state and federal corrections. In states with at least 500 women in prison in 1993, California had the highest inmate population, followed by Texas, New York, Florida, Ohio, and Michigan. The rate of incarceration for female prisoners sentenced to more than 1 year in prison was highest in the District of

Columbia at 119, or more than 3 times the incarceration rate of female prisoners nationwide, followed by Oklahoma, South Carolina, Alabama, and Arizona, at 95, 52, 50, and 49, respectively.

Sentenced Female Prisoners

In 1991 there were 39,928 sentenced female prisoners in the United States — or female inmates with sentences of more than one year (see Table 20-2). More than 72 percent of these were new court commitments, followed by conditional release violators, and escapees or AWOLs returned to prison. Most sentenced female prisoners were admitted to correctional facilities in the South, followed by the West, Midwest, and Northeast.

Sentenced female prisoners released from prison in 1991 totaled 30,240 inmates (see Table 20-3). Of those released conditionally, most were placed on parole or supervised mandatory release. Women prisoners given an unconditional release most often had their sentence expired. Female prisoners were most likely to be put on parole in the South, followed by Northeast, Midwest, and West; whereas female inmates were placed on probation most often in the South, Midwest, West, and Northeast, respectively.

WOMEN ON DEATH ROW

Women prisoners are rarely sentenced to death or executed in the United States (see chapter 6 for exceptions). In 1991, there were 34 female prisoners under sentence of death (see Table 20-4). Of the female death row inmates 22 were white and 12 were black. All had been convicted of murder. In two cases the inmate was removed from a sentence of death. The South had by far the most women on death row with 25, followed by the Midwest, West, and Northeast. By state, North Carolina had the most women under death sentence, followed by Alabama and Oklahoma.

RACE AND ETHNICITY OF FEMALE PRISONERS

Most female prison inmates are black, white, and/or non–Hispanic (see Figures 20-2 and 20-3). Black women made up 49.1 percent of

TABLE 20-1

Women in State or Federal Prisons, 1993

	Number of female inmates	Percent of all inmates	Percent change in female inmate population 1992–93	Incarceration rate 1993[a]
U.S. Total	55,365	5.8	9.6	38
Federal	6,891	7.7	7.7	4
State	48,474	5.6	9.9	34
States with at least 500 female inmates:				
California	7,580	6.3	12.3	43
Texas[b]	4,015	5.6	61.4	N/A
New York	3,528	5.5	0.8	37
Florida	2,696	5.1	3.7	38
Ohio	2,584	6.4	6.8	45
Michigan	1,801	4.6	-2.2	37
Georgia	1,760	6.3	21.0	47
Illinois	1,688	4.9	15.9	28
Oklahoma	1,582	9.6	13.0	95

State				
Virginia	1,219	5.3	4.8	36
Pennsylvania	1,194	4.6	8.0	19
New Jersey	1,134	4.8	3.6	28
Alabama	1,131	6.1	2.7	50
North Carolina	1,119	5.1	17.8	30
Louisiana	1,119	5.0	9.5	47
South Carolina	1,105	5.9	-2.0	52
Arizona	1,037	5.8	3.6	49
Connecticut	994	7.3	40.0	38
Maryland	976	4.8	2.3	33
Missouri	920	5.7	N/A	34
Indiana	778	5.4	5.4	26
District of Columbia	687	6.3	-4.6	119
Washington	666	6.4	7.8	25
Massachusetts	622	6.2	10.3	12
Mississippi	589	5.8	16.6	39
Kentucky	545	5.2	0.0	28
Colorado	542	5.7	2.8	30
Tennessee	521	4.1	-1.3	20

[a]The number of female prisoners with sentences of more than 1 year per 100,000 female residents on December 31, 1993
[b]Excludes 3,363 local jail backups.

Source: U.S. Department of Justice, *Prisoners in 1993* (Washington, D.C.: Government Printing Office, 1994), p. 5.

TABLE 20-2

Sentenced Female Prisoners Admitted to
State or Federal Jurisdiction,ᵃ by Type of Admission, 1991

Region and jurisdiction	Number of female prisoners 1/1/91	Number of sentenced female prisoners admitted during 1991						
		Total	New court commitments	Parole or other conditional release violators returned	Escapees and AWOLs returned	Returns from appeal or bond	Transfers from other jurisdictions	Other admissions
U.S. Total	40,564	39,928	28,829	9,812	580	98	149	460
Federal	3,858	b	b	b	b	b	b	b
State	36,706	39,928	28,829	9,812	580	98	149	460
Northeast	5,669	5,549	4,372	864	151	10	68	84
Midwest	7,484	6,772	5,607	976	82	12	20	75
South	14,479	16,646	13,207	2,877	185	74	41	262
West	9,074	10,961	5,643	5,095	162	2	20	39

ᵃFemale prisoners sentenced to more than 1 year.
ᵇNot reported.

Source: Adapted from U.S. Department of Justice, *Correctional Populations in the United States, 1991* (Washington, D.C.: Government Printing Office, 1993), p. 65.

TABLE 20-3
Sentenced Female Prisoners
Released Conditionally or Unconditionally
from State or Federal Jurisdiction,[a] by Type of Release, 1991

Region and jurisdiction	Conditional release					Unconditional release			
	Total	Parole	Probation	Supervised mandatory release	Other	Total	Expiration of sentence	Commutation	Other
U.S. Total	30,240	14,073	1,884	9,972	4,311	5,207	3,743	39	1,425
Federal[b]	—	—	—	—	—	—	—	—	—
State	30,240	14,073	1,884	9,972	4,311	5,207	3,743	39	1,425
Northeast	3,797	2,742	45	104	906	454	408	0	46
Midwest	4,337	2,037	812	1,369	119	1,461	1,351	4	106
South	12,315	7,912	834	758	2,811	2,693	1,408	35	1,250
West	9,791	1,382	193	7,741	475	599	576	0	23

[a]Female inmates sentenced to more than one year.
[b]Not reported.

Source: Adapted from U.S. Department of Justice, *Correctional Populations in the United States, 1991* (Washington, D.C.: Government Printing Office, 1993), p. 69.

TABLE 20-4

Movement of Female Prisoners
Under Sentence of Death, by Race, 1991

Region and State	Female Prisoners Under Sentence of Death								
	Received from court in 1991[b]			Death sentence removed in 1991[c]			Under death sentence 12/31/91		
	Total	White	Black	Total	White	Black	Total	White	Black
U.S. Total	4	3	1	2	1	1	34	22	12
Federal	0	0	0	0	0	0	0	0	0
State[a]	4	3	1	2	1	1	34	22	12
Northeast	0	0	0	0	0	0	1	0	1
Pennsylvania	0	0	0	0	0	0	1	0	1
Midwest	2	2	0	2	1	1	5	2	3
Missouri	2	2	0	1	1	0	2	2	0
Ohio	0	0	0	1	0	1	3	0	3
South	1	0	1	0	0	0	25	18	7
Alabama	0	0	0	0	0	0	5	3	2
Florida	0	0	0	0	0	0	2	2	0
Kentucky	0	0	0	0	0	0	1	1	0

Mississippi	0	0	0	0	0	2	0	2
North Carolina	0	1	0	0	0	6	5	1
Oklahoma	0	0	0	0	0	4	3	1
South Carolina	0	0	0	0	0	1	1	0
Tennessee	0	0	0	0	0	1	1	0
Texas	0	0	0	0	0	3	2	1
West	1	1	0	0	0	3	2	1
Arizona	1	1	0	0	0	1	1	0
California	0	0	0	0	0	1	1	0
Nevada	0	0	0	0	0	1	0	1

[a] The following states with death penalty statutes reported no women on death row in 1991: Connecticut, New Hampshire, Illinois, Indiana, Nebraska, South Dakota, Arkansas, Delaware, Georgia, Louisiana, Maryland, South Carolina, Virginia, Colorado, Idaho, Montana, New Mexico, Oregon, Utah, Washington, and Wyoming.

[b] All women received from court with a death sentence in 1991 had been convicted of murder.

[c] Dispositions of death sentences other than by execution included dismissal of indictment, reversal of judgment, commutation, resentencing, and ordering of a new trial. No woman was executed in 1991.

Source: Derived from U.S. Department of Justice, *Correctional Populations in the United States, 1991* (Washington, D.C.: Government Printing Office, 1993), p. 94.

FIGURE 20-2

Racial Distribution of State and Federal Female Prisoners, 1991

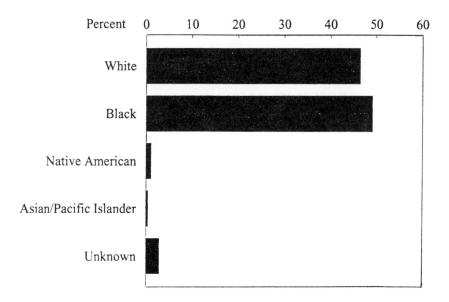

Source: Derived from U.S. Department of Justice, *Survey of State Prison Inmates,
1991: Women in Prison* (Washington, D.C.: Government Printing Office, 1994),
p. 59.

all women in state and federal prisons in 1991, while white women accounted for 46.4 percent of the female inmates. Native Americans and
Asian or Pacific Islanders made up less than 2 percent of the female
prison population.

Non–Hispanic female inmates constituted 66.9 percent of the
women in prison in 1991, with Hispanic women making up 11.6 percent of the inmates. The ethnic origin was unknown for about 21.5 percent of the female prisoners.

Among women in state correctional institutions in 1991, 45.5 percent were black non–Hispanic, 36.2 percent white non–Hispanic, and
14.2 percent Hispanic. Less than 4 percent of the female state prison
inmates were of other racial groups.

FIGURE 20-3

Ethnic Distribution of State
and Federal Female Prisoners, 1991

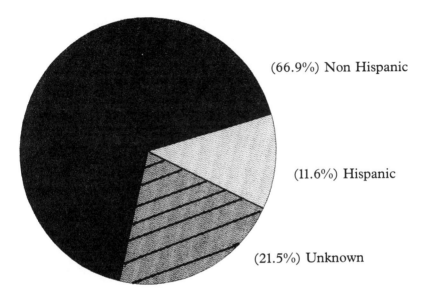

(66.9%) Non Hispanic

(11.6%) Hispanic

(21.5%) Unknown

Source: Derived from U.S. Department of Justice, *Survey of State Prison Inmates, 1991: Women in Prison* (Washington, D.C.: Government Printing Office, 1994), p. 60.

CHARACTERISTICS
OF FEMALES IN PRISON

Women in prison are most likely to be between 25 and 44 years of age, single, unemployed, with some high school education (see Table 20-5). Over 75 percent of the females in state prisons were aged 25 to 44 in 1991, while more than 50 percent fell between the ages of 25 and 34. The median age for a female state prisoner was 31 years old.

More than 8 out of 10 women in prison were unmarried or separated. Over 45 percent had never married, and nearly 20 percent were divorced. The majority of female inmates had at least attended high school, with nearly 40 percent having graduated from high school or gone to college.

TABLE 20-5

Characteristics of State
Female Prison Inmates, 1991

Characteristic	Percent of female inmates 1991
Age	
17 or younger	0.1
18-24	16.3
25-34	50.4
35-44	25.5
45-54	6.1
55 or older	1.7
Median age	31 yrs.
Marital status	
Married	17.3
Widowed	5.9
Divorced	19.1
Separated	12.5
Never married	45.1
Education [a]	
8th grade or less	16.0
Some high school	45.8
High school graduate	22.7
Some college or more	15.5
Pre-arrest employment	
Employed	46.7
Full-time	35.7
Part-time	11.0
Unemployed	53.3
Looking	19.2
Not looking	34.1
Number of Inmates	38,796

Note: Percentages may not add to total because of rounding.

[a] Based on highest grade completed.

Source: Derived from U.S. Department of Justice, *Survey of State Prison Inmates, 1991: Women in Prison* (Washington, D.C.: Government Printing Office, 1994), p. 2.

Less than 50 percent of the imprisoned women were employed at the time of their arrest. Of those unemployed, the majority were not actively seeking employment when arrested.

OFFENSES COMMITTED
BY INCARCERATED WOMEN

By and large, female prisoners tend to be incarcerated almost evenly for violent, property, and drug offenses. Table 20-6 distributes the most serious offenses for which women were sent to state prison in 1991. We can see that almost 33 percent of the female inmates were convicted of drug offenses and over 32 percent convicted of violent offenses, with property crime convictions just under 29 percent of all most serious offenses perpetrated. Less than 6 percent of the women were incarcerated for public-order offenses. Among individual crimes, approximately 1 in 5 female inmates was serving time for drug trafficking, with more than 10 percent of the women in prison for each of the following offenses: drug possession, murder, larceny-theft, and fraud.

For female new court commitments to state or federal prisons, the breakdown of offenses for which they were imprisoned differs somewhat from the female prison population in general as well as each other (see Figure 20-4). In 1991, new court commitments to state and federal institutions were more likely to be serving a sentence for a drug offense than female prisoners in general, with property offenses accounting for the second highest percentage of convictions rather than violent offenses. However, female new court commitments to state prison were more likely than those going to federal prison to be incarcerated for a violent offense. Conversely, nearly 4 times as many new court commitments to federal corrections were convicted of public-order offenses as new court commitments to state institutions.

FEMALE INMATES' HISTORY
OF DRUG AND/OR ALCOHOL USE

Most women in prison used and/or abused alcohol or drugs prior to entering prison. Almost 60 percent of the female state prison inmates had used alcohol in the year prior to committing the offense for which they were imprisoned, according to the Bureau of Justice Statistics.[2]

TABLE 20-6

Most Serious Offenses of
Women in State Prisons, 1991

Most Serious Offense	Percent of Female Prisoners
All offenses	100.0
Violent offenses	32.2
Murder[a]	11.7
Negligent manslaughter	3.4
Kidnapping	0.4
Rape	0.4
Other sexual assault	1.3
Robbery	7.8
Assault	6.2
Other violent[b]	1.1
Property offenses	28.7
Burglary	4.5
Larceny-theft	11.1
Motor vehicle theft	0.7
Arson	1.0
Fraud	10.2
Stolen property	1.0
Other property[c]	0.1
Drug offenses	32.8
Possession	11.8
Trafficking	19.8
Other/unspecified	1.3
Public-order offenses	5.7
Weapons	0.5
Other public-order[d]	5.1
Other offenses	0.6
Number of inmates	38,462

Note: Detail may not add to total due to rounding.

[a] Includes nonnegligent manslaughter.
[b] Includes blackmail, extortion, hit-and-run driving with bodily injury, child abuse, and criminal endangerment.
[c] Includes destruction of property, vandalism, hit-and-run driving without bodily injury, trespassing, and possession of burglary tools.
[d] Includes escape from custody, driving while intoxicated, offenses against morals and decency, and commercialized vice.

Source: Adapted from U.S. Department of Justice, *Survey of State Prison Inmates, 1991: Women in Prison* (Washington, D.C.: Government Printing Office, 1994), p. 3.

Nearly 20 percent of the women reported drinking alcohol daily, and another 17 percent at least once a week. Just under 50 percent of the female prisoners were under the influence of alcohol and/or drugs when perpetrating their crime, though only about 12 percent said they were under the influence of alcohol only.[3]

Previous drug use is even more prevalent among women in prison. Nearly 80 percent of female inmates in state prison in 1991 used drugs in their lifetime, over 65 percent used drugs regularly at some point, and more than 50 percent were daily drug users in the month before they perpetrated the offense they were imprisoned for.[4] Over 36 percent of the women inmates reported being under the influence of drugs when they committed their crime, while about 25 percent of the offenses were committed to get money to buy drugs.

Of the women who used drugs in the month before the offense they were convicted of, more than 36 percent used cocaine or crack cocaine, over 20 percent smoked marijuana, and almost 16 percent used heroin or other opiates (see Figure 20-5). Hallucinogens were the drugs least likely to be used by female inmates in the 30 days before committing their offense, with just over 2 percent of the inmates using them, followed by depressants and stimulants, used by 5 percent and just under 8 percent of the women, respectively.

Approximately 33 percent of the women in state prison had used a needle to inject illicit drugs at some stage, and nearly 20 percent had shared a needle. Hispanic and white female inmates were more likely than black female inmates to have been intravenous illegal drug users. Twenty-five percent of the white and Hispanic women had shared

FIGURE 20-4

Female New Court Commitments to State and Federal Prison, by Type of Offense Incarcerated For, 1991

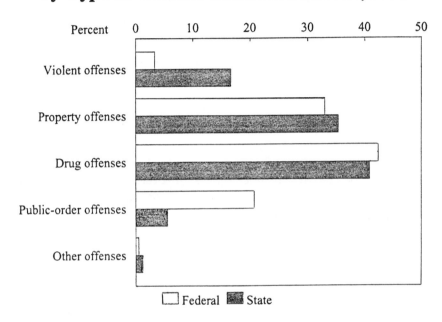

Source: Derived from U.S. Department of Justice, *National Corrections Reporting Program, 1991* (Washington, D.C.: Government Printing Office, 1994), pp. 12, 55.

a needle for illicit drugs, compared to about 10 percent of the black women in prison.

HIV, AIDS, AND WOMEN IN PRISON

In 1991, of the nearly 67 percent of women in prison who had ever been tested for the Human Immunodeficiency Virus (HIV) that causes AIDS and reported the results, 3.3 percent tested HIV-positive (this compares to a 2.1 infection rate for the 50.3 percent men tested and

FIGURE 20-5

Drugs Used by Women
State Prisoners in Month Before
Offense, by Type of Drug, 1991[a]

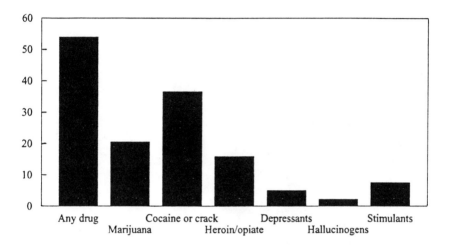

[a] Detail may not add to total because a prisoner may have been using one or more drugs.

Source: Calculated from U.S. Department of Justice, *Survey of State Prison Inmates, 1991: Women in Prison* (Washington, D.C.: Government Printing Office, 1994), p. 8.

reporting the results).[5] Hispanic women were the most likely to test positive for the virus at 6.8 percent, nearly double the 3.5 percent of black women HIV-positive, and more than three times the percentage of infected white women in prison at 1.9 percent.

Approximately 6.7 percent of the female inmates who had ever used a needle tested HIV-positive. Hispanic female IV drug users were most likely to test positive for HIV at 11.6 percent, followed by black females who used a needle to inject drugs at 8.3 percent, and white female IV drug users at 3.9 percent.[6]

FIGURE 20-6

Female Recidivists in State Prison, 1991

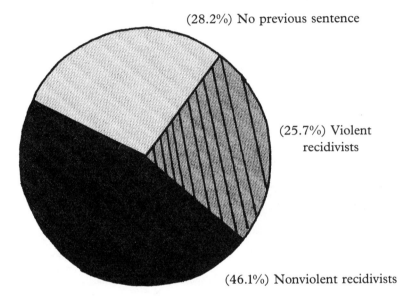

(28.2%) No previous sentence

(25.7%) Violent
recidivists

(46.1%) Nonviolent recidivists

Source: Adapted from U.S. Department of Justice, *Survey of State Prison Inmates,
1991: Women in Prison* (Washington, D.C.: Government Printing Office, 1994),
p. 4.

FEMALE RECIDIVISTS IN PRISON

The majority of imprisoned women had previously been incarcerated or on probation. More than 70 percent of women in state
prisons in 1991 were recidivists, or repeat convicted offenders (see Figure 20-6). Just over 46 percent of all female prisoners were currently
incarcerated for a nonviolent offense and had previously been convicted of nonviolent offenses. About 25 percent of the female recidivists were violent recidivists, while just over 28 percent of the women
in prison had no previous convictions or incarceration.

A correlation exists between adult female recidivism and juvenile
female delinquency. It is estimated that about 20 percent of women in
prison had a criminal record as a minor.[7]

SENTENCE LENGTH
FOR FEMALE INMATES

In general, women tend to serve less time in prison than men. Half the women inmates in 1991 had a maximum sentence length of 60 months or less, whereas half the men had a maximum sentence of 120 months or less. On average, women's sentences were 48 months shorter than sentences for men. Nearly 25 percent of all women in prison were serving sentences of less than 36 months, while just over 12 percent of the men received sentences of less than 36 months. Conversely, almost 28 percent of the imprisoned men had a maximum sentence length of 180 or more months, compared to under 18 percent of the imprisoned women. Approximately 7 percent of the female state prisoners and 9 percent of the male prisoners were sentenced to life in prison or death in 1991.[8]

FAMILY AND ABUSE
HISTORY OF WOMEN IN PRISON

Female prisoners often come from families fraught with dysfunction, absence of one or both parents, substance abuse, a cycle of criminality, and abusive treatment at the hands of parents. More than 50 percent of the imprisoned women in state correctional facilities in 1991 came from broken homes, where both parents were not present when the woman was growing up.[9] In addition, 39 percent of the inmates were raised in single mother households, while more than 9 percent were brought up by grandparents only. Black and Hispanic female inmates were more likely than white female inmates to have grown up in homes where one or both parents were missing.

Nearly 50 percent of the women in prison in 1991 had family members that were incarcerated at some point. For black women almost 53 percent reported family members ever being incarcerated, compared to under 40 percent of the white women. While growing up, 1 in 3 of the female state prisoners had parents who abused alcohol and/or drugs, with the vast majority of the abuse involving alcohol only or alcohol and drugs. White women imprisoned were more likely to have had substance abusing parents than black or Hispanic women incarcerated.

More than 40 percent of female inmates in state prison in 1991 reported being physically or sexually abused at some stage prior to entering prison.[10] Approximately one third of the inmates had been physically abused and about a third had been sexually abused. Either form of abuse was more likely to have come before the age of 18 than after. In over 55 percent of the sexual abuse episodes the inmate had been the victim of a completed rape. The abuser in almost 50 percent of the inmates' physical or sexual victimization was an intimate, such as a spouse or boyfriend; while nearly 38 percent of the perpetrators were parents or guardians. Female inmates who had a history of abuse were more likely to be in prison for homicide or sexual assault than female inmates who had never been abused.[11]

MOTHERS AND PREGNANT WOMEN IN PRISON

In 1991, more than 78 percent of the incarcerated women had children. It is estimated that 25,700 female prisoners were mothers to more than 56,000 children under the age of 18.[12] Imprisoned Hispanic women were most likely to have children under 18, followed by black women, then white women. Most children, irrespective of race, were currently living with grandparents.

Studies have shown that the incarcerated mother's separation from her children is the greatest hardship faced by a female inmate. One mother in prison cried out, "By taking away our rights to see our children, they're killing us."[13] Only 9 percent of the mothers in prison in 1991 received visits from their minor children. In many prisons children under the age of 16 are not allowed to visit. Imprisoned mothers also face the problem of inaccessibility as many prisons are located in isolated areas that are often reachable only by car.

Incarcerated mothers deprived of being with their children have been shown to experience feelings similar to those associated with loss due to death or divorce, including helplessness, anger, guilt, and fear of rejection.[14] Further problematic issues for mothers in prison are those that challenge their roles as mothers, such as parental rights, child placement, and visitation rights.

Women who enter prison pregnant may face even more problems. There is evidence that correctional officers are especially hostile and abusive toward pregnant inmates whom they regard as not "worthy enough to have children."[15] In some instances these women are coerced into having an abortion to prevent them from becoming "unworthy mothers." In other cases it has been reported that pregnant inmates who have wanted an abortion have been denied that right.[16] In many prisons, pregnant prisoners have complained about inadequate diet, posing risks to the unborn child as well as the lack of prenatal gynecological care.[17] Many pregnant, drug-addicted inmates are forced to withdraw "cold turkey" or are denied the use of methadone if they are heroin addicts, possibly endangering both mother and child.[18]

Further, some women have become pregnant after entering prison, due to consensual sex with or rape by a correctional officer. Few male correctional staff accused of such behavior ever face legal action. In a recent case of a Florida inmate who became pregnant after sexual relations with a prison guard, she was forced to go to court in order to keep her baby.[19]

LIFE FOR WOMEN IN PRISON

The prison world a female enters is often far more severe and restrictive than the world she left. After arriving at her assigned correctional facility, the new prisoner must go through a series of orientation or "get-acquainted" procedures. She usually comes in handcuffed and may be refingerprinted and photographed for prison records. Referred to as a "fish," the new female inmate soon "loses all remaining dignity when she is stripped and searched for contraband, showered, and issued prison attire and bedding."[20] Over the next several weeks the inmate, who is segregated during this period, undergoes a variety of medical and psychiatric examinations for everything from sexually transmitted diseases to mental illness.

By the time she joins the general prison population the female inmate has been instilled with the extensive rules and regulations of her imprisonment, including her new status of "institutional dependency." Though women's prisons tend to resemble college campuses compared to the more fortresslike men's penal institutions, some suggest that the actual rules and regulations female prisoners must abide by are stricter than those imposed on male prisoners.[21] Such rules and regulations, as well as disciplinary procedures, vary from one women's prison to another.

Major infractions include escapes, fighting, other violent acts, possession of contraband, property damage, and homosexuality. In a study of women's correctional programs, Ruth Glick and Virginia Neto found that homosexuality was considered a major infraction in 80 percent of women's prisons.[22] Other studies have found that homosexual acts are commonplace among female inmates and more or less accepted as part of prison life.[23] Penalties for major infractions typically include loss of privileges and isolation for up to 90 days and, in worst case scenarios, court prosecution.

Minor infractions include using foul language, yelling, having torn sheets, and walking on the grass. Disciplinary action for minor infractions ranges from being reprimanded to losing up to 60 days of "gain time"—or having that time deducted from the female inmate's sentence for good behavior.

Women in prison can be placed in solitary confinement or in the "hole" at any time for major or minor infractions. Kathryn Burkhart, an investigative reporter, gave a firsthand account of time spent in solitary confinement in a women's correctional institution:

> These cells are drearily the same in every jail I've visited—windowless and bare. Some have one thin, dirty and bloodstained mattress on the floor. Some have no mattress. Some jails provide blankets for the women confined, some do not. In some quarters, women locked in solitary are allowed to wear prison shifts—in others they are allowed to wear only their underwear or are stripped naked. Toilets are most often flushed from the outside, and women complain that on occasion sadistic matrons play games with flushing the toilets—either flushing them repeatedly until they overflow or not flushing them at all for a day or more at a time. ("If the toilet backs up, there's nothing you can do about it but live with the stench.") Food is passed into the room two or three times a day between the bottom of the dusty door and the unwashed floor, as are sanitary napkins if the woman is menstruating.[24]

Many women in prison regard the strict rules and regulations as deliberate attempts to "diminish their maturity" by treating them "like children and fostering dependency."[25] An example of such a rule can be found at the Pennsylvania State Correctional Institution for Women, where inmates were required to "recite the Lord's Prayer in unison at bedtime."[26]

Much of a female inmate's time in prison is spent being idle. With recreational facilities and vocational programs lacking in many women's prisons, inmates often find themselves with nothing to do other than perform menial chores or walk around their cell.

Health Care for Female Prisoners

Many women enter prison with gynecological, prenatal, and dental problems, along with other medical or psychiatric conditions such as diabetes, epilepsy, headaches, anxiety, hypertension, and alcohol and/or drug addiction. About 6 percent of the female inmates in 1991 were pregnant when admitted to prison. Nearly 25 percent of all female prisoners had participated in individual or group therapy for problems other than alcohol or drug abuse after admission. White women were more likely than black or Hispanic women to seek such counseling. Prior to entering prison, nearly 16 percent of female inmates in prison in 1991 had been admitted to a mental hospital or mental treatment program overnight. More than twice as many white female prisoners had stayed overnight in a mental hospital or mental treatment facility as black or Hispanic women in prison.[27]

The medical care women receive in prison can vary considerably from facility to facility, depending upon size, staff, budget, and the priority given to medical attention. In some prisons a female inmate can be close to death and still be denied treatment. For instance, medication may be withheld from an epileptic inmate until her condition is verified by a "couple of seizures." In other cases, women in prison may be doped or tranquilized as a means of social control rather than medical treatment. Burkhart wrote of the practice:

> More often, it seems, at Riker's and at other prisons, women inmates walk the halls in what seems to be a dazed, zombie-like state. Their words are slurred, their eyes are glazed, their clothes disheveled. Some women I have seen on one day having to be supported by other inmates even to walk, look like totally different people a day or two later when they said they "got off the medication." Some women complain that they are given Thorazine and Millaril against their will when they are upset about something; others complain they are unable to get tranquilizing medication when they want it.[28]

Vocational Training and
Rehabilitation Programs in Women's Prisons

There are few vocational training and rehabilitation programs offered to women in prison. Female inmates who already have advanced education have no real way to make use of their academic or occupational skills or to even further them. There are virtually no special programs or incentives available for female inmates who are mentally handicapped, educationally disadvantaged, or simply uninterested in vocational training.

Vocational training programs that do exist are often a reflection of traditional, low-paying female sex-role occupations, such as those in food service, or in clerical, sewing, or cosmetology fields. A federal report found that, on average, there were only 3 vocational programs in women's prisons for every 10 in men's prisons.[29] Even in large women's correctional facilities, rarely more than two or three vocational training programs are offered — and nearly all are geared toward "teaching women merely to cook, sew, and clean."[30]

In most women's prisons, inmates are required to perform "institutional maintenance." There is rarely any pay for this and what pay there is generally is very low and often less than that received by male inmates. In some instances this unskilled labor is referred to as vocational training. Women prisoners are often exploited by prison administrators and other state officials who use them as personal servants. Glick and Neto found that some female inmates in North Carolina and Georgia prisons worked in the governor's mansion as maids. In North Carolina, for instance, "eight women inmates were sent to the governor's home where their duties included cooking, cleaning, washing, and serving."[31] Notes one writer of this exploitation, "It's usually humiliating enough to be a house servant when you're being paid meager wages . . . but to have it be involuntary servitude gives me the plantation shudders."[32]

The Psychological Imprisonment
of Incarcerated Women

It is perhaps the psychological implications of imprisonment that may be most harmful to the woman inmate, for, in spite of the outward appearance of most women's prisons as cottages amidst trees and shrubbery, the effect can be confusing to female inmates and tends to "deaden any impetus for change."[33] In her study of women's corrections, Helen Gibson describes the psychological victimization of women present in the typical women's prison:

> While convention requires women's prisons to look like minimum security institutions, economic reality decrees that they cannot be minimum security. A minimum security institution can choose the

best risks, and send its failures somewhere else; a women's institution must accept every woman offender in the state. Because all women sentenced to prison must be housed in one institution, all must live by rules which are established for the control of a very few. ... The result is an atmosphere that in spite of attractive facilities and peaceful surroundings, is really very tense and oppressive. ... The reduction of women to a weak, dependent, and helpless status is brought about by more subtle means than by the gun or the high wall.[34]

Women in prison are further psychologically impaired by the outdated rules and regimens present in many institutions, limiting both their mobility and opportunity to better themselves for their return to the outside world. But what is likely more psychologically damaging to most female inmates than the prison establishment itself is the reality that women are often the victims of a double standard in terms of the crimes they are convicted of, time served, and avenues available for them both within the prison system and upon release. Few female prisoners can escape this form of psychological bondage once they come face to face with it.

Notes

Chapter 1. The Extent of Female Crime

1. Ronald Barri Flowers, *Demographics and Criminality: The Characteristics of Crime in America* (Westport, Conn.: Greenwood Press, 1989), p. 44.

2. Ibid., pp. 50–52.

3. Edwin W. Sutherland and Donald R. Cressey, *Criminology*, 10th ed. (Philadelphia: J.B. Lippincott, 1978), p. 29.

4. Charles H. Shireman and Frederic G. Reamer, *Rehabilitating Juvenile Justice* (New York: Columbia University Press, 1986), p. 20.

5. U.S. Department of Justice, Bureau of Justice Statistics Bulletin, *Prisoners in 1992* (Washington, D.C.: Government Printing Office, 1993), p. 4.

6. U.S. Department of Justice, Bureau of Justice Statistics Bulletin, *Jail Inmates 1992* (Washington, D.C.: Government Printing Office, 1993), p. 2.

7. U.S. Department of Justice, *Criminal Victimization in the United States, 1991: A National Crime Victimization Survey Report* (Washington, D.C.: Government Printing Office, 1992), p. 1.

Chapter 2. The Nature of Female Crime

1. Ronald B. Flowers, *Minorities and Criminality* (Westport, Conn.: Greenwood Press, 1988), pp. 40–46.

2. Marvin Wolfgang, *Patterns in Criminal Homicide* (Philadelphia: University of Pennsylvania, 1964).

3. Freda Adler, *Sisters in Crime: The Rise of the New Female Criminal* (New York: McGraw-Hill, 1975), p. 139.

4. R. M. Glick and V. V. Neto, *National Study of Women's Correctional Programs* (Washington, D.C.: Government Printing Office, 1977), p. 104.

5. Calculated from U.S. Department of Justice, *Correctional Populations in the United States, 1991* (Washington, D.C.: Government Printing Office, 1993), p. 59.

6. Ibid., p. 60.

7. Ronald B. Flowers, *Women and Criminality: The Woman as Victim, Offender, and Practitioner* (Westport, Conn.: Greenwood Press, 1987), p. 77.

8. Michael J. Hindelang, "Class and Crime," in Sanford H. Kadish, ed., *Encyclopedia of Crime and Justice*, vol. 1 (New York: Free Press, 1983), pp. 175–81.

9. John Braithwaite, "The Myth of Social Class and Criminality Reconsidered," *American Sociological Review* 46 (1981): 36–57.

10. Cited in Ronald B. Flowers, *Demographics and Criminality: The Characteristics of Crime in America* (Westport, Conn.: Greenwood Press, 1989), p. 106.

11. Flowers, *Demographics and Criminality*, pp. 134–35; U.S. Department of Justice, National Institute of Justice, *Characteristics of Different Types of Drug-Involved Offenders* (Washington, D.C.: Government Printing Office, 1988), pp. 9–10, 20–21.

Chapter 3. Female Crime in Comparison to Male Crime

1. U.S. Department of Justice, *Criminal Victimization in the United States, 1992: A National Crime Victimization Survey Report* (Washington, D.C.: Government Printing Office, 1994), pp. 59, 63.

2. U.S. Federal Bureau of Investigation, *Crime in the United States: Uniform Crime Reports 1992* (Washington, D.C.: Government Printing Office, 1993), pp. 229, 231.

3. Nancy Wise, "Juvenile Delinquency Among Middle-Class Girls," in Edmund Vaz, ed., *Middle Class Juvenile Delinquency* (New York: Harper & Row, 1967).

4. F. Ivan Nye and James F. Short, "Scaling Delinquent Behavior," *American Sociological Review* 22 (1958): 326–32.

5. Stephen A. Cernkovich and Peggy C. Giordano, "A Comparative Analysis of Male and Female Delinquency," *Sociological Quarterly* 20 (1979): 131–45.

6. Peter Kratcoski and John E. Kratcoski, "Changing Patterns in the Delinquent Activities of Boys and Girls: A Self-Reported Delinquency Analysis," *Adolescence* 10 (1975): 38–91.

7. Freda Adler, *Sisters in Crime: The Rise of the New Female Criminal* (New York: McGraw-Hill, 1975), p. 15.

8. Darrell J. Steffensmeir, "Sex Differences in Patterns of Adult Crime, 1965–77: A Review and Assessment," *Social Forces* 58 (1980): 1098–99.

9. Carol Smart, "The New Female Criminal: Reality or Myth," *British Journal of Criminology* 19 (1979): 50–59.

10. Rita James Simon, *Women and Crime* (Lexington, Mass.: D. C. Heath, 1975), p. 42.

11. George W. Noblit and Janie M. Burcart, "Women and Crime: 1960–1970," *Social Science Quarterly* 56 (1976): 656–57.

12. Martin Gold and David J. Reimer, "Changing Patterns of Delinquent Behavior Among Americans 13 Through 16 Years Old: 1967–72," *Crime and Delinquency* 7 (1975): 483–517.

13. Cernkovich and Giordano, "A Comparative Analysis," pp. 131–45.

14. Douglas Smith and Christy A. Visher, "Sex and Involvement in Deviance/Crime: A Quantitative Review of the Empirical Literature," *American Sociological Review* 45 (1980): 691–701.

15. Kratcoski and Kratcoski, "Changing Patterns in the Delinquent Activities of Boys and Girls," p. 88.

16. Darrell J. Steffensmeir and Renee Hoffman Steffensmeir, "Trends in

Female Delinquency: An Examination of Arrest, Juvenile Court, Self-Report, and Field Data," *Criminology* 18 (1980): 22–23.

17. Michael Hindelang, "Age, Sex, and the Versatility of Delinquency Involvement," *Social Problems* 18 (1971): 533.

18. R. Barri Flowers, *The Adolescent Criminal: An Examination of Today's Juvenile Offender* (Jefferson, N.C.: McFarland & Co., 1990), p. 78.

Chapter 4. Theories on Female Criminality

1. Cesare Lombroso and William Ferrero, *The Female Offender* (New York: Appleton, 1900).

2. Joy Pollock, "Early Theories of Female Criminality," in Lee H. Bowker, *Women, Crime, and the Criminal Justice System* (Lexington, Mass.: Lexington Books, 1978), p. 29.

3. Ronald B. Flowers, *Women and Criminality: The Woman as Victim, Offender, and Practitioner* (Westport, Conn.: Greenwood Press, 1987), p. 92.

4. Ibid.

5. Ibid.

6. T. C. Gibbens, "Female Offenders," *British Journal of Hospital Medicine* 6 (1971): 279–86.

7. Flowers, *The Adolescent Criminal*, p. 79. *See also* J. Cowie, B. Cowie, and E. Slater, *Delinquency in Girls* (London: Heinemann, 1968).

8. *See, for example*, K. Dalton, "Menstruation and Crime," *British Medical Journal* 2 (1961): 1752–53; R. M. Carney and B. D. Williams, "Premenstrual Syndrome: A Criminal Defense," *Notre Dame Law Review* 59 (1983): 253–69.

9. Cited in R. Barri Flowers, "Violent Women: Are They Catching up to Violent Men or Have They Surpassed Them?" *ERIC Documents Reproduction Service* No ED 301 496 (1989): 1–19.

10. Sigmund Freud, *New Introductory Lectures on Psychoanalysis* (New York: W. W. Norton, 1933).

11. Elissa P. Benedek, "Women and Homicide," in Bruce L. Danto, John Bruhns, and Austin H. Kutscher, eds., *The Human Side of Homicide* (New York: Columbia University Press, 1982), p. 154.

12. Julia A. Sherman, *On the Psychology of Women* (Springfield, Ill.: Charles C Thomas, 1971), p. 48.

13. Flowers, *Women and Criminality*, p. 94.

14. Flowers, *The Adolescent Criminal*, p. 80; Gisela Konopla, *The Adolescent Girl in Conflict* (Englewood Cliffs, N.J.: Prentice-Hall, 1966).

15. *See, for example*, Emily Werner and Ruth S. Smith, *Kauai's Children Come of Age* (Honolulu: University Press of Hawaii, 1977).

16. Coramae Richey Mann, *Female Crime and Delinquency* (University, Ala.: University of Alabama Press, 1984), p. 57. *See also* William I. Thomas, *Sex and Society: Studies in the Social Psychology of Sex* (Boston: Little, Brown, 1907).

17. Morris Janowitz, *W. I. Thomas* (Chicago: University of Chicago Press, 1966), p. xxvii. *See also* William I. Thomas, *The Unadjusted Girl: With Cases and Standpoint for Behavior Analysis* (New York: Harper & Row, 1923).

18. Pollock, "Early Theories of Female Criminality," p. 45.

19. Ibid.

20. Sheldon Glueck and Eleanor Glueck, *Five Hundred Delinquent Women* (New York: Alfred A. Knopf, 1934).

21. Otto Pollak, *The Criminality of Women* (Philadelphia: University of Philadelphia Press, 1950).

22. Flowers, *Women and Criminality*, p. 97.

23. Ibid.

24. Ibid., pp. 83–84; Laura Crites, ed., *The Female Offender* (Lexington, Mass.: Lexington Books, 1976).

25. Carol Engel Temin, "Discriminatory Sentencing of Women Offenders: The Argument for ERA in a Nutshell," *American Criminal Law Review* 11 (1973): 353–72; Barbara Allen Babcock, "Introduction: Women and the Criminal Law," *American Criminal Law Review* 11 (1973): 291–94.

26. Eileen B. Leonard, *Women, Crime, and Society: A Critique of Theoretical Criminology* (New York: Longman, 1982), p. 5.

27. Ronald B. Flowers, *Demographics and Criminality: The Characteristics of Crime in America* (Westport, Conn.: Greenwood Press, 1989), p. 88.

28. Ibid.; Rebecca Emerson Dobash and Russell Dobash, *Violence Against Wives* (New York: Free Press, 1979).

29. Richard A. Cloward and Lloyd Ohlin, *Delinquency and Opportunity* (New York: Free Press, 1960).

30. Susan K. Datesman, Frank R. Scarpitti, and Richard M. Stephenson, "Female Delinquency: An Application of Self and Opportunity Theories," *Journal of Research in Crime and Delinquency* 12 (1975): 120.

31. Stephen A. Cernkovich and Peggy C. Giordano, "Delinquency, Opportunity, and Gender," *Journal of Criminal Law and Criminology* 70 (1979): 150.

32. Leonard, *Women, Crime, and Society*, p. 11.

33. Ibid.

34. Dorie Klein, "The Etiology of Female Crime: A Review of the Literature," *Issues in Criminology* 8 (1973): 6.

35. Mann, *Female Crime and Delinquency*, p. 96.

36. Jennifer James, "Motivations for Entrance into Prostitution," in Crites, ed., *The Female Offender*, p. 202.

37. Rita James Simon, *The Contemporary Woman and Crime* (Washington, D.C.: Government Printing Office, 1975), p. 48.

38. Laura Crites, "Women Offenders: Myth or Reality," in Crites, *The Female Offender*.

39. Joseph G. Weis, "Liberation and Crime: The Invention of the New Female Criminal," *Crime and Social Justice* 6 (1976): 17–27.

Chapter 5. Factors in Female Delinquency and Crime

1. Cited in R. Barri Flowers, *The Adolescent Criminal: An Examination of Today's Juvenile Offender* (Jefferson, N.C.: McFarland & Co., 1990), p. 138.

2. Maura G. Crowley, "Female Runaway Behavior and Its Relationship to Prostitution," Masters thesis, Sam Houston State University, Institute of Contemporary Corrections and Behavioral Sciences, 1977, p. 63.

3. Sparky Harlan, Luanne L. Rodgers, and Brian Slattery, *Male and Female Adolescent Prostitution: Huckleberry House Sexual Minority Youth Services Project* (Washington, D.C.: U.S. Department of Health and Human Services, 1981), p. 14.

4. U.S. Department of Justice, Bureau of Justice Statistics Special Report,

Survey of Youth in Custody, 1987 (Washington, D.C.: Government Printing Office, 1988), p. 3.

5. U.S. Department of Justice, Bureau of Justice Statistics Special Report, *Women in Jail 1989* (Washington, D.C.: Government Printing Office, 1992), p. 10; U.S. Department of Justice, Bureau of Justice Statistics Special Report, *Survey of State Prison Inmates, 1991: Women in Prison* (Washington, D.C.: Government Printing Office, 1994), p. 1.

6. *Women in Jail 1989*, p. 9; *Women in Prison*, pp. 1, 6.

7. Linda S. King, "Responding to Spouse Abuse: The Mental Health Profession," *In Response to Family Violence* 4, 5 (1981): 7–9.

8. Vincent J. Fontana, *The Maltreated Child: The Maltreatment Syndrome in Children* (Springfield, Ill: Charles C Thomas, 1964).

9. H. E. Simmons, *Protective Services for Children*, 2nd ed. (Sacramento: Citadel Press, 1970).

10. Cited in Glenn Collins, "The Violent Child: Some Patterns Emerge," *New York Times* (September 27, 1982), p. B10 (L).

11. Crowley, "*Female Runaway Behavior*," p. 63; Harlan, Rodgers, and Slattery, *Male and Female Adolescent Prostitution*, p. 15.

12. Martin R. Haskell and Lewis Yablonsky, *Crime and Delinquency*, 2nd ed. (Chicago: Rand McNally, 1974).

13. *Women in Jail 1989*, p. 10; *Women in Prison*, p. 5.

14. Harlan, Rodgers, and Slattery, *Male and Female Adolescent Prostitution*, p. 21.

15. Mimi H. Silbert, "Delancey Street Study: Prostitution and Sexual Assault," Summary of results (San Francisco: Delancey Street Foundation, 1982), p. 3.

16. Flowers, *The Adolescent Criminal*, p. 50; Patricia Hersch, "Coming of Age on City Streets," *Psychology Today* (January 1988), p. 32.

17. Ronald B. Flowers, *Women and Criminality: The Woman as Victim, Offender, and Practitioner* (Westport, Conn.: Greenwood Press, 1987), p. 63.

18. Cited in "Preventing Sexual Abuse of Children," *Parade Magazine* (May 26, 1985), p. 16.

19. *Women in Jail 1989*, p. 10; *Women in Prison*, p. 5.

20. Cited in Jeanne Thornton, "Family Violence Emerges from the Shadows," *U.S. News & World Report* (January 23, 1984), p. 66.

21. Richard J. Gelles, "The Myth of Battered Husbands," *MS.* (October 1979), pp. 65–66, 71–72.

22. K. Yllo and Murray A. Straus, "Interpersonal Violence Among Married and Cohabitating Couples." Paper presented at the annual meeting of the National Council on Family Relations, Philadelphia, 1978.

23. Flowers, *Women and Criminality*, pp. 23–24, 108–9.

24. Ibid., p. 108; Sandy Nelson, "Women Who Kill," *Sacramento Bee* (December 30, 1986), p. B9.

25. *Women in Prison*, p. 3.

26. Ibid.

27. Ronald B. Flowers, *Children and Criminality: The Child as Victim and Perpetrator* (Westport, Conn.: Greenwood Press, 1986), pp. 49–59.

28. Richard L. Dugdale, *The Jukes: A Study in Crime, Pauperism, and Heredity* (New York: Putnam, 1877).

29. Henry H. Goddard, *Feeblemindedness, Its Causes and Consequences* (New York: Macmillan, 1914).

30. Christopher Ounsted, Rhoda Oppenheimer, and Janet Lindsay, "The Psychopathology and Psychotherapy of the Families, Aspects Bounding Failure," in A. Franklin, ed., *Concerning Child Abuse* (London: Churchill Livingston, 1975).

31. E. Rathbone and R. Pierce, "Intergenerational Treatment Approach," in Robert J. Hunner and Yvonne E. Walker, eds., *Exploring the Relationship Between Child Abuse and Delinquency* (Montclair, N.J.: Allanheld, Osmun and Co., 1981), p. 66; Norman A. Polansky, Christine De Saix, and Shlomo A. Sharlin, *Child Neglect: Understanding and Reaching the Parents* (New York: Child Welfare League of America, 1972).

32. Maria Roy, "A Current Survey of 150 Cases," in Maria Roy, ed., *Battered Women: A Psychosociological Study of Domestic Violence* (New York: Van Nostrand Reinhold, 1977).

33. J. Gayford, "Wife-Battering: A Preliminary Survey of 100 Cases," *British Medical Journal* 1 (1975): 194–97.

34. *Women in Prison*, p. 5; *Flowers, The Adolescent Criminal*, pp. 133–35.

35. Ronald B. Flowers, *Demographics and Criminality: The Characteristics of Crime in America* (Westport, Conn.: Greenwood Press, 1989), pp. 132–33; U.S. Department of Justice, National Institute of Justice, *Characteristics of Different Types of Drug-Involved Offenders* (Washington, D.C.: Government Printing Office, 1988), pp. 20–21.

36. Flowers, *Women and Criminality*, pp. 126–28; Flowers, *The Adolescent Criminal*, pp. 59–60.

37. D. Kelly Weisberg, *Children of the Night: A Study of Adolescent Prostitution* (Lexington, Mass.: Lexington Books, 1985), pp. 117–19; Mimi H. Silbert, *Sexual Assaults of Prostitutes: Phase One* (Washington, D.C.: National Institute of Mental Health, 1980), p. 48.

38. Flowers, *Demographics and Criminality*, pp. 153–54; Michael J. Martin and James Walters, "Familial Correlates of Selected Types of Child Abuse and Neglect," *Journal of Marriage and the Family* 5 (1982): 267–76.

39. Patricia Mrazek, "The Nature of Incest: A Review of Contributing Factors," in Patricia Beezley Mrazek and C. Henry Kempe, eds., *Sexually Abused Children and Their Families* (New York: Pergamon Press, 1981), p. 99.

40. Brandt F. Steele, "Violence Within the Family," in Ray E. Helfer and C. Henry Kempe, eds., *Child Abuse and Neglect: The Family and the Community* (Cambridge: Ballinger Publishing Co., 1976), p. 12.

41. *Women in Prison*, p. 7.

42. Flowers, *The Adolescent Criminal*, pp. 49–50, 56; Flowers, *Women and Criminality*, pp. 124–27.

43. Flowers, *Women and Criminality*, p. 129; *Women in Jail 1989*, p. 3; Ronald B. Flowers, *Minorities and Criminality* (Westport, Conn.: Greenwood Press, 1988), pp. 86, 98.

44. Cited in Flowers, *Demographics and Criminality*, p. 155. *See also* Murray A. Straus, Richard J. Gelles, and Suzanne K. Steinmetz, *Behind Closed Doors: Violence in the American Family* (New York: Doubleday, 1980).

45. Flowers, *Children and Criminality*, pp. 66–67; Flowers, *Demographics and Criminality*, p. 152.

46. Flowers, *Women and Criminality*, p. 129; Flowers, *Minorities and Criminality*, pp. 83–102.

47. *See, for example*, D. T. Lunde, "Hot Blood's Record Month: Our Murder Boom," *Psychology Today* 9 (1975), pp. 35–42; Adele Mayer, *Incest: A Treatment*

Manual for Therapy with Victims, Spouses, and Offenders (Holmes Beach, Fla.: Learning Publications, Inc., 1983), p. 22.

48. S. Zalba, "The Abused Child: A Survey of the Problem," *Social Work* 11, 4 (1966): 3–16.

49. Cited in Hersch, "Coming of Age," pp. 31–32.

50. Weisberg, *Children of the Night*, pp. 101–3; V. W. Wilson, "A Psychological Study of Juvenile Prostitutes," *International Journal of Social Psychiatry* 5, 1 (1959): 69.

51. Flowers, *Women and Criminality*, p. 114.

52. Saleem Shah and Loren Roth, "Biological and Psychological Factors in Criminality," in Daniel Glaser, ed., *Handbook of Criminology* (Chicago: Rand McNally, 1974), p. 145.

53. J. H. Morton, H. Addison, R. G. Hunt, and J. J. Sullivan, "A Clinical Study of Premenstrual Tension," *Journal of Obstetrics and Gynecology* 162 (1953): 1182–91.

54. K. Dalton, "Menstruation and Crime," *British Medical Journal* 2 (1961): 1752–53.

55. Julie Horney, "Menstrual Cycles and Criminal Responsibility," *Law and Human Behavior* 2, 1 (1978): 25–36.

56. Flowers, *Women and Criminality*, pp. 108–9; Flowers, *Children and Criminality*, pp. 49–59.

57. Flowers, *The Adolescent Criminal*, p. 50.

58. Ibid., pp. 57–58; Flowers, *Demographics and Criminality*, p. 133; Flowers, *Women and Criminality*, pp. 108–14.

59. Flowers, *Children and Criminality*, pp. 50–55; Flowers, *Demographics and Criminality*, pp. 151–57; Richard J. Gelles, *The Violent Home* (Beverly Hills: Sage Publications, 1987).

60. U.S. Department of Justice, *Criminal Victimization in the United States, 1992: A National Crime Victimization Survey Report* (Washington, D.C.: Government Printing Office, 1994), p. 63.

61. *Women in Prison*, p. 4.

62. Ibid.

Chapter 6. Homicidal Women

1. U.S. Federal Bureau of Investigation, *Crime in the United States: Uniform Crime Reports 1992* (Washington, D.C.: Government Printing Office, 1993), p. 19.

2. Ibid., p. 222.

3. Ibid., p. 234.

4. Cited in Sandy Nelson, "Women Who Kill," *Sacramento Bee* (December 30, 1986), p. B1.

5. Ibid., p. B9.

6. G. Rasko, "The Victim of the Female Killer," *Victimology: An International Journal* 1 (1976): 396–402.

7. J. Totman, *The Murderess: A Psychosocial Study of the Process* (Ann Arbor: University Microfilms, 1971).

8. Cited in Nelson, "Women Who Kill," p. B9.

9. D. Ward, M. Jackson, and R. Ward, "Crimes of Violence by Women," in D. Mulvill, M. M. Tumin, and L. A. Curtis, ed., *Crimes of Violence* (Washington, D.C.: Government Printing Office, 1969).

10. Theo Solomon, "History and Demography of Child Abuse," *Pediatrics* 51, 4 (1973): 773–76.

11. Ronald B. Flowers, *Children and Criminality: The Child as Victim and Perpetrator* (Westport, Conn.: Greenwood Press, 1986), p. 4.

12. *The Holy Bible*, Book of Joshua, 6:17–21.

13. Solomon, "History and Demography of Child Abuse," p. 773.

14. C. Morris, *The Tudors* (London: Fontana, 1967).

15. J. E. Oliver, "The Epidemiology of Child Abuse," in Selwyn M. Smith, ed., *The Maltreatment of Children* (Baltimore, Md.: University Park Press, 1978), p. 95.

16. Shirley O'Brien, Child Abuse: *Commission and Omission* (Provo, Ut.: Brigham Young University Press, 1980), p. 5.

17. Carol Smart, *Women, Crime, and Criminology: A Feminist Critique* (Boston: Routledge and Kegan Paul, 1977), p. 6.

18. Ibid.; Ronald B. Flowers, *Women and Criminality: The Woman as Victim, Offender, and Practitioner* (Westport, Conn.: Greenwood Press, 1987), p. 110.

19. W. Sage, "Violence in the Children's Room," *Human Behavior* 4 (1975): 42.

20. *Uniform Crime Reports 1992*, p. 16.

21. D. T. Lunde, "Hot Blood's Record Month: Our Murder Boom," *Psychology Today* 9 (1975): pp. 35–42.

22. Maria W. Piers, *Infanticide* (New York: W. W. Norton, 1978), p. 14.

23. Cited in Nick Jordan, "Till Murder Us Do Part," *Psychology Today* 19 (July 1985), p. 7.

24. Ibid.

25. Ibid.

26. Elissa P. Benedek, "Women and Homicide," In Bruce L. Danto, John Bruhns, and Austin H. Kutscher, eds., *The Human Side of Homicide* (New York: Columbia University Press, 1982), p. 155.

27. Flowers, *Women and Criminality*, p. 109.

28. Lenore E. Walker, *The Battered Woman Syndrome* (New York: Springer, 1984), p. 40.

29. *Uniform Crime Reports*, p. 17.

30. Ibid., p. 19.

31. Ibid.; Suzanne K. Steinmetz, "The Battered Husband Syndrome," *Victimology* 2 (1978): 499–509.

32. Quoted in Nelson, "Women Who Kill," p. B1.

33. Ibid., p. B9.

34. Quoted in Glenn Collins, "A Study Assesses Traits of Women Who Kill," *New York Times* (July 7, 1986), p. C18.

35. Quoted in Nelson, "Women Who Kill," p. B9.

36. Kay M. Porterfield, "Are Women as Violent as Men?" *Cosmopolitan* 197 (September 1984), p. 297.

37. Cited in Julie Horney, "Menstrual Cycles and Criminal Responsibility," *Law and Human Behavior* 2, 1 (1978): 25–36.

38. Ibid.

39. Ibid.; Saleem Shah and Loren Roth, "Biological and Psychological Factors in Criminality," in Daniel Glaser, ed., *Handbook of Criminology* (Chicago: Rand McNally, 1974), p. 145.

40. "British Legal Debate: Premenstrual Tension and Criminal Behavior," *New York Times* (December 29, 1981), p. C3.

41. Ibid.
42. Flowers, *Women and Criminality*, pp. 94–101.

Chapter 7. Women and Domestic Violence

1. U.S. Department of Justice, Bureau of Justice Statistics Special Report, *Family Violence* (Washington, D.C.: Government Printing Office, 1984), p. 2.

2. U.S. Federal Bureau of Investigation, *Crime in the United States: Uniform Crime Reports 1992* (Washington, D.C.: Government Printing Office, 1993), p. 231.

3. Ibid., p. 222.

4. P.L. 93–247; P.L. 95–266.

5. *Fact Sheet: Child Abuse and Neglect Data* (Englewood, Co.: American Humane Association, 1993), p. 1.

6. U.S. Department of Health and Human Services, *Child Maltreatment 1992: Reports from the States to the National Center on Child Abuse and Neglect* (Washington, D.C.: Government Printing Office, 1994), p. 10.

7. Richard J. Gelles, *The Violent Home* (Beverly Hills: Sage Publications, 1987), p. 55.

8. Brandt F. Steele and C. Pollock, "A Psychiatric Study of Parents Who Abuse Infants and Small Children," in Ray E. Helfer and C. Henry Kempe, eds., *The Battered Child* (Chicago: University of Chicago Press, 1968), pp. 89–133.

9. David G. Gil, *Violence Against Children: Physical Child Abuse in the United States* (Cambridge: Harvard University Press, 1970).

10. S. Zalba, "Battered Children," *Trans-Action* 8 (1971): 58–61; Ronald B. Flowers, *Children and Criminality: The Child as Victim and Perpetrator* (Westport, Conn.: Greenwood Press, 1986), p. 65.

11. Blair Justice and Rita Justice, *The Abusing Family* (New York: Human Sciences Press, 1976), p. 90.

12. Gil, *Violence Against Children*, p. 109.

13. Ronald B. Flowers, *Demographics and Criminality: The Characteristics of Crime in America* (Westport, Conn.: Greenwood Press, 1989), pp. 152–53.

14. U.S. Department of Health and Human Services, *Study Findings: National Study of the Incidence and Severity of Child Abuse and Neglect* (Washington, D.C.: Government Printing Office, 1981).

15. Cited in Flowers, *Children and Criminality*, p. 117.

16. Gil, *Violence Against Children*, p. 117.

17. Peggy Smith and Marvin Bohnstedt, *Child Victimization Study Highlights* (Sacramento: Social Research Center of the American Justice Institute, 1981).

18. Flowers, *Children and Criminality*, p. 65; Ronald B. Flowers, *Women and Criminality: The Woman as Victim, Offender, and Practitioner* (Westport, Conn.: Greenwood Press, 1987), p. 113.

19. Michael J. Martin and James Walters, "Familial Correlates of Selected Types of Child Abuse and Neglect," *Journal of Marriage and the Family* 5 (1982): 267–76.

20. G. C. Murdock, "The Abused Child and the School System," *American Journal of Public Health* 60 (1970): 105.

21. Flowers, *Children and Criminality*, pp. 87–88; M. S. Dine, "Tranquilizer Poisoning: An Example of Child Abuse," *Pediatrics* 36 (1965): 782–85; Jerry P. Flanzer, *The Many Faces of Family Violence* (Springfield, Ill.: Charles C Thomas, 1982), pp. 36–38.

22. Flowers, *Demographics and Criminality*, p. 154.

23. Ibid.

24. Robert Langley and Richard C. Levy, *Wife Beating: The Silent Crisis* (New York: E. P. Dutton, 1977).

25. Suzanne K. Steinmetz, "The Battered Husband Syndrome," *Victimology* 2 (1978): 507.

26. Cited in Jeanne Thornton, "Family Violence Emerges from the Shadows," *U.S. News & World Report* (January 23, 1984), p. 66.

27. Richard J. Gelles, "The Myth of Battered Husbands," *Ms.* (October 1979), pp. 65–66, 71–72.

28. Gelles, *The Violent Home*, pp. 50–52.

29. M. Bulcroft and M. Straus, "Validity of Husband, Wife, and Child Reports of Conjugal Violence and Power," cited in Lewis Okun, *Woman Abuse: Facts Replacing Myths* (New York: State University of New York Press, 1985), pp. 38, 261.

30. Cited in Steinmetz, "The Battered Husband Syndrome."

31. D. A. Gaquin, "Spouse Abuse: Data from the National Crime Survey," *Victimology* 2 (1977–1978): 632–43.

32. Bulcroft and Straus, "Validity of Husband, Wife, and Child Reports."

33. Murray A. Straus, Richard J. Gelles, and Suzanne K. Steinmetz, *Behind Closed Doors: Violence in the American Family* (New York: Doubleday, 1980).

34. J. E. O'Brien, "Violence in Divorce-Prone Families," *Journal of Marriage and the Family* 33 (1971): 692–98.

35. Straus, Gelles, and Steinmetz, *Behind Closed Doors*.

36. Gelles, *The Violent Home*.

37. Flowers, *Demographics and Criminality*, p. 157.

38. Bonnie E. Carlson, "Battered Women and Their Assailants," *Social Work* 22 (1977): 456.

39. Flowers, *Children and Criminality*, p. 44; Gil, *Violence Against Children*.

40. Richard J. Gelles, "Child Reformation," *American Journal of Orthopsychiatry* 43 (1973): 611–21.

41. Justice and Justice, *The Abusing Family*, pp. 55–80.

42. William N. Friedrick and Jerry A. Boriskin, "The Role of the Child in Abuse: A Review of the Literature, in Gertrude J. Williams and John Money, eds., *Traumatic Abuse and Neglect of Children at Home* (Baltimore, Md.: Johns Hopkins University Press, 1980), p. 194; J. Milowe and R. Lourie, "The Child's Role in the Battered Child Syndrome," *Journal of Pediatrics* 65 (1964): 1079–81.

Chapter 8. Incestuous Women

1. *The Holy Bible*, Book of Numbers 26:59; Exodus 6:20.

2. *The Holy Bible*, Book of Genesis 29:15–30; 20:12.

3. Ronald B. Flowers, *Children and Criminality: The Child as Victim and Perpetrator* (Westport, Conn.: Greenwood Press, 1986), p. 8.

4. Patricia Mrazek, "Definitions and Recognition of Sexual Child Abuse: Historical and Cultural Perspectives," in Patricia Beezley Mrazek and C. Henry Kempe, eds., *Sexually Abused Children and Their Families* (New York: Pergamon Press, 1981), p. 7.

5. Cited in Carol L. Mithers, "Incest: The Crime That's All in the Family," *Mademoiselle* 96 (June 1984), p. 127.

6. Heidi Vanderbilt, "Incest—A Chilling Report," *Lear's* (February 1992), p. 52.

7. Marshall D. Schechter and Leo Roberge, "Sexual Exploitation," in Ray E. Helfer and C. Henry Kempe, eds., *Child Abuse and Neglect: The Family and the Community* (Cambridge: Ballinger Publishing Co., 1976), p. 129.

8. Quoted in Vanderbilt, "Incest—A Chilling Report," p. 63.

9. Ibid., p. 62.

10. Adele Mayer, *Incest: A Treatment Manual for Therapy with Victims, Spouses and Offenders* (Holmes Beach, Fla.: Learning Publications, 1983), p. 22.

11. Cited in Vanderbilt, "Incest—A Chilling Report," p. 62.

12. Quoted in Ibid.

13. Ibid.

14. Ibid., p. 63.

15. Quoted in Ibid., p. 62.

16. Ibid., p. 63.

17. R. Medlicott, "Parent-Child Incest," *Australian Journal of Psychiatry* 1 (1967): 180.

18. R. Lidz and T. Lidz, "Homosexual Tendencies in Mothers of Schizophrenic Women," *Journal of Nervous Mental Disorders* 149 (1969): 229.

19. Vanderbilt, "Incest—A Chilling Report," p. 63.

20. Quoted in Ibid.

21. Ibid., p. 54.

Chapter 9. Women and Prostitution

1. Nathan C. Heard, *Howard Street* (New York: Dial Press, 1970), p. 86.

2. Marshall B. Clinard, *Sociology of Deviant Behavior* (New York: Holt, Rinehart & Winston, 1957), p. 249.

3. Edwin M. Lemert, *Social Pathology* (New York: McGraw-Hill, 1951).

4. Charles Winick and Paul M. Kinsie, *The Lively Commerce* (Chicago: Quadrangle Books, 1971), p. 3.

5. Paul J. Goldstein, *Prostitution and Drugs* (Lexington, Mass.: Lexington Books, 1979), p. 33.

6. Abraham Flexner, *Prostitution in Europe* (New York: Century Co., 1914), p. 11.

7. *U.S. v. Bitty*, 208 U.S. 393, 401 (1908); Charles Rosenbleet and Barbara J. Pariente, "The Prostitution of the Criminal Law," *American Criminal Law Review* 11 (1973): 373.

8. Howard B. Woolston, *Prostitution in the United States* (New York: Century Co., 1921), p. 35.

9. *State v. Perry*, 249 Oregon 76, 81, 436 (1968); Rosenbleet and Pariente, "The Prostitution of the Criminal Law," p. 381.

10. Kate Millett, "Prostitution: A Quartet for Female Voices," in Vivian Gornick and Barbara K. Moran, eds., *Women in a Sexist Society* (New York: New American Library, 1971), p. 79.

11. U.S. Federal Bureau of Investigation, *Crime in the United States: Uniform Crime Reports 1992* (Washington, D.C.: Government Printing Office, 1993), pp. 229, 231.

12. Marilyn G. Haft, "Hustling for Rights," in Laura Crites, ed., *The Female Offender* (Lexington, Mass.: Lexington Books, 1976), pp. 212–13.

13. Jennifer James, *Entrance into Juvenile Prostitution* (Washington, D.C.: National Institute of Mental Health, 1980), p. 19; Mimi H. Silbert, *Sexual Assault of Prostitutes: Phase One* (Washington, D.C.: National Institute of Mental Health, 1980), p. 10.

14. Haft, "Hustling for Rights," p. 212.

15. Ibid.

16. Ibid.

17. Cited in Ronald B. Flowers, *Women and Criminality: The Woman as Victim, Offender, and Practitioner* (Westport, Conn.: Greenwood Press, 1987), p. 129.

18. *Uniform Crime Reports 1992*, p. 222; D. Kelly Weisberg, *Children of the Night: A Study of Adolescent Prostitution* (Lexington, Mass.: Lexington Books, 1985), pp. 124–28.

19. Harry Benjamin and R. E. L. Masters, *Prostitution and Morality* (New York: Julian Press, 1964).

20. Goldstein, *Prostitution and Drugs*, pp. 34–37.

21. Cited in Linda Lee, "The World (and Underworld) of the Professional Call Girl," *New Woman* (January 1983), p. 61.

22. Jennifer James, "Two Domains of Streetwalker Argot," *Anthropological Linguistics* 14 (1972): 174–75; Jennifer James, "Prostitutes and Prostitution," in Edward Sagarin and Fred Montanino, eds., *Deviants: Voluntary Actors in a Hostile World* (Morrison, N.J.: General Learning Press, 1977), pp. 390–91.

23. Lee H. Bowker, *Women, Crime, and the Criminal Justice System* (Lexington, Mass.: Lexington Books, 1978), p. 154.

24. Bowker, *Women, Crime, and the Criminal Justice System*, p. 155; Jennifer James, "Prostitute-Pimp Relationships," *Medical Aspects of Human Sexuality* 7 (1973): 147–63.

25. Bowker, *Women, Crime, and the Criminal Justice System*, p. 155.

26. James, "Prostitutes and Prostitution," pp. 390–91.

27. Flowers, *Women and Criminality*, p. 126; Silbert, *Sexual Assault of Prostitutes*, p. 60; Weisberg, *Children of the Night*, pp. 96–97.

28. Quoted in Rolaine Hochstein, "Prostitutes: Happy Hookers or Society's Victims?" *Glamour* 83 (May 1985), p. 184.

29. Robert Karen, "The World of the Middle Class Prostitute," *Cosmopolitan* 202 (January 1987), p. 205.

30. Ibid.

31. Ibid., p. 206.

32. Quoted in Ibid., p. 205.

33. Ibid., p. 206.

34. Ibid., p. 207.

35. Lee, "The World (and Underworld) of the Professional Call Girl," p. 61. *See also* Mary Reinholz, "An Intimate Look at the Life of a Call Girl," *Cosmopolitan* (August 1994), pp. 110, 114; Barbara Ignoto, *Confessions of a Part-Time Call Girl* (New York: Dell, 1986); Sydney Barrows and William Novak, *Mayflower Madam: The Secret Life of Sydney Biddle Barrows* (New York: Arbor House, 1986).

36. Quoted in Lee, "The World (and Underworld) of the Professional Call Girl," p. 61.

37. Ibid.

38. Freda Adler, *Sisters in Crime: The Rise of the New Female Criminal* (New York: McGraw-Hill, 1975), p. 73.

39. Coramae Richey Mann, "White-Collar Prostitution," Unpublished paper, 1974.

40. Cited in Lee, "The World (and Underworld) of the Professional Call Girl," p. 62.

41. Harold Greenwald, *The Elegant Prostitute: A Social and Psychoanalytic Study* (New York: Walker and Co., 1970).

42. Ibid., p. xx.

43. Ibid., p. 242; Bowker, *Women, Crime, and the Criminal Justice System,* pp. 151–52.

44. Karen E. Rosenblum, "Female Deviance and the Female Sex Role: A Preliminary Investigation," *British Journal of Sociology* 26 (1975): 173–78.

45. James H. Bryan, "Apprenticeship in Prostitution," *Social Problems* 12 (1965): 287–97.

46. Ibid.; Bowker, *Women, Crime, and the Criminal Justice System*, p. 152.

47. James H. Bryan, "Occupational Ideologies and Individual Attitudes of Call Girls," *Social Problems* 13 (1966): 441–50.

48. Quoted in Lee, "The World (and Underworld) of the Professional Call Girl," p. 63.

49. Jennifer James, "Motivations for Entrance into Prostitution," in Laura Crites, ed., *The Female Offender* (Lexington, Mass.: Lexington Books, 1976), p. 194; Kingsley Davis, "The Sociology of Prostitution," *American Sociological Review* 2 (1937): 744–55.

50. Hochstein, "Prostitutes: Happy Hookers or Society's Victims?" p. 187.

51. Norma Jean Almodovar as quoted in Karen, "The World of the Middle Class Prostitute," p. 207.

52. Flowers, *Women and Criminality*, p. 128.

53. Cited in R. Barri Flowers, *The Adolescent Criminal: An Examination of Today's Juvenile Offender* (Jefferson, N.C.: McFarland & Co., 1990), p. 63.

54. Ibid.

55. Cited in Lee, "The World (and Underworld) of the Professional Call Girl," p. 62.

56. Ibid.

57. Ibid.

Chapter 10. Women and Drug Abuse

1. Walter R. Cuskey, T. Premkumar, and Lois Siegel, "Survey of Opiate Addiction Among Females in the U.S. Between 1850 and 1970," in Freda Adler and Rita J. Simon, eds., *The Criminology of Deviant Women* (Boston: Houghton Mifflin, 1979).

2. Anne Geller and Helene MacLean, "Substance Abuse," Helene MacLean, ed., *Every Woman's Health: The Complete Guide to Body and Mind*, 5th ed. (Garden City, N.Y.: Guild American Books, 1993), p. 409.

3. Jose E. Sanchez and Bruce D. Johnson, "Women and the Drugs-Crime Connection: Crime Rates Among Drug-Abusing Women at Rikers Island," *Journal of Psychoactive Drugs* 19, 2 (1987): 205–16; U.S. Department of Justice, National Institute of Justice, *Characteristics of Different Types of Drug-Involved Offenders* (Washington, D.C.: Government Printing Office, 1988), pp. 20–21.

4. Ronald B. Flowers, *Women and Criminality: The Woman as Victim, Offender, and Practitioner* (Westport, Conn.: Greenwood Press, 1987), p. 143; R. Barri Flowers, *The Adolescent Criminal: An Examination of Today's Juvenile Offender* (Jefferson, N.C.: McFarland & Co., 1990), pp. 59–60.

5. Centers for Disease Control, *Morbidity and Mortality Weekly Report* (March 27, 1987); U.S. Department of Justice, *Survey of State Prison Inmates, 1991: Women in Prison* (Washington, D.C.: Government Printing Office, 1993), p. 25.

6. These include arrests for driving under the influence, liquor law violations, and drunkenness. U.S. Federal Bureau of Investigation, *Crime in the United States: Uniform Crime Reports 1992* (Washington, D.C.: Government Printing Office, 1993), p. 231.

7. Geller and MacLean, "Substance Abuse," p. 385.

8. Ibid.

9. *Uniform Crime Reports 1992*, p. 231.

10. U.S. Department of Health and Human Services, *National Household Survey on Drug Abuse: Population Estimates 1991* (Rockville, Md.: National Institute on Drug Abuse, 1991).

11. U.S. Department of Justice, *Women in Prison* (Washington, D.C.: Government Printing Office, 1994), p. 3.

12. Ibid., p. 7.

13. Ibid., pp. 7–9; Flowers, *Women and Criminality*, p. 143.

14. Geller and MacLean, "Substance Abuse," p. 408.

15. Ibid.

16. Ibid.

17. Ibid.

18. Ibid.

19. *Women in Prison*, p. 8.

20. Quoted in "Turning Increasingly to Cocaine," *Time* (April 2, 1984): 87.

21. Ibid.

22. Ibid.

23. "Cocaine Deaths are Accelerating," *Sacramento Bee* (July 11, 1986), p. A22.

24. "Turning Increasingly to Cocaine."

25. Flowers, *Women and Criminality*, p. 143; *Characteristics of Different Types of Drug-Involved Offenders*, p. 21; Ronald B. Flowers, *Demographics and Criminality: The Characteristics of Crime in America* (Westport, Conn.: Greenwood Press, 1990), pp. 132–33.

26. Cited in Flowers, *Demographics and Criminality*, p. 130.

27. William E. McAuliffe and Robert A. Gordon, "A Test of Lindesmith's Theory of Addiction: The Frequency of Euphoria Among Long-Term Addicts," *American Journal of Sociology* 79 (1974): 795–840.

28. *Characteristics of Different Types of Drug-Involved Offenders*, p. 21; *Women in Prison*, p. 9; Flowers, *Women and Criminality*, pp. 128, 143.

29. *Characteristics of Different Types of Drug-Involved Offenders*, p. 21.

30. Ibid., p. 6.

31. Geller and MacLean, "Substance Abuse," p. 403.

32. Ibid., p. 402.

33. Ibid.

34. Flowers, *Women and Criminality*, p. 142.

35. Ibid.

36. Ibid.

37. Marvin R. Burt, Thomas J. Glynn, and Barbara J. Sowder, *Psychosocial Characteristics of Drug-Abusing Women* (Rockville, Md.: U.S. Department of Health, Education, and Welfare, 1979).

Chapter 11. Female White-Collar Criminals

1. U.S. Federal Bureau of Investigation, *Crime in the United States: Uniform Crime Reports 1992* (Washington, D.C.: Government Printing Office, 1993), pp. 229, 231.
2. Cited in Ronald B. Flowers, *Women and Criminality: The Woman as Victim, Offender, and Practitioner* (Westport, Conn.: Greenwood Press, 1987), p. 140.
3. Ibid.; Larry Miller, "The Lady Is A (White-Collar) Criminal," *Cosmopolitan* (July 1983), pp. 227–30.
4. Quoted in Flowers, *Women and Criminality*, p. 141.
5. Ted Gest, "Women Expand Their Roles in Crime, Too," *U.S. News & World Report* (November 12, 1984), p. 62.
6. Quoted in Miller, "The Lady Is A (White-Collar) Criminal," p. 227.
7. Ibid.
8. Ibid., p. 229.
9. Ibid.
10. Quoted in Ibid., p. 230.
11. Ibid.
12. Flowers, *Women and Criminality*, pp. 83–84.
13. Ibid., p. 140; Gest, "Women Expand Their Roles in Crime"; U.S. Department of Justice, Bureau of Justice Statistics Special Report, *Tracking Offenders: White-Collar Crime* (Washington, D.C.: Government Printing Office, 1986).
14. Miller, "The Lady Is A (White-Collar) Criminal," p. 230.

Chapter 12. Female Rapists and Con Artists

1. U.S. Federal Bureau of Investigation, *Crime in the United States: Uniform Crime Reports 1992* (Washington, D.C.: Government Printing Office, 1993), p. 222.
2. Ronald B. Flowers, *Women and Criminality: The Woman as Victim, Offender, and Practitioner* (Westport, Conn.: Greenwood Press, 1987), p. 133.
3. Ibid., p. 134.
4. Diana E. Russell, *Rape in Marriage* (New York: Macmillan, 1982), pp. 280–82.
5. Flowers, *Women and Criminality*, p. 114; Heidi Vanderbilt, "Incest—A Chilling Report," *Lear's* (February 1992), p. 63.
6. Quoted in "Sex Researcher's Report: The Men Raped by Women," *San Francisco Chronicle* (March 15, 1982), p. 5.
7. Ibid.
8. Kay M. Porterfield, "Are Women as Violent as Men?" *Cosmopolitan* 197 (September 1984), p. 276.
9. Quoted in "Sex Researcher's Report."
10. Ibid.
11. Stuart J. Miller, "Foreword," in Anthony M. Scacco, Jr., ed., *Male Rape: A Casebook of Sexual Aggression* (New York: AMS Press, 1982), p. ix.
12. Diana E. Russell, *Sexual Exploitation: Rape, Child Sexual Abuse, and Workplace Harassment* (Beverly Hills: Sage Publications, 1984), p. 67.
13. Dorothy West, "I Was Afraid to Shut My Eyes," in Scacco, Jr., *Male Rape*, p. 171.
14. Flowers, *Women and Criminality*, pp. 37–42.

15. Ibid., pp. 113–114; Russell, *Sexual Exploitation*; U.S. Department of Justice, *Survey of State Prison Inmates, 1991: Women in Prison* (Washington, D.C.: Government Printing Office, 1994), p. 3.

16. *Uniform Crime Reports 1992*, p. 222; U.S. Federal Bureau of Investigation, *Crime in the United States: Uniform Crime Reports 1960* (Washington, D.C.: Government Printing Office, 1961).

17. Flowers, *Women and Criminality*, p. 138.

18. Quoted in John Kobler, "Con Women of the World," *Cosmopolitan* 196 (April 1984), p. 248.

19. Ibid.

20. Ibid.

21. Ibid.

22. Ibid., pp. 248–49.

23. Ibid., p. 249.

24. Ibid., p. 288.

25. Quoted in Ibid., p. 248.

26. Ibid., p. 289.

27. Ibid.

Chapter 13. Runaway Girls

1. Ronald B. Flowers, *Children and Criminality: The Child as Victim and Perpetrator* (Westport, Conn.: Greenwood Press, 1986), p. 132.

2. Patricia Hersch, "Coming of Age on City Streets," *Psychology Today* (January 1988), pp. 31, 34.

3. Cited in Flowers, Children and Criminality, pp. 132–33.

4. Suburban areas includes suburban city and county law enforcement agencies within metropolitan areas. U.S. Federal Bureau of Investigation, *Crime in the United States: Uniform Crime Reports 1992* (Washington, D.C.: Government Printing Office, 1993), p. 220.

5. James A. Hildebrand, "Why Runaways Leave Home," *Police Science* 54 (1963): 211–16.

6. Robert Shellow, "Suburban Runaways of the 1960s," *Monographs of the Society for Research in Child Development* 32 (1967): 17.

7. Louise Homer, "Criminality-Based Resource for Runaway Girls," *Social Casework* 10 (1973): 474.

8. R. Barri Flowers, *The Adolescent Criminal: An Examination of Today's Juvenile Offender* (Jefferson, N.C.: McFarland & Co., 1990), pp. 49–51.

9. Cited in John Zaccaro, Jr., "Children of the Night," *Woman's Day* (March 29, 1988), p. 138.

10. Cited in Hersch, "Coming of Age," pp. 31–32.

11. Ibid.

12. Flowers, *Children and Criminality*, p. 133.

13. C. J. English, "Leaving Home: A Typology of Runaways," *Society* 10 (1973): 22–24.

14. "'Runaways', 'Throwaways,' 'Bag Kids'—An Army of Drifter Teens," *U.S. News & World Report* (March 11, 1985), p. 53.

15. "'Rat Pack' Youth: Teenage Rebels in Suburbia," *U.S. News & World Report* (March 11, 1985), p. 54.

16. Cited in Hersch, "Coming of Age," p. 31.

17. Robin Lloyd, *For Money or Love: Boy Prostitution in America* (New York: Ballantine, 1976), pp. 58–72.

18. "Prostitutes: The New Breed," *Newsweek* (July 12, 1971), p. 78.

19. Ibid.

20. Hersch, "Coming of Age," p. 32.

21. As quoted in Dotson Rader, "I Want to Die So I Won't Hurt No More," *Parade Magazine* (August 18, 1985), p. 4.

22. Hersch, "Coming of Age," pp. 32, 35.

23. Cited in Zaccaro, Jr., "Children of the Night," p. 137.

Chapter 14. Girl Prostitutes

1. Henry Benjamin and R. E. L. Masters, *Prostitution and Morality* (New York: Julian Press, 1964), p. 161.

2. Ronald B. Flowers, *Children and Criminality: The Child as Victim and Perpetrator* (Westport, Conn.: Greenwood Press, 1986), p. 7; Reay Tannahill, *Sex in History* (New York: Stein and Day, 1980), p. 374.

3. Cited in Michael Satchel, "Kids for Sale," *Parade Magazine* (July 20, 1986), p. 4.

4. R. Barri Flowers, *The Adolescent Criminal: An Examination of Today's Juvenile Offender* (Jefferson, N.C.: McFarland & Co., 1990), pp. 54–55.

5. Ibid., p. 55.

6. Sam Meddis, "Teen Prostitution Rising, Study Says," *USA Today* (April 23, 1984), p. 3A.

7. *See, for example,* Flowers, *Children and Criminality,* pp. 80–81; Flowers, *The Adolescent Criminal,* pp. 55–57; Maura G. Crowley, "Female Runaway Behavior and Its Relationship to Prostitution," Masters thesis, Sam Houston State University, Institute of Contemporary Corrections and Behavior Sciences, 1977; Judianne Densen-Gerber and S. F. Hutchinson, "Medical-Legal and Societal Problems Involving Children-Child Prostitution, Child Pornography and Drug-Related Abuse; Recommended Legislation," in Selwyn M. Smith, ed., *The Maltreatment of Children* (Baltimore, Md.: University Park Press, 1978), pp. 317–50.

8. Jennifer James, *Entrance into Juvenile Prostitution* (Washington, D.C.: National Institute of Mental Health, 1980), p. 17.

9. Ibid., p. 29; D. Kelly Weisberg, *Children of the Night: A Study of Adolescent Prostitution* (Lexington, Mass.: Lexington Books, 1985), p. 94.

10. Ellen Hale, "Center Studies Causes of Juvenile Prostitution," *Gannett News Service* (May 21, 1981).

11. Mimi H. Silbert, *Sexual Assault of Prostitutes: Phase One* (Washington, D.C.: National Institute of Mental Health, 1980), p. 15.

12. James, *Entrance into Juvenile Prostitution,* p. 18; Jennifer James, *Entrance into Juvenile Prostitution: Progress Report, June 1978* (Washington, D.C.: National Institute of Mental Health, 1978), p. 53.

13. The Enablers, *Juvenile Prostitution in Minnesota: The Report of a Research Project* (St. Paul: The Enablers, 1978), p. 18.

14. Sparky Harlan, Luanne L. Rodgers, and Brian Slattery, *Male and Female Adolescent Prostitution: Huckelberry House Sexual Minority Youth Services Project* (Washington, D.C.: U.S. Department of Health and Human Services, 1981), p. 7.

15. James, *Entrance into Juvenile Prostitution,* p. 19.

16. Ibid.; The Enablers, *Juvenile Prostitution in Minnesota*, p. 18; Flowers, *The Adolescent Criminal*, p. 56.

17. Silbert, *Sexual Assault of Prostitutes*, p. 10; James, *Entrance into Juvenile Prostitution*, p. 10.

18. Crowley, "Female Runaway Behavior," p. 63.

19. Harlan, Rodgers, and Slattery, *Male and Female Adolescent Prostitution*, p. 14.

20. James, *Entrance into Juvenile Prostitution*, p. 88.

21. Harlan, Rodgers, and Slattery, *Male and Female Adolescent Prostitution*, p. 15.

22. Diana Gray, "Turning Out: A Study of Teenage Prostitution," Masters thesis, University of Washington, 1971, p. 25.

23. Crowley, "Female Runaway Behavior," pp. 77–74.

24. *See, for example,* Katherine MacVicar and Marcia Dillon, "Childhood and Adolescent Development of Ten Female Prostitutes," *Journal of the American Academy of Child Psychiatry* 19, 1 (1980): 148–49; Frances Newman and Paula J. Caplan, "Juvenile Female Prostitution as a Gender Consistent Response to Early Deprivation," *International Journal of Women's Studies* 5, 2 (1981): 131.

25. Harlan, Rodgers, and Slattery, *Male and Female Adolescent Prostitution*, p. 21.

26. Mimi H. Silbert, "Delancey Street Study: Prostitution and Sexual Assault," Summary of results (San Francisco: Delancey Street Foundation, 1982), p. 3.

27. Flowers, *The Adolescent Criminal*, p. 58; Flowers, *Children and Criminality*, pp. 82–83.

28. Crowley, "Female Runaway Behavior," p. 63; Harlan, Rodgers, and Slattery, *Male and Female Adolescent Prostitution*, p. 15.

29. Flowers, *The Adolescent Criminal*, pp. 59–60; The Enablers, *Juvenile Prostitution in Minnesota*, p. 89; Weisberg, *Children of the Night*, pp. 117–19.

30. Paul W. Haberman and Michael M. Baden, *Alcohol, Other Drugs and Violent Death* (New York: Oxford University Press, 1978), pp. 18–19.

31. Crowley, "Female Runaway Behavior," p. 80; Flowers, *The Adolescent Criminal*, p. 59; Weisberg, *Children of the Night*, p. 118.

32. Flowers, *Children and Criminality*, p. 97; Densen-Gerber and Hutchinson, "Medical-Legal and Societal Problems Involving Children-Child Prostitution," p. 322.

33. The Enablers, *Juvenile Prostitution in Minnesota*, p. 75.

34. John G. Hubbell, "Child Prostitution: How It Can Be Stopped," *Reader's Digest* (June 1984), pp. 202, 205.

35. Jennifer James, "Prostitute-Pimp Relationships," *Medical Aspects of Human Sexuality* 7 (1973): 147–63.

36. Dorothy H. Bracey, *"Baby-Pros: Preliminary Profiles of Juvenile Prostitutes* (New York: John Jay Press, 1979), p. 23.

37. Freda Adler, *Sisters in Crime: The Rise of the New Female Criminal* (New York: McGraw-Hill, 1975), p. 72.

38. The Enablers, *Juvenile Prostitution in Minnesota*, p. 57.

39. Bracey, *"Baby-Pros,"* p. 23.

40. Ibid.

41. Quoted in Hale, "Center Studies Causes of Juvenile Prostitution."

42. "Prostitutes: The New Breed," *Newsweek* (July 12, 1971), p. 78.

43. Quoted in Clemens Bartolas, *Juvenile Delinquency* (New York: John Wiley & Sons, 1985), p. 342.

44. James, *Entrance Into Juvenile Prostitution: Progress Report.*

45. Flowers, *The Adolescent Criminal*, p. 58; V. W. Wilson, "A Psychological Study of Juvenile Prostitutes," *International Journal of Social Psychiatry* 5, 1 (1959): 69.

46. Crowley, "Female Runaway Behavior," p. 63; Joseph J. Peters, "Children Who Are Victims of Sexual Assault and the Psychology of Offenders," *American Journal of Psychotherapy* 30 (1976): 398–421; John Zaccaro, Jr., "Children of the Night," *Woman's Day* (May 29, 1988), p. 138.

47. James, *Entrance Into Juvenile Prostitution*, p. 68.

48. Ibid., p. 80; Silbert, *Sexual Assault of Prostitutes*, p. 56.

49. Quoted in Patricia Hersch, "Coming of Age on City Streets," *Psychology Today* (January 1988), pp. 32, 35.

50. Bracey, *"Baby-Pros,"* pp. 61–62; Flowers, *The Adolescent Criminal*, p. 60.

51. Flowers, *The Adolescent Criminal*, pp. 62–63; Ronald B. Flowers, *Women and Criminality: The Woman as Victim, Offender, and Practitioner* (Westport, Conn.: Greenwood Press, 1987), p. 129.

52. Cited in Hersch, "Coming of Age," p. 37.

53. Ibid., p. 31.

Chapter 15. Girls, Alcohol, and Drugs

1. The offenses include drug abuse violations, driving under the influence, liquor laws, and drunkenness. U.S. Federal Bureau of Investigation, *Crime in the United States: Uniform Crime Reports 1992* (Washington, D.C.: Government Printing Office, 1993), p. 231.

2. Ibid., p. 226.

3. Ibid., p. 235; Ronald B. Flowers, *Demographics and Criminality: The Characteristics of Crime in America* (Westport, Conn.: Greenwood Press, 1990), pp. 128, 133–34.

4. Cited in Paul W. Haberman and Michael M. Baden, *Alcohol, Other Drugs and Violent Death* (New York: Oxford University Press, 1978), pp. 18–19.

5. U.S. Department of Health, Education, and Welfare, *The Special Report to the U.S. Congress on Alcohol and Drugs* (Washington, D.C.: Government Printing Office, 1978).

6. Peter C. Kratcoski and John E. Kratcoski, "Changing Patterns in the Delinquent Activities of Boys and Girls: A Self-Reported Delinquency Analysis," *Adolescence* 10, 37 (1975): 87.

7. The age for legal drinking and purchase of alcohol varies from state to state, ranging from 18 to 21.

8. Cited in R. Barri Flowers, *The Adolescent Criminal: An Examination of Today's Juvenile Offender* (Jefferson, N.C.: McFarland & Co., 1990), p. 90.

9. Paul H. Hahn, *The Juvenile Offender and the Law*, 3rd ed. (Cincinnati: Anderson, 1984), p. 109.

10. U.S. Department of Justice, National Institute of Justice, *Characteristics of Different Types of Drug-Involved Offenders* (Washington, D.C.: Government Printing Office, 1988), pp. 9–10.

11. James Thorton, *Delinquency and Justice* (Glenview, Ill.: Scott Foresman and Co., 1982), p. 296.

12. Kratcoski and Kratcoski, "Changing Patterns in the Delinquent Activities of Boys and Girls," p. 87.

13. Nechama Tec, *Grass Is Green in Suburbia* (Roslyn Heights, N.Y.: Libra Publishers, 1974), p. 46.

14. *Characteristics of Different Types of Drug-Involved Offenders*, p. 9; Lloyd D. Johnston, Patrick M. O'Malley, and Gerald G. Bachman, *Drug Use Among American High School Students, College Students, and Other Young Adults, National Trends Through 1985* (Rockville, Md.: National Institute on Drug Abuse, 1986).

15. Denise B. Kandel and Kazuo Yamaguchi, "Developmental Patterns of Use of Legal, Illegal, and Medically Prescribed Psychotropic Drugs from Adolescence to Adulthood," in C. L. Jones and R. J. Battjes, eds., *Etiology of Drug Abuse: Implications for Prevention* (Rockville, Md.: National Institute on Drug Abuse, 1985), pp. 193–235.

16. *Characteristics of Different Types of Drug-Involved Offenders*, p. 9.

17. Ibid., pp. 9–14; Flowers, *The Adolescent Criminal*, pp. 90–91; U.S. Department of Health and Human Services, *A Drug Retrospective: 1961–1980* (Washington, D.C.: Government Printing Office, 1980).

18. Quoted in "Crack: A Cheap and Deadly Cocaine Is A Spreading Menace," *Time* 127 (June 2, 1986), p. 18.

19. *Characteristics of Different Types of Drug-Involved Offenders*, p. 10–11.

20. Cheryl Carpenter, Barry Glassner, Bruce D. Johnson, and Julia Loughlin, *Kids, Drugs, and Crime* (Lexington, Mass.: Lexington Books, 1988), pp. 220–21.

21. Quoted in Clemens Bartollas, *Juvenile Delinquency* (New York: John Wiley & Sons, 1985), p. 341.

22. Ibid.; *Characteristics of Different Types of Drug-Involved Offenders*, p. 10.

23. Flowers, *The Adolescent Criminal*, pp. 59–60, 95; Delbert S. Elliott, Suzanne S. Ageton, David Huizinga, Brian Knowles, and Rochelle J. Canter, *The Prevalence and Incidence of Delinquent Behavior, 1976–1980* (Boulder, Co.: Behavioral Research Institute, 1983).

24. *Characteristics of Different Types of Drug-Involved Offenders*, p. 10; Carpenter, Glassner, Johnson, and Loughlin, *Kids, Drugs, and Crime*, pp. 85–100.

25. Flowers, *The Adolescent Criminal*, pp. 51–52, 59–60.

26. Ibid., p. 60; Ronald B. Flowers, *Children and Criminality: The Child as Victim and Perpetrator* (Westport, Conn.: Greenwood Press, 1986), p. 97.

27. Flowers, *Children and Criminality*, p. 88; Alfred Kadushin and Judith A. Martin, *Child Abuse: An Interactional Event* (New York: Columbia University Press, 1981), pp. 125–28; Patricia Hersch, "Coming of Age on City Streets," *Psychology Today* (January 1988), pp. 31–32; John Zaccaro, Jr., "Children of the Night," *Woman's Day* (March 29, 1988), p. 138.

28. Ronald B. Flowers, *Women and Criminality: The Woman as Victim, Offender, and Practitioner* (Westport, Conn.: Greenwood Press, 1987), pp. 141–43; Denise B. Kandel, Ora Simcha-Fagan, and Mark Davies, "Risk Factors for Delinquency and Illicit Drug Use From Adolescence to Young Adulthood," *Journal of Drug Issues* Winter (1986): 67–90.

29. *Characteristics of Different Types of Drug-Involved Offenders*, p. 10; Flowers, *The Adolescent Criminal*, p. 90.

Chapter 16. Girl Thieves

1. Ronald B. Flowers, *Demographics and Criminality: The Characteristics of Crime in America* (Westport, Conn.: Greenwood Press, 1989), pp. 86–87.

2. Cited in Ronald B. Flowers, *Children and Criminality: The Child as Victim and Perpetrator* (Westport, Conn.: Greenwood Press, 1986), p. 139.

3. Cheryl Carpenter, Barry Glassner, Bruce D. Johnson, and Julia Loughlin, *Kids, Drugs, and Crime* (Lexington, Mass.: Lexington Books, 1988), p. 140.

4. R. Barri Flowers, *The Adolescent Criminal: An Examination of Today's Juvenile Offender* (Jefferson, N.C.: McFarland & Co., 1990), pp. 78–79.

5. Kathryn Harrison, "The Thrill of the Steal," *Mademoiselle* (October 1993), p. 186.

6. Anne Campbell, *Girl Delinquents* (New York: St. Martin's Press, 1981), p. 131.

7. Flowers, *The Adolescent Criminal*, p. 94.

8. Carpenter, Glassner, Johnson, and Loughlin, *Kids, Drugs, and Crime*, p. 85.

9. U.S. Department of Justice, National Institute of Justice, *Characteristics of Different Types of Drug-Involved Offenders* (Washington, D.C.: Government Printing Office, 1988), p. 10.

10. Ibid., pp. 10–13; Flowers, *The Adolescent Criminal*, pp. 93–94.

11. Flowers, *Children and Criminality*, pp. 131–35.

12. Flowers, *The Adolescent Criminal*, pp. 57–60.

13. Ronald B. Flowers, *Women and Criminality: The Woman as Victim, Offender, and Practitioner* (Westport, Conn.: Greenwood Press, 1987), pp. 78–87.

14. Cited in Harrison, "The Thrill of the Steal," p. 186.

15. Ibid.

16. Ibid.

17. Ibid., p. 224.

18. Flowers, *Women and Criminality*, pp. 99, 143.

Chapter 17. Girls in Gangs

1. "On the Wild Side: Women in Gangs," *New York Times* (January 2, 1986), p. C8.

2. Ibid.

3. R. Barri Flowers, *The Adolescent Criminal: An Examination of Today's Juvenile Offender* (Jefferson, N.C.: McFarland & Co., 1990), p. 100.

4. Walter B. Miller, *Violence by Youth Gangs and Youth Groups as a Crime Problem in Major American Cities* (Washington, D.C.: Government Printing Office, 1975).

5. Flowers, *The Adolescent Criminal*, p. 101; "On the Wild Side."

6. Ronald B. Flowers, *Women and Criminality: The Woman as Victim, Offender, and Practitioner* (Westport, Conn.: Greenwood Press, 1987), p. 138; Peter C. Buffum, "Homosexuality in Female Institutions," in Anthony M. Scacco, Jr., ed., *Male Rape: A Casebook of Sexual Aggressions* (New York: AMS Press, 1982), pp. 165–67.

7. Flowers, *The Adolescent Criminal*, pp. 101–2; Ronald B. Flowers, *Minorities and Criminality* (New York, N.Y.: Praeger Publishers, 1990), pp. 138–39.

8. Howard L. Myerhoff and Barbara G. Myerhoff, "Field Observations of Middle Class Gangs," *Social Forces* 42 (1964): 328–36; Dale G. Hardman, "Small Town Gangs," *Journal of Criminal Law, Criminology and Police Science* 60, 2 (1969): 176–77.

9. "On the Wild Side."

10. Peggy C. Giordano, "Girls, Guys, and Gangs: The Changing Social Concept of Female Delinquency," *Journal of Criminal Law and Criminology* 69 (1978): 130.

11. Waln K. Brown, "Black Female Gangs in Philadelphia," *International Journal of Offender Therapy and Comparative Criminology* 21 (1970): 221–29.

12. Hardman, "Small Town Gangs," pp. 176–77.

13. Freda Adler, *Sisters in Crime: The Rise of the New Female Criminal* (New York: McGraw-Hill, 1975), p. 99.

14. Quoted in Sheila Weller, "Girls in the Gang: A Nineties Nightmare," *Cosmopolitan* (August 1994), p. 168.

15. "On the Wild Side;" Anne Campbell, *Girl Delinquents* (New York: St. Martin's Press, 1981).

16. Weller, "Girls in the Gang," p. 167.

17. Miller, *Violence by Youth Gangs.*

18. Weller, "Girls in the Gang," p. 168.

19. Ibid.

20. Ibid.

21. Ibid.

22. Ibid., pp. 168–69.

23. Quoted in "On the Wild Side."

24. Weller, "Girls in the Gang," p. 168.

25. "On the Wild Side."

26. Weller, "Girls in the Gang," p. 168.

27. Albert K. Cohen, *Delinquent Boys: The Culture of the Gang* (New York: Free Press, 1955).

28. Ibid., pp. 36–44.

29. Flowers, *The Adolescent Criminal*, p. 105.

30. Ibid.

31. Albert K. Cohen and James F. Short, Jr., "Research on Delinquent Subcultures," *Journal of Social Issues* 14, 3 (1958): 20–37.

32. Richard A. Cloward and Lloyd E. Ohlin, *Delinquency and Opportunity: A Theory of Delinquent Gangs* (New York: Free Press, 196).

33. Flowers, *The Adolescent Criminal*, p. 106.

34. Cloward and Ohlin, *Delinquency and Opportunity*, p. 80.

35. Ibid., p. 148.

36. Walter B. Miller, "Lower-Class Culture as a Generating Milieu of Gang Delinquency," *Journal of Social Issues* 14 (1958): 5–19.

37. Flowers, *The Adolescent Criminal*, p. 108.

Chapter 18. Girls in Custody

1. U.S. Department of Justice, *Public Juvenile Facilities, 1989: Children in Custody* (Washington, D.C.: Government Printing Office, 1991), p. 4.

2. U.S. Department of Justice, Bureau of Justice Statistics Special Report, *Survey of State Prison Inmates, 1991: Women in Prison* (Washington, D.C.: Government Printing Office, 1994), p. 2; U.S. Department of Justice, Bureau of Justice Statistics Special Report, *Women in Jail 1989* (Washington, D.C.: Government Printing Office, 1992), p. 3.

3. *Women in Jail 1989*, p.3; *Women in Prison*, p. 2.

4. Ronald B. Flowers, *Demographics and Criminality: The Characteristics of Crime in America* (Westport, Conn.: Greenwood Press, 1989), p. 176.

5. R. Barri Flowers, *The Adolescent Criminal: An Examination of Today's Juvenile Offender* (Jefferson, N.C.: McFarland & Co., 1990), p. 168.

6. Ibid.

7. John J. Downey, "Why Children Are in Jail and How to Keep Them Out," *Children* 17 (1970): 3–4.

8. See Flowers, *The Adolescent Criminal*, p. 168; Thomas J. Cottle, *Children in Jail: Seven Lessons in American Justice* (Boston: Beacon Press, 1977), pp. viii–ix.

9. Downey, "Why Children Are in Jail."

10. Cited in Flowers, *The Adolescent Criminal*, p. 168.

11. "Jailing Youth With Adults: A National Catastrophe," *Justice Assistance News* 1 (1980): 3.

12. William G. Nagle, "Prison Architecture and Prison Violence," in Albert K. Cohen, George F. Cole, and Robert G. Bailey, eds., *Prison Violence* (Lexington, Mass.: D. C. Heath, 1976), p. 105.

13. "When Children Go to Jail," *Newsweek* (May 27, 1985), pp. 87–89.

14. *Children in Custody*, p. 6.

15. Flowers, *Demographics and Criminality*, p. 176; U.S. Department of Justice, *Survey of Youth in Custody, 1987* (Washington, D.C.: Government Printing Office, 1988), p. 6.

16. *Survey of Youth in Custody, 1987*, p. 3.

17. Ibid., p. 4; Flowers, *The Adolescent Criminal*, pp. 171–79; Ronald B. Flowers, *Children and Criminality: The Child as Victim and Perpetrator* (Westport, Conn.: Greenwood Press, 1986), pp. 88, 101–2.

18. Flowers, *The Adolescent Criminal*, pp. 133–39.

19. Ibid., pp. 182–83; Christopher M. Sieverdes and Clemens Bartollas, "Modes of Adaptation and Game Behavior at Two Juvenile Institutions," in Paul C. Friday and V. Lorne Stewart, eds., *Youth Crime and Juvenile Justice: International Perspectives* (New York: Holt, Rinehart and Winston, 1977), pp. 27–35.

20. This case study was adapted from Mary Barbera-Hogan, "Teens Who Turn to Trouble: Inside Juvenile Hall," *Teen* (July 1986): pp. 42–45.

21. Ibid.

22. Ibid., p. 44.

23. Ibid.

24. Flowers, *The Adolescent Criminal*, p. 186.

25. R. M. Emerson, *Judging Delinquents: Context and Process in Juvenile Court* (Chicago: Aldine-Atherton, 1969), p. 219.

26. Cited in Flowers, *The Adolescent Criminal*, p. 187.

27. Howard N. Snyder and Terrence A. Finnegan, *Delinquency in the United States 1983* (Pittsburgh: National Center for Juvenile Justice, 1987), p. 11.

28. Flowers, *The Adolescent Criminal*, pp. 188–90.

Chapter 19. Women as Jail Inmates

1. U.S. Department of Justice, Bureau of Justice Statistics Bulletin, *Jail Inmates 1992* (Washington, D.C.: Government Printing Office, 1993), p. 2.

2. Ibid.

3. Ronald B. Flowers, *Women and Criminality: The Woman as Victim, Offender, and Practitioner* (Westport, Conn.: Greenwood Press, 1987), p. 161.

4. U.S. Department of Justice, *Women in Jail 1989* (Washington, D.C.: Government Printing Office, 1992), p. 3.

5. Ibid., p. 3.

6. Ibid., p. 9.

7. Ibid.

8. Ibid., p. 10.

9. Ibid.

10. Ibid.

11. Ibid.

12. Flowers, *Women and Criminality*, p. 161.

13. Ibid.

14. *Women in Jail 1989*, p. 2.

15. Flowers, *Women and Criminality*, p. 162.

16. Patsy Sims, "Women in Southern Jails," in Laura Crites, ed., *The Female Offender* (Lexington, Mass.: Lexington Books, 1976), p. 141.

17. Flowers, *Women and Criminality*, p. 162.

18. *Women in Jail 1989*, p. 8.

19. Ibid.

20. Sims, "Women in Southern Jails," p. 137.

21. Flowers, *Women and Criminality*, p. 162.

22. Sims, "Women in Southern Jails," p. 140.

Chapter 20. Women Prisoners

1. Sentenced inmates refers to prisoners with sentences of more than one year. U.S. Department of Justice, Bureau of Justice Statistics Bulletin, *Prisoners in 1993* (Washington, D.C.: Government Printing Office, 1994), p. 4.

2. U.S. Department of Justice, Bureau of Justice Statistics Special Report, *Survey of State Prison Inmates, 1991: Women in Prison* (Washington, D.C.: Government Printing Office, 1994), p. 9.

3. Ibid.

4. Ibid., p. 7.

5. U.S. Department of Justice, Bureau of Justice Statistics, *Survey of State Prison Inmates, 1991* (Washington, D.C.: Government Printing Office, 1993), p. 25.

6. *Women in Prison*, p. 9.

7. Ibid., p. 4.

8. Ibid.

9. Ibid., pp. 4–5.

10. Ibid., p. 5.

11. Ibid., pp. 3–6.

12. Ibid., p. 6.

13. Ronald B. Flowers, *Women and Criminality: The Woman as Victim, Offender, and Practitioner* (Westport, Conn.: Greenwood Press, 1987), p. 159.

14. Ibid.; Brenda G. McGowan and Karen L. Blumenthal, "Children of Women Prisoners: A Forgotten Minority," in Laura Crites, ed., *The Female Offender* (Lexington, Mass.: Lexington Books, 1976), p. 128.

15. Gerald A. McHugh, "Protection of the Rights of Pregnant Women in Prisons and Detention Facilities," *New England Journal on Prison Law* 6 (1980): 235–37.

16. Flowers, *Women and Criminality*, p. 160.

17. Ibid.

18. Ibid.

19. Coramae Richey Mann, *Female Crime and Delinquency* (University, Ala.: University of Alabama Press, 1984), pp. 230–31.

20. Flowers, *Women and Criminality*, p. 155.

21. Linda Singer, "Women and the Correctional Process," *American Criminal Law Review* 11 (1973): 301.

22. Ruth W. Glick and Virginia V. Neto, *National Study of Women's Correctional Programs* (Washington, D.C.: Government Printing Office, 1977), pp. 41–42.

23. Tom Goldstein, "Behind Prison Walls," *Cosmopolitan* 198 (November 1984): 261.

24. Kathryn Burkhart, *Women in Prison* (Garden City, N.Y.: Doubleday, 1973), p. 148.

25. Mann, *Female Crime and Delinquency*, p. 210.

26. Richard Deming, *Women: The New Criminals* (Nashville, Tenn.: Thomas Nelson, Inc., 1977), p. 159.

27. *Survey of State Prison Inmates, 1991: Women in Prison*, p. 10.

28. Burkhart, *Women in Prison*, p. 333.

29. Cited in Flowers, *Women and Criminality*, p. 157.

30. Marilyn G. Haft, "Women in Prison—Discriminatory Practices and Some Legal Solutions," *Clearinghouse Review* 8 (1974): 1–2.

31. Flowers, *Women and Criminality*, p. 159; Glick and Neto, *National Study of Women's Correctional Programs*, p. 79; Joan Potter, "In Prison, Women are Different," *Corrections Magazine* 4 (1978): 20.

32. Burkhart, *Women in Prison*, p. 303.

33. Helen E. Gibson, "Women's Prisons: Laboratories for Penal Reform," in Crites, ed., *The Female Offender*, p. 99.

34. Ibid.

Selected Bibliography

Adler, Freda. *Sisters in Crime: The Rise of the New Female Criminal*. New York: McGraw-Hill, 1975.

————, and Rita James Simon, eds. *The Criminology of Deviant Women*. Boston: Houghton Mifflin, 1979.

Ageton, Suzanne. "The Dynamics of Female Delinquency, 1976–1980." *Criminology* 21 (1983): 555–84.

Babcock, Barbara Allen. "Introduction: Women and the Criminal Law." *American Criminal Law Review* 11 (1973): 291–94.

Barrows, Sydney, and William Novak. *Mayflower Madam: The Secret Life of Sydney Biddle Barrows*. New York: Arbor House, 1986.

Benedek, Elissa P. "Women and Homicide." In Bruce L. Danto, John Bruhns, and Austin H. Kutscher, eds. *The Human Side of Homicide*. New York: Columbia University Press, 1982.

Benjamin, Henry, and R. E. L. Masters. *Prostitution and Morality*. New York: Julian Press, 1964.

Bowker, Lee H., ed. *Women, Crime, and the Criminal Justice System*. Lexington, Mass.: Lexington Books, 1978.

Bracey, Dorothy H. *"Baby-Pros": Preliminary Profiles of Juvenile Prostitutes*. New York: John Jay Press, 1979.

Braithwaite, John. "The Myth of Social Class and Criminality Reconsidered." *American Sociological Review* 46 (1981): 36–57.

"British Legal Debate: Premenstrual Tension and Criminal Behavior." *New York Times* (December 29, 1981): C3.

Brown, Waln K. "Black Female Gangs in Philadelphia." *International Journal of Offender Therapy and Comparative Criminology* 21 (1970): 221–29.

Bryan, James H. "Apprenticeship in Prostitution." *Social Problems* 12 (1965): 287–97.

————. "Occupational Ideologies and Individual Attitudes of Call Girls." *Social Problems* 13 (1966): 441–50.

Buffum, Peter C. "Homosexuality in Female Institutions." In Anthony M. Scacco, Jr., ed., *Male Rape: A Casebook of Sexual Aggressions*. New York: AMS Press, 1982.

Burkhart, Kathryn. *Women in Prison*. Garden City, N.Y.: Doubleday, 1973.

Burt, Marvin R., Thomas J. Glynn, and Barbara J. Sowder. *Psychosocial Character-istics of Drug-Abusing Women*. Rockville, Md.: U.S. Department of Health, Education, and Welfare, 1979.

Campbell, Anne. *Girl Delinquents*. New York: St. Martin's, 1981.

Carney, R. M., and B. D. Williams. "Premenstrual Syndrome: A Criminal De-fense." *Notre Dame Law Review* 59 (1983): 253–69.

Carpenter, Cheryl, Barry Blassner, Bruce D. Johnson, and Julia Loughlin. *Kids, Drugs, and Crime*. Lexington, Mass.: Lexington Books, 1988.

Cernkovich, Stephen A., and Peggy C. Giordano. "A Comparative Analysis of Male and Female Delinquency." *Sociological Quarterly* 20 (1979): 131–45.

Chapman, June Roberts. *Economic Realities and the Female Offender*. Lexington, Mass.: Lexington Books, 1980.

Cloward, Richard A., and Lloyd E. Ohlin. *Delinquency and Opportunity: A Theory of Delinquent Gangs*. New York: Free Press, 1960.

Cohen, Albert K. *Delinquent Boys: The Culture of the Gang*. New York: Free Press, 1955.

Collins, Glenn. "A Study Assesses Traits of Women Who Kill." *New York Times* (July 7, 1986): C18.

Cottle, Thomas J. *Children in Jail: Seven Lessons in American Justice*. Boston: Beacon Press, 1977.

Cowie, J., B. Cowie, and E. Slater. *Delinquency in Girls*. London: Heinemann, 1968.

Crites, Laura, ed. *The Female Offender*. Lexington, Mass.: Lexington Books, 1976.

Crowley, Maura G. "Female Runaway Behavior and Its Relationship to Prostitu-tion." M.S. thesis, Sam Houston State University, Institute of Contemporary Corrections and Behavioral Sciences, 1977.

Cuskey, Walter R., T. Premkumar, and Lois Siegel. "Survey of Opiate Addiction Among Females in the U.S. Between 1850 and 1970." In Freda Adler and Rita James Simon, eds., *The Criminology of Deviant Women*. Boston: Houghton Mifflin, 1979.

Dalton, K. "Menstruation and Crime." *British Medical Journal* 2 (1961): 1752–53.

Datesman, Susan K. "Women, Crime and Drugs." In James Inciardi, ed. *The Drugs-Crime Connection*. Beverly Hills: Sage Publications, 1981.

————, Frank R. Scarpitti, and Richard M. Stephenson. "Female Delinquency: An Application of Self and Opportunity Theories." *Journal of Research in Crime and Delinquency* 12 (1975): 120ff.

Davis, Kingsley. "The Sociology of Prostitution." *American Sociological Review* 2 (1937): 744–55.

Deming, Richard. *Women: The New Criminals*. Nashville, Tenn.: Thomas Nelson, 1977.

Densen-Gerber, Judianne, and S. F. Hutchinson. "Medical-Legal and Societal Problems Involving Children-Child Prostitution, Child Pornography, and Drug-Related Abuse: Recommended Legislation." In Selwyn M. Smith, ed., *The Male Treatment of Children*. Baltimore: University Park Press, 1978.

Dugdale, Richard L. *The Jukes: A Study in Crime, Pauperism, and Heredity*. New York: Putnam, 1877.

Elliott, Delbert S., Suzanne S. Ageton, David Huizinga, Brian Knowles, and Rochelle J. Canter. *The Prevalence and Incidence of Delinquent Behavior, 1976–1980*. Boulder, Colo.: Behavioral Research Institute, 1983.

Enablers, The. *Juvenile Prostitution in Minnesota: The Report of a Research Project*. St. Paul: The Enablers, 1978.

English, C. J. "Leaving Home: A Typology of Runaways." *Society* 10 (1973): 22–24.

Flanzer, Jerry P. *The Many Faces of Family Violence.* Springfield, Ill.: Charles C Thomas, 1982.

Flexner, Abraham. *Prostitution in Europe.* New York: Century, 1914.

Flowers, R. Barri. *The Adolescent Criminal: An Examination of Today's Juvenile Offender.* Jefferson, N.C.: McFarland, 1990.

————. *The Sex Slave Murders: The Brutal Odyssey of Gerald and Charlene Gallego.* Miami, Fla.: J. Flores Publications, 1995.

————. *The Victimization and Exploitation of Women and Children: A Study of Physical, Mental and Sexual Maltreatment in the United States.* Jefferson, N.C.: McFarland, 1994.

————. "Violent Women: Are They Catching Up to Violent Men or Have They Surpassed Them?" *ERIC Documents Reproduction Service,* No ED 301 496 (1989).

Flowers, Ronald Barri. *Children and Criminality: The Child as Victim and Perpetrator.* Wesport, Conn.: Greenwood, 1986.

————. *Demographics and Criminality: The Characteristics of Crime in America.* Westport, Conn.: Greenwood, 1989.

————. *Minorities and Criminality.* Westport, Conn.: Greenwood, 1988.

————. *Women and Criminality: The Woman as Victim, Offender, and Practitioner.* Westport, Conn.: Greenwood, 1987.

Freud, Sigmund. *New Introductory Letters on Psychoanalysis.* New York: W. W. Norton, 1933.

Geller, Anne, and Helene MacLean, "Substance Abuse." In Helene MacLean, ed. *Every Woman's Health: The Complete Guide to Body and Mind.* 5th edition. Garden City, N.Y.: Guild America Books, 1993.

Gelles, Richard J. *The Violent Home.* Beverly Hills: Sage Publications, 1987.

Gest, Ted. "Women Expand Their Roles in Crime, Too." *U.S. News and World Report* (November 12, 1984): 62.

Gibbens, T. C. "Female Offenders." *British Journal of Hospital Medicine* 6 (1971): 279–86.

Gibson, Helen E. "Women's Prisons: Laboratories for Penal Reform." In Laura Crites, ed., *The Female Offender.* Lexington, Mass.: Lexington Books, 1976.

Gil, David G. *Violence Against Children: Physical Child Abuse in the United States.* Cambridge: Harvard University Press, 1970.

Giordano, Peggy C. "Girls, Guys, and Gangs: The Changing Social Concept of Female Delinquency." *Journal of Criminal Law and Criminology* 69 (1978): 130ff.

Glick, Ruth W., and Virginia V. Neto. *National Study of Women's Correctional Programs.* Washington, D.C.: Government Printing Office, 1977.

Glueck, Sheldon, and Eleanor Glueck. *Five Hundred Delinquent Women.* New York: Knopf, 1934.

Goddard, Henry H. *Feeblemindedness, Its Causes and Consequences.* New York: Macmillan, 1914.

Goldstein, Paul J. *Prostitution and Drugs.* Lexington, Mass.: Lexington Books, 1979.

Gray, Diana. "Turning Out: A Study of Teenage Prostitution." M.S. thesis, University of Washington, 1971.

Greenwald, Harold. *The Elegant Prostitute: A Social and Psychoanalytic Study.* New York: Walker & Co., 1970.

Haberman, Paul W., and Michael M. Baden. *Alcohol, Other Drugs, and Violent Death*. New York: Oxford University Press, 1978.

Haft, Marilyn G. "Hustling For Rights." In Laura Crites, ed., *The Female Offender*. Lexington, Mass.: Lexington Books, 1976.

Harlan, Sparky, Luanne L. Rodgers, and Brian Slattery. *Male and Female Adolescent Prostitution: Huckleberry House Sexual Minority Youth Services Project*. Washington, D.C.: U.S. Department of Health and Human Services, 1981.

Harrison, Kathryn. "The Thrill of the Steal." *Mademoiselle* (October 1993): 186–87, 223–24.

Heidensohn, Frances M. *Women and Crime: The Life of the Female Offender*. New York: New York University Press, 1985.

Hersch, Patricia. "Coming of Age on City Streets." *Psychology Today* (January 1988): 28–37.

Hochstein, Rolaine. "Prostitutes: Happy Hookers or Society's Victims?" *Glamour* 83 (May 1985): 184–91.

Homer, Louise. "Criminality-Based Resource for Runaway Girls." *Social Casework* 10 (1973): 474ff.

Horney, Julie. "Menstrual Cycles and Criminal Responsibility." *Law and Human Behavior* 2, 1 (1978): 25–36.

Ignoto, Barbara. *Confessions of a Part-Time Call Girl*. New York: Dell, 1986.

Inciardi, James A. "Women, Heroin, and Property Crime." In Susan K. Datesman and Frank R. Scarpetti, eds. *Women, Crime, and Justice*. New York: Oxford University Press, 1980.

Inciardi, James A., and Anne E. Pottieger. "Drug Use and Crime Among Women Narcotics Users: An Empirical Assessment." *Journal of Drug Issues* 16, 1 (1986): 91–106.

James, Jennifer. *Entrance into Juvenile Prostitution*. Washington, D.C.: National Institute of Mental Health, 1980.

―――――. "Motivations for Entrance into Prostitution." In Laura Crites, ed. *The Female Offender*. Lexington, Mass.: Lexington Books, 1976.

―――――. "Prostitute-Pimp Relationships." *Medical Aspects of Human Sexuality* 7 (1973): 147–63.

Janowitz, Morris. *W. I. Thomas*. Chicago: University of Chicago Press, 1966.

Johnston, Lloyd D., Patrick M. O'Malley, and Jerald G. Bachman. *Drug Use Among High School Students, College Students, and Other Young Adults, National Trends Through 1985*. Rockville, Md.: National Institute on Drug Abuse, 1986.

Kandel, Denise B., Ora Simcha-Fagan, and Mark Davies. "Risk Factors for Delinquency and Illicit Drug Use from Adolescence to Young Adulthood." *Journal of Drug Issues* (Winter 1986): 67–90.

Karen, Robert. "The World of the Middle Class Prostitute." *Cosmopolitan* 202 (January 1987): 202–7.

Klein, Dorie. "The Etiology of Female Crime: A Review of the Literature." *Issues in Criminology* 8 (1973): 6ff.

Kobler, John. "Con Women of the World." *Cosmopolitan* 196 (April 1984): 247–49, 288–89.

Konopla, Gisela. *The Adolescent Girl in Conflict*. Englewood Cliffs, N.J.: Prentice-Hall, 1966.

Kratcoski, Peter C., and John E. Kratcoski. "Changing Patterns in the Delinquent Activities of Boys and Girls: A Self-Reported Delinquency Analysis." *Adolescence* 10, 37 (1975): 38–91.

Lee, Linda. "The World (and Underworld) of the Professional Call Girl." *New Woman* (January 1988): 60–63.

Leonard, Eileen B. *Women, Crime, and Society: A Critique of Theoretical Criminology.* New York: Longman, Inc., 1982.

Lidz, R., and T. Lidz. "Homosexual Tendencies in Mothers of Schizophrenic Women." *Journal of Nervous Mental Disorders* 149 (1969): 229ff.

Lombroso, Cesare, and William Ferrero. *The Female Offender.* New York: Appleton, 1900.

Lund, D. T. "Hot Blood's Record Month: Our Murder Boom." *Psychology Today* 9 (1975): 35–42.

McAuliffe, William E., and Robert A. Gordon. "A Test of Lindesmith's Theory of Addiction: The Frequency of Euphoria Among Long-term Addicts." *American Journal of Sociology* 79 (1974): 795–840.

McHugh, Gerald A. "Protection of the Rights of Pregnant Women in Prisons and Detention Facilities." *New England Journal on Prison Law* 6 (1980): 235–37.

MacVicar, Katherine, and Marcia Dillon. "Childhood and Adolescent Development of Ten Female Prostitutes." *Journal of the American Academy of Child Psychiatry* 19, 1 (1980): 148–49.

Mann, Coramae Richey. *Female Crime and Delinquency.* University, Ala.: University of Alabama Press, 1984.

Mayer, Adele. *Incest: A Treatment Manual for Therapy with Victims, Spouses, and Offenders.* Holmes Beach, Fla.: Learning Publications, 1982.

"The Men Raped by Women." *San Francisco Chronicle* (March 15, 1982): 5.

Miller, Larry. "The Lady is a White-Collar Criminal." *Cosmopolitan* 195 (July 1983): 227–30.

Miller, Walter B. "Lower-Class Culture as a Generating Milieu of Gang Delinquency." *Journal of Social Issues* 14 (1958): 5–19.

Millett, Kate. "Prostitution: A Quartet for Female Voices." In Vivian Gornick and Barbara K. Moran, eds., *Women in a Sexist Society.* New York: New American Library, 1971.

Morris, C. *The Tudors.* London: Fontana, 1967.

Morton, J. H., H. Addison, R. G. Hunt, and J. J. Sullivan. "A Clinical Study of Premenstrual Tension." *Journal of Obstetrics and Gynecology* 162 (1953): 1182–91.

Mrazek, Patricia B. "The Nature of Incest: A Review of Contributing Factors." In Patricia B. Mrazek and C. Henry Kempe, eds., *Sexually Abused Children and Their Families.* New York: Pergamon, 1981.

Nagel, Ilene H., and John Hagan. "Gender and Crime: Offense Patterns and Criminal Court Sanctions." In Michael Tonry and Norval Morris, eds. *Crime and Justice: An Annual Review of Research.* Vol. 4. Chicago: University of Chicago Press, 1983.

Nelson, Sandy. "Women Who Kill." *Sacramento Bee* (December 30, 1986): B1.

Newman, Frances, and Paula J. Caplan. "Juvenile Female Prostitution as a Gender Consistent Response to Early Deprivation." *International Journal of Women's Studies* 5, 2 (1981): 128–37.

Noblit, George W., and Janie M. Burcart. "Women and Crime, 1960–70." *Social Science Quarterly* 56 (1976): 656–57.

"On the Wild Side: Women in Gangs." *New York Times* (January 2, 1985): C8.

Piers, Maria W. *Infanticide.* New York: Norton, 1978.

Pollak, Otto. *The Criminality of Women.* Philadelphia: University of Philadelphia Press, 1950.

Pollock, Joy. "Early Theories of Female Criminality." In Lee H. Bowker, ed. *Women, Crime, and the Criminal Justice System.* Lexington, Mass.: Lexington Books, 1978.

Porterfield, Kay M. "Are Women as Violent as Men?" *Cosmopolitan* 197 (September 1984): 276–79.

Potter, Joan. "In Prison, Women Are Different." *Corrections Magazine* 4 (1978): 20ff.

Rasko, G. "The Victim of the Female Killer." *Victimology: An International Journal* 1 (1976): 396–402.

Reinholz, Mary. "An Intimate Look at the Life of a Call Girl." *Cosmopolitan* (August 1994): 110, 114.

Rosenbaum, Marsha. "Women Addicts' Experience of the Heroin World: Risk, Chaos, and Inundation." *Urban Life* 10, 1 (1981): 65–91.

Rosenblum, Karen E. "Female Deviance and the Female Sex Role: A Preliminary Investigation." *British Journal of Sociology* 26 (1975): 173–78.

Russell, Diana E. *Rape in Marriage.* New York: Macmillan, 1982.

Sanchez, Jose E., and Bruce D. Johnson. "Women and the Drugs-Crime Connection: Crime Rates Among Drug-Abusing Women at Rikers Island." *Journal of Psychoactive Drugs* 19, 2 (1987): 205–16.

Scacco, Anthony M., Jr., ed. *Male Rape: A Casebook of Sexual Aggressions.* New York: AMS Press, 1982.

Schlossman, Steven, and Stephanie Wallach. "The Crime of Precocious Sexuality: Female Juvenile Delinquency in the Progressive Era." *Harvard Educational Review* 48 (1978): 65–94.

"Sex Researcher's Report: The Men Raped by Women." *San Francisco Chronicle* (March 15, 1982): 5.

Shah, Saleem, and Loren Roth. "Biological and Psychological Factors in Criminality." In Daniel Glaser, ed. *Handbook of Criminology.* Chicago: Rand McNally, 1974.

Silbert, Mimi H. "Delancey Street Study: Prostitution and Sexual Assault." Summary of results. San Francisco: Delancey Street Foundation, 1982.

————. *Sexual Assault of Prostitutes: Phase One.* Washington, D.C.: National Institute of Mental Health, 1980.

Simon, Rita James. *Women and Crime.* Lexington, Mass.: D. C. Heath, 1975.

Sims, Patsy. "Women in Southern Jails." In Laura Crites, ed. *The Female Offender.* Lexington, Mass.: Lexington Books, 1976.

Singer, Linda. "Women and the Correctional Process." *American Criminal Law Review* 11 (1973): 301ff.

Smart, Carol. *Women, Crime and Criminology: A Feminist Critique.* London: Routledge & Kegan Paul, 1977.

Smith, Douglas, and Christy A. Visher. "Sex and Involvement in Deviance/Crime: A Quantitative Review of the Empirical Literature." *American Sociological Review* 45 (1980): 691–701.

Steele, Brandt F., and C. Pollock. "A Psychiatric Study of Parents Who Abuse Infants and Small Children." In Ray E. Helfer and C. Henry Kempe, eds. *The Battered Child.* Chicago: University of Chicago Press, 1968.

Steffensmeir, Darrell J., and Renee Hoffman Steffensmeir. "Trends in Female Delinquency: An Examination of Arrest, Juvenile Court, Self-Report and Field Data." *Criminology* 18 (1980): 62–85.

Steinmetz, Suzanne K. "The Battered Husband Syndrome." *Victimology: An International Journal* 2 (1978): 499–509.

Straus, Murray A., Richard J. Gelles, and Suzanne K. Steinmetz. *Behind Closed Doors: Violence in the American Family*. New York: Doubleday, 1980.

Tannahill, Reay. *Sex in History*. New York: Stein and Day, 1980.

Tec, Nechama. *Grass Is Green in Suburbia*. Roslyn Heights, N.Y.: Libra, 1974.

Temin, Carol Engel. "Discriminatory Sentencing of Women Offenders: The Argument for ERA in a Nutshell." *American Criminal Law Review* 11 (1973): 353–72.

Thomas, William I. *The Unadjusted Girl: With Cases and Standpoint for Behavior Analysis*. New York: Harper & Row, 1923.

Totman, J. *The Murderess: A Psychosocial Study of the Process*. Ann Arbor: University Microfilms, 1971.

U.S. Department of Health and Human Services. *Child Maltreatment 1992: Reports from the States to the National Center on Child Abuse and Neglect*. Washington, D.C.: Government Printing Office, 1994.

_____. *A Drug Retrospective: 1961-1980*. Washington, D.C.: Government Printing Office, 1980.

_____. *National Household Survey on Drug Abuse: Population Estimates 1991*. Rockville, Md.: National Institute on Drug Abuse, 1991.

_____. Substance Abuse and Mental Health Services Administration. *Preliminary Estimates from the 1992 National Household Survey on Drug Abuse*. Washington, D.C.: Government Printing Office, 1993.

U.S. Department of Justice. Bureau of Justice Statistics. *A National Report: Drugs, Crime, and the Justice System*. Washington, D.C.: Government Printing Office, 1992.

_____. Bureau of Justice Statistics. *Correctional Populations in the United States, 1991*. Washington, D.C.: Government Printing Office, 1993.

_____. Bureau of Justice Statistics. *Criminal Victimization in the United States, 1992: A National Crime Victimization Report*. Washington, D.C.: Government Printing Office, 1994.

_____. Bureau of Justice Statistics. *National Corrections Reporting Program, 1991*. Washington, D.C.: Government Printing Office, 1994.

_____. Bureau of Justice Statistics. *Sourcebook of Criminal Justice Statistics— 1992*. Washington, D.C.: Government Printing Office, 1993.

_____. Bureau of Justice Statistics. *Survey of State Prison Inmates, 1991*. Washington, D.C.: Government Printing Office, 1993.

_____. Bureau of Justice Statistics Bulletin. *Jail Inmates 1992*. Washington, D.C.: Government Printing Office, 1993.

_____. Bureau of Justice Statistics Bulletin. *Prisoners in 1993*. Washington, D.C.: Government Printing Office, 1994.

_____. Bureau of Justice Statistics Special Report. *HIV in U.S. Prisons and Jails*. Washington, D.C.: Government Printing Office, 1993.

_____. Bureau of Justice Statistics Special Report. *Survey of State Prison Inmates, 1991: Women in Prison*. Washington, D.C.: Government Printing Office, 1994.

_____. Bureau of Justice Statistics Special Report. *Survey of Youth in Custody, 1987*. Washington, D.C.: Government Printing Office, 1988.

_____. Bureau of Justice Statistics Special Report. *Tracking Offenders: White-Collar Crime*. Washington, D.C.: Government Printing Office, 1986.

_____. Bureau of Justice Statistics Special Report. *Women in Jail 1989*. Washington, D.C.: Government Printing Office, 1992.

_____. Juvenile Justice Bulletin. *Public Juvenile Facilities, 1987: Children in Custody*. Washington, D.C.: Government Printing Office, 1988.

————. Juvenile Justice Bulletin. *Public Juvenile Facilities, 1989: Children in Custody*. Washington, D.C.: Government Printing Office, 1991.

————. National Institute of Justice. *Characteristics of Different Types of Drug-Involved Offenders*. Washington, D.C.: Government Printing Office, 1988.

U.S. Federal Bureau of Investigation. *Crime in the United States: Uniform Crime Reports 1992*. Washington, D.C.: Government Printing Office, 1993.

Vanderbilt, Heidi. "Incest: A Chilling Report." *Lear's* (February 1992): 50–76.

Walker, Lenore E. *The Battered Woman Syndrome*. New York: Springer, 1984.

Ward, D., M. Jackson, and R. Ward. "Crimes of Violence by Women." In D. Mulvill, M. M. Tumin, and L. A. Curtis, eds. *Crimes of Violence*. Washington, D.C.: Government Printing Office, 1969.

Weis, Joseph G. "Liberation and Crime: The Invention of the New Female Criminal." *Crime and Social Justice* 6 (1976): 17–27.

Weisberg, D. Kelly. *Children of the Night: A Study of Adolescent Prostitution*. Lexington, Mass.: Lexington Books, 1985.

Weller, Sheila. "Girls in the Gang: A Nineties Nightmare." *Cosmopolitan* (August 1994): 167–69.

West, Dorothy. "I Was Afraid to Shut My Eyes." In Anthony M. Scacco, Jr., ed. *Male Rape: A Casebook of Sexual Aggressions*. New York: AMS Press, 1982.

"When Children Go to Jail." *Newsweek* (May 27, 1985): 87–89.

Winick, Charles, and Paul M. Kinsie. *The Lively Commerce: Prostitution in the United States*. Chicago: Quadrangle Books, 1971.

Wise, Nancy. "Juvenile Delinquency Among Middle-Class Girls." In Edmund Vaz, ed. *Middle-Class Juvenile Delinquency*. New York: Harper & Row, 1967.

Woolston, Howard B. *Prostitution in the United States*. New York: Century, 1921.

Zaccaro, John, Jr. "Children of the Night." *Woman's Day* (March 29, 1988): 80–81.

Index

Abuse 90, 95, 98, 195; alcohol 35, 75, 93, 116, 153, 157, 161–63, 165–67, 174, 187, 195, 209–13, 227, 229–30, 233; child 72, 73, 75–77, 87–88, 90, 113, 115, 137, 177; conjugal 74; cycle of 74–75, 233; drug 8, 10, 25, 35, 40, 47, 49, 52, 75, 77, 93, 115–24, 141, 144, 153, 157, 160, 163, 165–67, 174, 187, 195, 196, 209–13, 227, 229–30, 233; family 74, 95; parent 90; physical 88, 98, 144, 146, 149, 152, 189, 212, 214, 234; psychological 77; sexual 73–75, 91, 98, 111, 113, 133–34, 144–45, 149, 177, 189, 195, 212, 214, 234; spouse 90, 93; substance 40, 62, 72, 75, 87–88, 95, 112–13, 121, 137, 145–47, 153, 158–60, 165–66, 174, 199, 233; tranquilizer 93; *see also* Child abuse; Child neglect; Domestic violence; Drug abuse; Drug addicts; Family violence
Adler, Alfred 67
Adler, Freda 55, 57, 154, 179
Aftercare 198
Aggravated assault 8, 10, 13, 38, 49, 55, 193
AIDS (Acquired Immune Deficiency Syndrome) 101, 113–14, 115, 121, 141, 147–48, 156, 230
Alcohol abuse 35, 75, 93, 116, 153, 157, 161–63, 165–67, 174, 187, 195, 209–13, 227, 229–30, 233; *see also* Alcohol-related crimes

Alcohol-related crimes 39–40, 49, 52, 157–60, 195
All other offenses 8, 35
American Humane Association (AHA) 92
American Indians 27, 202; *see also* Native Americans
American Journal of Obstetrics and Gynecology 89
Arrest(s) 5, 10, 13–20, 26–27, 58, 62, 76; for alcohol-related crimes 39–40, 52, 157–60; by community size 11–13; Crime Index 13, 26; for drug abuse violations 10, 40, 47, 52, 116, 158, 160; for drug-related offenses 39–40, 52, 157–60; female 8, 13, 26, 46, 49, 51, 58, 82; for female sex offenses 43; frequency of 35; of juveniles 53–55, 62, 158–60; larceny-theft 168–71, 175; male 44, 46–49, 51, 58; for murder and nonnegligent manslaughter 82–84; for offenses against family and children 90–91; and preferential treatment 69; property crime 36–37, 47, 51, 55, 58, 62; for prostitution and commercialized vice 43, 104–5, 141, 148, 150; rate of female 10, 58; ratios and gender 46–49; of runaways 27, 141; statistics 5, 38, 90, 134, 157–60; trends 13, 16–20, 58, 62, 83–84, 126, 131, 134, 141, 159, 171, 175; violent crime 26–27, 38, 47, 49, 55, 58, 62, 120, 131; for

white-collar offenses 38–39, 126–27,
130; *see also* Alcohol abuse; Child
abuse; Crime(s); Delinquency;
Domestic violence; Drug abuse;
Female crime; Homicide; Juveniles;
Murder; Official statistics; Property
crimes; Prostitutes; Prostitution;
Uniform Crime Reports (UCR); Violent crimes
Arson 8, 35, 51, 89
Asians 27, 35, 84, 179, 202, 224
Assaults 8, 10, 76, 89, 113, 126; aggravated 8, 10, 13, 38, 49, 55; minor
62; other 8, 10, 13, 55; physical 189,
214; sexual 132–34, 189, 199, 214;
simple 8, 23, 193; *see also* Victimization; Violence; Violent crime(s)
Atavism 66

Barfield, Margie Velma 81
Barrows, Sydney 110, 113
Battered men 93
Battered women 72, 74, 86–87, 93
Battered women's syndrome 87
Baunach, Phyllis 128
Bechtel, J. A. 142
Benedek, Elissa P. 86
Benjamin, Harry 105
Biological theories 65–67
Blacks 27, 35, 76, 84, 92, 105, 110,
118, 136, 143–44, 151, 160, 179, 192,
202, 209, 212, 217, 224, 229–31,
233–34, 237
Bohnstedt, Marvin 92
Borden, Lizzie 81, 89
"Born criminals" 65–66
The Boujoo 135–36
Bowman, Barbara 128
Bracey, Dorothy H. 154
Broken homes 72, 111, 137, 152, 212,
234
Brown, Sandra 128–29
Brown, Waln K. 179
Bryan, James H. 111
Bucy, June 147
Bulcroft, M. 94
Burcart, Janie M. 58
Bureau of Justice Statistics, (BJS) 23,
27, 128, 212, 227
Bureau of the Census 23

Burglary 8, 23, 36, 58, 71, 171, 175
Burkhart, Kathryn 236–37

Call girls 101, 110–14; high class 110–
11, 114; *see also* Prostitutes; Prostitution
Campbell, Anne 173, 180
Canton, Carol 144
Carpenter, Cheryl 166–67, 174
Centers for Disease Control (CDC)
113
Cernkovich, Stephen A. 55, 62, 70
Child abandonment 93
Child abuse 72–77, 87, 88, 90–93,
95, 98, 113, 115, 137, 152, 177; age
and abusive women 91–92; causes of
95; characteristics of abusive women
92–93; and drug use 115, 121; female
child abusers 91–92; physical 73; and
prostitution 152; race, ethnicity, and
92; *see also* Abuse; Sexual abuse;
Victimization
Child Abuse Prevention and Treat-
ment Act (CAPTA) 91
Child maltreatment 75–76, 91–93, 95;
causes of 95
Child molestation 145
Child neglect 73, 74, 88, 91–92, 95,
113, 177
Child pornography 148, 152
Child prostitution 142, 148
Child sexual abuse 73–75, 133–34
Chivalry 130
Cloward, Richard A. 182–83
Cohen, Albert K. 181–82
Commercialized vice 8, 27, 43–44,
47, 53, 142; *see also* Prostitutes;
Prostitution
Con artists 134–37, 196
Confidence games 120, 131, 134–37
Conflict theory 68
Conformists 196
Conjugal abuse 74
Cooke, W. R. 89
Covenant House 147, 156
Cowie, J. 66
Cox, Frances 128
Cressey, Donald R. 20
Crime, juvenile 53–55; *see also* Delin-
quency

Crime in the United States: Uniform Crime Reports 5

Crime Index 8, 10, 13, 18, 26–27, 35, 49, 62, 168–69

Crime(s): aggravated assault 8, 10, 13, 38, 49, 55, 193; alcohol-related 39–40, 49, 52, 157–60, 195; all other offenses 8, 35, 49; arson 8, 35, 51; assaults 8, 10, 13, 37, 55, 62; burglary 8, 23, 36, 71, 171, 175; and class 35; con games 120, 134–37; curfew and loitering law violations 55, 142; disorderly conduct 49, 55; distribution of female 8–9; domestic violence 70, 75–77, 87, 90–95, 134, 195; driving under the influence 8, 27, 40, 158, 160, 162; drug abuse violations 8, 10, 40, 47, 49, 52, 116, 158–60; drug-related 39–40, 43, 49, 52, 157–60, 195, 199; drug trafficking 75, 116, 227; drunkenness 40, 52, 158, 160, 162; embezzlement 38, 58, 125–27, 171; extent of 5–25; female 5–27, 37; forcible rape 8, 38, 43, 47, 49, 131; forgery and counterfeiting 38–39, 58, 125–27; fraud 8, 38–39, 43, 58, 125–27, 136, 227; frequency of female 35; gambling 35; gender and juvenile 53–55, 59–62; hidden 69, 91; homicide 43, 75, 82–84, 87; incest 96–100, 112; *Index* 8, 10, 13, 18, 26–27, 35, 49, 62, 126, 168–69; infanticide 69, 76, 84–86; kidnapping 25, 81; larceny 23, 58, 71, 126; larceny-theft 8, 10, 35–36, 43, 51, 130, 145, 153, 168–71, 174–75, 193, 227; liquor law violations 40, 52, 158, 160, 162; motor vehicle theft 8, 10, 13, 23, 36–37, 49, 58, 171, 176; murder 8, 25, 35, 38, 76, 81–89, 141, 193, 217, 227; nature of female 26–43; nonindex 19, 27, 47; non-negligent manslaughter 8, 35, 82, 84; nonviolent 35; petty 147, 153, 168; property 8, 10, 36–37, 44, 47, 49, 55, 58, 62, 75, 120, 125, 157, 166, 188, 193, 203, 209, 227; prostitution and commercialized vice 8, 25, 27, 44, 47, 53, 70, 101–15, 120, 141–42, 148–57, 166–67, 177; rape 8, 23, 70, 109, 131–34, 141, 148, 156; rates 10–11; reported 8, 20; robbery 8, 23, 38, 43, 49, 71, 113, 120, 126, 153; runaways 8, 13, 27, 44, 47, 53, 62, 72, 75–77, 111, 113, 141–47, 149, 157, 166–67, 174, 195; sex 6, 40, 75, 166; shoplifting 62, 66, 69, 120, 166, 168, 172–74, 176–77; simple assaults 8, 23, 193; stolen property-related 51, 58, 171, 175–76; street 35; suspicion 35; vagrancy 8, 35; vandalism 8, 36, 49, 51, 58, 145, 193; victimless 25; violent 8, 10, 13, 18–19, 23, 27, 35, 37–38, 44, 47, 49, 55, 88, 62, 75–76, 89, 115, 120, 125, 131, 141, 157, 166, 188, 203, 209, 227; white-collar 38–39, 125–31; *see also* Drug abuse; Female crime; Property crime(s); Prostitutes; Prostitution; Rape; Runaways; Violent crime(s); White-collar crimes

Criminal justice system 69, 76, 121, 166

Criminal laws 157, 162

Criminal Victimization in the United States: A National Crime Victimization Survey 23

Criminality 5, 44, 55, 58, 65–71, 137; adult 74; age and female 26–27; black female 27; and class 35; and criminal subculture 137; delinquency 5, 44, 55, 62; dynamics of 5–78; extent of female 22; factors linked to female 72–78; female 5–25, 44, 58, 62, 66–67, 70–72, 75–76, 88; female homicide 82–89; male 5; and menstruation 66–67, 76–77, 88–89; and mental illness 76; nature of female 22; property 58; scope of female 5–8; theories on female 65–71; trends in female 13, 16–20; violent 89; white female 27; women's 71; *see also* Crime(s); Delinquency; Female crime; Inmates; Prisoners

The Criminality of Women (Pollak) 68

Crites, Laura 71

Crowley, Maura G. 72, 73, 152

Curfew and loitering law violations 55, 142

Datesman, Susan K. 70
Delinquency 5, 20, 35, 44, 55, 59,
61–62, 74, 77, 157, 166–67, 181, 195;
cycle of 75, 195; factors in female
72–78; and family cycle of abuse
74–75; female 5, 20, 59, 62, 66–67,
70, 75, 157; and gangs 178–81;
genetics and female 66; juvenile 55,
59, 62, 166–67; male 62, 70; male-
female ratio of 62; nature of 59–62;
rates of 35, 62; and self-report
surveys 55, 62, 70; and substance
abuse 166–67; theories on female
65–71; trends 59–62; see also Juvenile
detention; Juveniles; Runaways;
Status offenses
Delinquents: boy 72; female 66, 72;
girl 72, 195; juvenile 147 and
recidivism, 77–78.
Disorderly conduct 49, 55
Diversionary programs 198
Division of Adolescent Medicine at the
Children's Hospital of Los Angeles
144
Domestic violence 70, 74–77, 87,
90–95, 134, 195; causes of 94–95; see
also Child abuse; Violence
Driving under the influence 8, 27, 40,
49, 158, 160, 162
Drug abuse 25, 35, 77, 93, 115–24,
141, 153, 157, 160, 163–67, 174, 187,
195–196, 209–13, 227, 229–30, 233;
and AIDS 121; and alcohol abuse
157, 163, 165–67, 195, 209–13; and
child abuse 121; and drug addicts
107, 115, 117–21, 128, 156, 163, 166,
174; and drug dealers 77, 115,
165–66; female inmates and 209–13,
227, 229–30; and gangs 182; and
girl inmates 195; girls and 157,
163–67; and girls' theft crimes 194;
illegal drugs and 116–19; and juvenile
delinquency 166–67; of parents 195,
212–13, 233; prescription 121, 124;
and prostitution 109–10, 153,
166–67; scope of women's 115–16;
women and cocaine 119–20; women
offenders and 120–21; see also
Alcohol abuse; Drug abuse violations; Drug-related offenses;
Substance abuse

Drug abuse violations 8, 10, 40, 47,
49, 52, 116, 158–60; see also Drug
abuse; Substance abuse
Drug addicts 107, 115, 117–20, 128,
156, 163, 166, 174, 182
Drug dealing 77, 115, 121, 156,
165–66, 209, 227
Drug-related offenses 39–40, 43, 49,
52, 157–60, 195, 199, 203
Drug trafficking 75, 116, 227
Drunkenness 40, 52, 158, 160, 162
Dugdale, Richard L. 74
Duncan, Elizabeth Ann 81

Embezzlement 38, 58, 125–27, 171
Emerson, R. M. 197
English, C. J. 145
English, Christine 89
Ethnicity 27, 35, 75–76, 92, 105, 151,
217
Evert, Kathy 97, 99
Exhibitionism 69, 97

Faison, Claudette 181
Family abuse 74, 95; see also Child
abuse; Domestic violence
Family offenses 75, 90
Family violence 74–75, 88, 90, 94
Federal Bureau of Investigation (FBI)
5, 87, 90, 104
Female crime 5–78; alcohol-related
39–40, 49, 52, 157–60, 195; arrest
trends 13–20, 62; and class 35;
comparison of 11–13; in comparison
to male crime 44–62; con artists
134–37; distribution of 8–9; domestic violence 70, 75–77, 87, 90–95;
and drug abuse 120–21, 157, 163–65;
drug-related 39–40, 43, 49, 52,
157–60, 195; extent of 5–25; factors
in 72–78; frequency of 35; gender
and 53–55; girls in gangs 178–80;
hidden 69, 91; homicidal women
81–89; incestuous women 96–100;
and the menstrual cycle 66–67,
76–77, 88–89; and mental illness 76;
nature of 26–43; property crimes
36–37, 43, 51, 55, 58, 62, 125–30,
166, 193, 203, 209, 227; prostitution

and commercialized vice 43–44, 53, 101–14, 148–56, 166–67, 177; race and ethnicity 27, 35, 75–76, 92, 105, 151, 217; rapists 131–34; rates 10–11, 58; runaways 8, 13, 27, 44, 47, 53, 62, 72, 75–77, 111, 113, 141–47, 157; status offenses 141, 147, 157, 162, 187–88, 195; and substance abuse 75; and theft crimes 168–77, 193; theories on 65–71; violent crime 37–38, 43, 49, 55, 58, 62, 74–77, 89, 115, 131, 166, 193, 203, 209, 227; *see also* Alcohol abuse; Arrests; Crime(s); Drug abuse; Offenses; Prisoners; Prostitutes; Prostitution
Female pedophiles 99
Female rapists 131–34
Females in custody 21–22; *see also* Inmates; Jail; Juvenile detention; Prisoners; Prison(s)
Ferrero, William 65–66, 89
Fleiss, Heidi 101
Flexner, Abraham 102
Flowers, Ronald Barri 87
Fontana, Vincent J. 73
Ford, Gerald 81
Forgery and counterfeiting 38–39, 58, 125–27
Fraud 8, 10, 38–39, 43, 58, 125–27, 136, 227
"Frayed-collar" crimes 129
French, Deloris 111
Freud, Sigmund 67, 69
Fromme, Lynette "Squeaky" 81
Frosch, William 137

Gallego, Charlene Williams 81
Gambling 35
Gangs 146, 178–84; conflict 183; criminal 183; and ethnicity 179; extent of girls in 178–79; girls in 178–84; juvenile 178–84; nature of girl gang members 179–81; and race 179; retreatist 183; and social status 179; why girls join gangs 181; *see also* Delinquency; Juveniles
Gayford, J. 75
Gelles, Richard J. 91, 93–95
Gibbens, T. C. 66
Gibson, Helen E. 238

Gil, David G. 91–92, 95
Giordano, Peggy C. 55, 62, 70, 179
Glick, Ruth W. 27, 235, 238
Glueck, Eleanor 68
Glueck, Sheldon 68
Goddard, Henry H. 74
Gold, Martin 62
Goldstein, Paul J. 102, 105–6
Gray, Diana 152
Greenwald, Harold 111
Groth, Nicholas 97, 133

Handkerchief switch, the 135–36
Hardman, Dale G. 179
Harris, Jean 81
Haskell, Martin R. 73
Hersch, Patricia 147, 156
Hidden crime 69, 91
Hildebrand, James A. 144
Hindelang, Michael 62
Hispanics 35, 76, 84, 92, 110, 118, 136, 143, 151, 160, 179, 192, 202, 224, 229, 231, 233, 237
Holzer, Adela 128
Homer, Louise 144
Homicidal women 81–89
Homicide 43, 75, 82–84, 87, 126, 234
Horney, Karen 67
Howard Street (Heard) 102
Huckleberry House 72–73, 152
Hudson, Mary 128
Human Immunodeficiency Virus (HIV) 113, 156, 230–31
Humphrey, John 88

Immigration charges 43
Incarceration 22, 76, 103, 120, 199, 203, 212; and ethnicity 76, 202, 217, 224; for prostitution 103; and race 76, 202–3, 217, 224; rate of 22, 199, 215–17; and white-collar offenders 130; *see also* Inmates; Inmates, black; Inmates, Hispanic; Inmates, non-Hispanic; Inmates, white; Jail(s); Juvenile detention; Prison(s); Prisoners; Prostitutes; Prostitution
Incest 73, 76, 96–100, 112, 132, 148, 152; defining 96–97; extent of 97; and girl prostitutes 152; mother-

daughter 99; mother-son 99; nature
of female 97–98; *see also* Child
abuse; Sexual abuse
Incestuous women 96–100; *see also*
Incest
Infanticide 69, 76, 84–86
Inmates 21–22, 44, 78, 116, 150, 179,
195; background dysfunction and
abuse of female jail 212–13; background factors of girl 195; black 35,
192, 203, 212, 217, 224, 229–30,
233–34, 237; characteristics of
female jail 202–3; characteristics of
female prison 225–27; on death row
217; and drug use/abuse 116, 120,
209–12, 227, 229–30; female 21–22,
44, 73–76, 78, 116, 134, 199; as first-
time offenders 209; girl 195; girl jail
187–88; Hispanic 35, 192, 202, 224,
229, 231, 233–34, 237; HIV and
AIDS 230–31; jail 21, 44, 187, 199–
215; juvenile 188–92; life of female
235–36; male 44, 233; non–Hispanic
202, 217, 224; offenses incarcerated
for 227; prison 21–22, 44, 187; prison
gangs 179; and recidivism 195, 232;
runaways as 150; sentence length for
female 233; and status offenses
187–88; white 35, 192, 202–3, 209,
212, 217, 224, 229, 233–34, 237;
women 116, 120, 133, 199–214,
215–39; *see also* Drug abuse; Drug
addicts; Incarceration; Juvenile
detention; Prisoners; Runaways;
Status offenses

Jail(s) 22, 44, 130, 187–89, 199–214;
criminal history of jailed women
203–9; drug and alcohol abuse
history of women 209–12; extent of
women in 199–200; females in 22,
44, 187–89, 199–214; girls in 187–89;
male inmates 44; women in 22, 72,
73, 103, 199–215; women's sexual
and physical abuse in 199, 214; *see
also* Inmates; Prisoners; Prison(s)
James, Jennifer 71, 107–8, 111–12, 150,
152, 154–55
Justice, Blair 91–92, 95
Justice, Rita 92, 95

Juvenile delinquency 55, 59, 62,166–
67, 232; and girls' substance abuse
166–67; *see also* Delinquency; Delinquents; Status offenses
Juvenile detention 22, 54, 72, 147,
187, 189–92; girls in private juvenile
facilities 21–22, 189–92; girls in
public juvenile facilities 21–22, 72,
187, 189–92, 195; in long-term
juvenile facilities 72, 195; males in
private juvenile facilities 54, 72, 191;
males in public juvenile facilities 54,
72, 191; *see also* Jail(s); Prison(s)
Juvenile gangs 178–84
Juvenile justice system 69, 166, 198
Juveniles 35, 53–55, 61–62, 78, 111,
157, 160, 163, 182; female 53–55,
61–62, 157, 160, 162–63, 187, 232;
gangs 178–84; institutionalized 193;
male 53–55, 61–62, 163, 181; *see also*
Delinquency; Delinquents; Juvenile
detention

Kennedy, Jim 156
Kidnapping 25, 81, 154
King Nimrod 85
Kinsie, Paul M. 102
Kirkpatrick, John 88
Klein, Dorie 70
Konopla, Gisela 67
Kratcoski, John E. 55, 161, 163
Kratcoski, Peter C. 55, 161, 163
Kumili, Kurt 179, 181

Langley, Robert 93
Larceny 23, 58, 71, 126; *see also*
Larceny-theft
Larceny-theft 8, 10, 35–36, 43, 51, 55,
69, 130, 145, 153, 166, 168–71, 174–75,
193, 227; *see also* Property Crime(s)
Law enforcement 91, 130, 166, 168, 179
Lee, Linda 110
Lemert, Edwin M. 102
Levy, Richard C. 93
Lewis, D. 73
Lidz, R. 100
Lidz, T. 100
Liquor law violations 40, 52, 158, 160,
162

Little, Joanne 214
Lombroso, Cesare 65–67, 69, 89
Los Angeles's Central Juvenile Hall 196
Lourie, R. 95
Lower-class culture theory 181, 184
Lower-class prostitutes 110, 113; *see also* Streetwalkers
Lunde, D. T. 85

Mann, Coramae 111
Manslaughter 84, 88–89
Marital violence 93–94; *see also* Battered women; Domestic violence
Markson, Lillian 128
Martin, Michael J. 93
Masters, R. E. L. 105
Masters, William 132–33
Mathews, Ruth 98–99
Mayer, Adele 98
Medlicott, R. 100
Menstrual cycle 66–67, 76–77, 88–89
Mental illness 72, 76, 87, 88, 146
Metropolitan Statistical Areas (MSAs) 11
Middle-class prostitutes 108–10, 112; *see also* Prostitutes; Prostitution
Miller, Stuart J. 133
Miller, Walter B. 179–80, 184
Millett, Kate 103
Milowe, J. 95
Moore, Sara Jane 81
Morton, J. H. 76
Motor vehicle theft 8, 10, 13, 23, 36–37, 49, 58, 171, 176
Mrazek, Patricia 75
Murder 8, 25, 35, 38, 76, 81–89, 141, 193, 217, 227; *see also* Homicide; Nonnegligent manslaughter

National Cocaine Hotline 165
National Committee for Prevention of Child Abuse (NCPCA) 91
National Crime Victimization Survey (NCVS) 23, 25, 46, 77, 90
National Institute for Mental Health 126
National Institute of Justice (NIJ) 120–21

National Institute on Drug Abuse (NIDA) 117, 162
National Network of Runaway and Youth Services 146–47
National Task Force on Prostitution 113
Native Americans 35, 84, 118, 151, 160, 224
Neto, Virginia V. 27, 235, 238
New Testament 84
New York Police Department 109
New York Psychiatric Institute 76, 144
New York Youth at Risk 181
Noblit, George W. 58
Nonnegligent manslaughter 8, 35, 82, 84
Nonresidential day treatment programs 198
North Carolina Correctional Center for Women 84
Nye, F. Ivan 55

O'Brien, J. E. 94
Offenders 22–23, 44, 46, 66, 190, 197–98; criminal 175; and drug abuse 120–21; female 23, 44, 46, 65–66, 82, 121, 175; female juvenile 22; first-time 209; girl 168, 187, 197–98; juvenile 187, 190; male 23, 44, 46; multiple 23, 46; noninstitutional dispositions for girl 197–98; repeat 215, 232; sex 98–100; single 23, 46; white-collar 130; women 115, 120–21; *see also* Delinquents; Prisoners
Offenses 5, 8, 35, 49, 57; against family and children 13, 69, 75, 90–91; against persons 193; aggravated assault 8, 10, 13, 38, 49, 55, 193; alcohol abuse 35; alcohol-related 39–40, 49, 52, 157–60, 195; arson 8, 35, 51; assaults 8, 10, 13, 37, 55, 62; burglary 8, 23, 36, 58, 71, 171, 175; con games 120, 134–37; Crime Index 8, 10, 13, 18, 26–27, 35, 49, 62, 126, 168–69; criminal 96, 193; curfew and loitering law violations 55, 142; disorderly conduct 49; domestic violence 70, 75–77, 87, 90–95; driving under the influence 8, 27, 40, 158, 160, 162; drug 203, 209, 212, 227; drug

abuse violations 8, 10, 40, 47, 49, 52, 116, 158–60; drug-related 39–40, 43, 49, 52, 157–60, 195 199; drug trafficking 75, 227; drunkenness 40, 52, 158, 160, 162; embezzlement 38, 58, 125–27, 171; forcible rape 8, 13, 38, 43, 47, 49, 131; forgery and counterfeiting 38–39, 58, 125–27; fraud 8, 10, 38–39, 43, 58, 125–27, 136, 227; frequency of 35; gambling 35; homicide 43, 75, 82–84, 87; immigration charges 43; incest 96–100, 112; infanticide 69, 76, 84–86; larceny 23, 58, 71, 126; larceny-theft 8, 10, 35–36, 43, 51, 55, 130, 145, 153, 168–71, 174–75, 193, 227; liquor law violations 40, 52, 158, 160, 162; motor vehicle theft 8, 10, 13, 23, 36–37, 49, 58, 171, 176, 193; murder and nonnegligent manslaughter 8, 25, 35, 38, 76, 81–89, 193, 217, 227; nonindex 8, 13, 19, 27, 47; property 120, 157, 166, 193, 227; prostitution and commercialized vice 8, 25, 43–44, 47, 53, 70, 101–15, 120, 141–42, 148–57, 166–67, 177; public-order 43, 125, 203, 227; rape 8, 23, 70, 109, 131–34, 141, 148, 156; robbery 8, 23, 38, 43, 49, 71, 113, 120, 126, 153; runaways 8, 13, 44, 47, 53, 55, 62, 75, 111, 113, 141–47, 157, 174; sex 43; shoplifting 62, 66, 69, 120, 166, 168, 172–74, 176–77; simple assaults 23, 193; status 141, 147, 157, 162, 187– 88, 195; stolen property-related 51, 58, 171, 175–76; substance abuse 158; suspicion 35; vagrancy 8, 35; vandalism 8, 36, 47, 49, 51, 58, 145, 193; violent 120, 130, 157, 203, 227; weapons-related charges 43, 47; white-collar 38–39, 125–31; see also Arrests; Crime(s); Delinquency; Drug abuse; Drug abuse violations; Drug dealing; Drug-relateld offenses; Homicide; Murder; Nonnegligent manslaughter; Property crime(s); Prostitutes; Prostitution; Rape; Runaways; Sex crimes; Sexual abuse; Violent crimes; White-collar crimes
Offenses against family and children 13, 69, 75, 90–91; see also Child abuse; Child neglect; Domestic violence
Official statistics 20, 27, 55, 57–59, 69, 92; see also Arrest(s), statistics; National Crime Victimization Survey (NCVS); Self-report surveys; Uniform Crime Reports (UCR)
Ohlin, Lloyd E. 182–83
Old Testament 84
Opportunistic theory 70, 129, 181–84
Ounsted, Christopher 75

Pacific Islanders 35, 224; see also Asians, Native Americans
Parent abuse 90; see also Child abuse; Domestic violence
Parker, Bonnie 81
Parole 217
Paternalism 130
Penn, Frances 128
Pennsylvania State Correctional Institution for Women 236
Physical abuse 88, 98, 144, 146, 149, 152, 189, 212, 214, 234; see also Child abuse; Domestic violence
Piers, Maria W. 85
Pimps 77, 107–9, 135, 146–48, 153–54, 156; see also Prostitutes; Prostitution; Streetwalkers
Pincus, C. 91
Pocketbook drop, the 135
Polansky, Norman A. 75
Pollak, Otto 68–69
Powell, Bernadette 81
Premenstrual syndrome (PMS) 66–67, 76–77, 88–89
Prisoners 5, 21–22, 35, 43–44, 65, 77, 215–39; American Indian 202; Asian 35, 202, 224; black 192, 202–3, 209, 217, 224, 230, 234, 237; black female 27, 35, 209, 212, 229–31, 233; characteristics of female 225–27; and child abuse 73; and drug-related offenses 116, 120, 195, 199, 203, 209, 212, 227; and drug trafficking 116, 227; and drug use/abuse 75, 116, 120, 209–12, 227, 229–30; extent of female 21–22, 215–17; family and abuse history of female 233–34;

federal 22, 35, 43–44, 215–16, 224; female 22, 27, 35, 43, 65, 134; health care for female 237; Hispanic 35, 192, 202, 224, 229, 231, 233, 237; HIV, AIDS, and women 230–31; incarcerated mothers 234–35; in jail 22, 44, 72, 187–89, 199–215; life in prison for women 235–36; in long-term juvenile facilities 72, 187, 195; male 215; Native American 35, 224; new court commitments 43; non–Hispanic 202, 217, 224; offenses committed by female 227; Pacific Islander 35, 224; and physical abuse 212, 214, 234; pregnant 234–35; in private juvenile facilities 22, 54, 189–92; and property crimes 120, 188, 193, 203, 227; psychological imprisonment of female 238–39; in public juvenile facilities 22, 54, 189–92; and public-order offenses 43, 203, 209, 227; rate of incarceration 22, 199, 215–17; recidivists 195, 232; and risk of rape 133–34; sentenced female 22, 215, 217; and sexual abuse 74, 199, 212, 214, 234; state 22, 35, 43–44, 75, 78, 116, 120, 215–16, 224; and status offenses 188, 195; and substance abuse 192, 212, 233; by type of offense perpetrated 43, 193–95; and violent crimes 120, 188, 193, 195, 203, 209, 217, 227; white 192, 202–3, 209, 217, 224, 233–34, 237; white female 35, 209, 212, 229, 231, 233; women 22, 77, 116, 214–39; women on death row 217; *see also* Alcohol abuse; Child abuse; Delinquents; Drug abuse; Drug abuse violations; Drug addicts; Drug dealing; Family violence; Inmates; Juvenile detention; Juveniles; Native Americans; Property crime(s); Sexual abuse; Substance abuse; Violent crime(s)

Prison(s) 22, 35, 43, 116, 120, 187–89; characteristics of females in 225–27; family and abuse history of women in 233–34; federal 35, 43, 215–16, 224; females in 22, 35, 43; girls in 187–89; HIV and AIDS in 230–31; juvenile 73; mothers in 215, 234–35;

pregnant women in 234–35; psychological implications for women in 238–39; state 35, 43, 75, 78, 116, 120, 215–16, 224; vocational training and rehabilitation programs in women in 73–74, 116, 120, 214–39; women's 237–38; *see also* Jail(s); Prisoners

Probation 78, 195, 197, 215, 217, 232

Property crime(s) 8, 10, 13, 18–19, 36–37, 43–44, 47, 49, 55, 58, 62, 75, 120, 125–26, 130, 157, 166, 188, 193, 203, 209, 227; arrest rate for 10, 58; arson 8, 51; burglary 8, 23, 36, 58, 171, 175; by community size 13; embezzlement 38, 58, 125–27, 171; forgery and counterfeiting 38–39, 58, 125–27; fraud 8, 10, 38–39, 43, 58, 125–27, 136, 227; larceny 23, 58, 71, 126; larceny-theft 8, 10, 43, 51, 55, 69, 130, 145, 153, 166, 168–71, 174–75, 193, 227; motor vehicle theft 8, 10, 13, 23, 36–37, 49, 58, 171, 176; shoplifting 62, 66, 120, 172–74, 176–77; stolen property-related offenses 51, 58, 171, 175–76; vandalism 8, 36, 49, 51, 145, 193; white-collar 38–39, 125–31; *see also* Drug abuse; Drug-related offenses

Prostitutes 65, 68–69, 73, 77, 81, 101–14, 120; adult female 101, 113; adventure and promiscuity 154–55; ages of girl 150; and AIDS 113–14, 148, 150, 156; black 105, 151; and broken homes 72; call girls 101, 110–14; child 149; and child abuse 73; child sexual and physical abuse 152; and con games 135; and drug abuse/addiction 109–10, 120, 157; and ethnicity 75–76, 151; exploitation of 152, 156; extent of girl 149; family circumstances of girl 152; female 73, 102, 105, 114; girl 72, 75, 107, 113, 148–56; lower-class 110, 113; male 105; middle-class 108–10, 112; and pimps 77, 107–9, 135, 148, 153–54, 156; and race 75–76, 105, 151; race and ethnic composite of girl 150–51; reasons girls become 155–56; and runaways 111, 113, 142, 146–47,

149, 166; and sexual assault 73; and sexually transmitted diseases 109, 112; social class of girl 150; street-walkers 107–8, 111–13; and substance abuse 75; types of women 105–7; upper-class 110, 113; and victimization 113–14, 156; violent girl 153; white 105, 150–51; *see also* Drug abuse; Prostitution

Prostitution 8, 25, 27, 43–44, 47, 49, 70–71, 74–75, 77, 101–15, 120, 141, 148–57, 166–67, 177; and AIDS 113–14, 148, 150, 156; arrested for 104–5, 141; child 142, 148; defining girl 148–49; definitions of 101–3, 148; and drug use 115, 157, 166; incarceration for 103; juvenile 53; magnitude of women's 103–5; money and women's 112–13; substance abuse and girl 153, 166–67; and theft crimes 153, 168, 177; theories on 65–66, 68, 71; white-collar 111; women and 101–14; *see also* Drug abuse; Prostitutes; Sex crimes

Psychological abuse 77; *see also* Battered women

Psychological theories 67

Public-order offenses 43, 125, 203, 209, 227

Queen Mary 85

Race 27, 35, 75–76, 92, 105, 151, 217

Rape 8, 23, 70, 109, 131–34, 141, 148, 156; defined 132–33; forcible 8, 13, 38, 43, 47, 49, 131

Rapists 131–34, 136; female 131–34; imprisoned 133; male 132; rape of females 133–34; rape of males 132–33; reasons women rape 134; *see also* Sex offenders; Sexual abuse

Rasko, G. 84

Rat packers 145

Reaction-formation theory 181–82

Reamer, Frederic G. 20

Recidivism 77–78, 195, 212

Reimer, David J. 62

Residential treatment programs 198

Retreatists 196

Robbery 8, 23, 38, 43, 49, 71, 120, 126, 153

Roberts, Julia 101

Rosenblum, Karen E. 111

Roy, Maria 75

Runaways 8, 13, 27, 44, 47, 53, 62, 72, 75–77, 111, 113, 141–47, 149, 157, 166–67, 174, 195; and age of females 142–43; and AIDS 147; and alcohol abuse 166–67; arrests as 27, 44; characteristics of runaway girls 143–44; and drug abuse 144, 157, 166–67; and ethnicity 75–76; extent of female 141–42; motivating factors for 146; and pimps 146–47; and prostitution 111, 113, 142, 146–47, 149, 166–67; and race 75–76; realities of life for 146–47; and sexually transmitted diseases 147; and substance abuse 147, 166; and theft crimes 168, 174; types of girl 145; *see also* Alcohol abuse; Drug abuse; Status offenses

Russell, Diana E. 133

Sarrel, Philip 132–33

Schizophrenia 76

Self-report surveys 55, 62, 70, 71; and juvenile crime 55, 62; *see also* Official statistics; *Uniform Crime Reports (UCR)*

Sex crimes 75, 166

Sex offenders 98–100

Sex offenses 43

Sexual abuse 73–74, 91, 98, 111, 133, 144–45, 149, 167, 177, 189, 212, 214, 234

Sexual assaults 132–33, 189, 199, 214

Sexual exploitation 91, 101, 147; *see also* Prostitution

Sexual slavery 153

Sexually transmitted diseases 109, 112, 147, 156

Shaffer, David 144

Shellow, Robert 144

Shireman, Charles H. 20

Shoplifting 62, 66, 69, 120, 166, 168, 172–74, 176–77

Short, James F. 55

Silbert, Mimi H. 73, 150, 152

Simmons, H. E. 73

Simon, Rita James 58, 71, 130
Simple assaults 8, 23, 193, 195
Sims, Patsy 213–14
Sisters in Crime: The Rise of the New Female Criminal (Adler) 55
Smart, Carol 57
Smith, Douglas 62
Smith, Peggy 92
Smith, Sandie 89
Smith, Susan 81
Socioeconomic theories 70–71
Sociological theories 68–70
Spousal violence 93–95; *see also* Family violence
Spouse abuse 90, 93; education and 94; female spouse abusers 93; socioeconomics and 94; *see also* Battered women; Domestic violence
Status offenses 141, 147, 157, 162, 187–88, 195
Steele, Brandt F. 75, 91
Steffensmeir, Darrell J. 57, 62
Steffensmeir, Renee Hoffman 62
Steinmetz, Suzanne K. 93
Stolen property-related offenses 51, 58, 171, 175–76
Straus, Murray A. 74, 93–94
Streetwalkers 101, 106–8, 111–13; *see also* Prostitutes; Prostitution
Substance abuse 40, 62, 72, 75, 87, 95, 112–13, 121, 137, 145–47, 158–59, 165–67, 174, 199, 212, 234; and female inmates 199, 212; and girls' theft crimes 174; and juvenile delinquency 166–67; *see also* Alcohol abuse; Drug abuse
Suicide 75–76, 147, 157, 167, 180, 189
Sutherland, Edwin W. 20

Tec, Nechama 163
Thomas, William I. 68
Throwaways 77, 145, 156
Totman, J. 84
Tranquilizer abuse 93
Treadwell, Mary 128
Truancy 195

The Unadjusted Girl: With Cases and Standpoint for Behavior Analysis (Thomas) 68

Uniform Crime Reporting Program 5, 20
Uniform Crime Reports (UCR) 5, 8, 10, 20–21, 57, 82, 104, 168; criticism of 20–21; *see also* National Crime Victimization Survey (NCVS); Official statistics
U.S. Department of Justice 23
U.S. Supreme Court 103
Upper-class prostitutes 110, 113; *see also* Call girls; Prostitution

Vagrancy 8, 35
Vandalism 8, 36, 47, 49, 51, 58, 145, 193
Vanderbilt, Heidi 100
Venereal diseases 113, 147; *see also* Sexually transmitted diseases
Victimization 5, 21, 23, 87, 90, 112–14, 141, 156, 234; child abuse 87, 195, 212, 234; data 5; and female inmates 195, 212, 234; multiple-offender 23, 46; and prostitution 112–14, 156; rates of 113; reported 25; single-offender 23, 46; surveys 23, 46; *see also* Child abuse; Domestic Violence; Sexual abuse
Violence 23, 49, 74–75, 86, 90, 94–95, 120, 148, 152, 154, 181, 195; crimes of 23, 49, 77, 113, 131, 178; domestic 70, 75–77, 87, 90–95, 134, 195; family 74–75, 88, 90, 94; female 89, 131; marital, 93–94; and prostitution 148, 152–54; spousal 93–95; by women 120; *see also* Violent crime(s)
Violent crime(s) 8, 10, 13, 18–19, 23, 35, 37–38, 43–44, 47, 49, 55, 58, 62, 70, 75–76, 89, 113, 115, 120, 125–26, 131, 141, 157, 166, 188, 203, 209, 227; aggravated assault 8, 10, 13, 38, 49, 55, 193; arrest rate for 10; arrests for 13, 18, 26–27, 58; domestic violence 70, 75–77, 87, 90–95; forcible rape 8, 13, 38, 43, 47, 49, 131; homicide 43, 75, 82–84, 87, 126; kidnapping 25, 81; multiple-offender 46; murder and nonnegligent manslaughter 8, 25, 35, 38, 76, 81–89, 141, 193, 217, 227;

rape 8, 23, 70, 109, 131–34, 141; robbery 8, 23, 38, 43, 49, 71, 113, 120, 126, 153; single-offender 46; victimizations 46; see also Crime(s); Homicide; Offenses; Violence
Visher, Christy A. 62

Walker, Lenore E. 87
Walters, James 93
Weapons charges 8, 13, 43, 47
Weis, Joseph G. 71
Weller, Sheila 180
White-collar crimes 38–39, 125–30, 131; arrests for 125–27, 130; chivalry, paternalism and female 130; defining 125; dimensions of female 125–27; explanations for women's 129; male 125; nature of 127–28; types of female white-collar criminals 127–28; see also Property crime(s)

White-collar prostitution 111; see also Call girls
Whites 27, 35, 75, 84, 105, 118, 143–44, 151, 179, 192, 202, 209, 212, 217, 224, 229, 231, 233–34, 237
Wife battering 86, 177; see also Battered women; Domestic violence
Winick, Charles 102
Wise, Nancy 55
Wolfgang, Marvin E. 27
Women's liberation movement 55, 58, 71
Woolston, Howard B. 103
Wuornos, Aileen Carol 81

Yablonsky, Lewis 73
Yllo, K. 74

Zalba, S. 76